WORKING MEN'S COLLEGE.

LIBRARY REGULATIONS.

The Library is open every week-day evening (except Saturday), from 6.30 to 10 o'clock.

This book may be kept for three weeks. If not returned within that period, the borrower will be liable to a fine of one penny per week.

If lost or damaged, the borrower will be required to make good such loss or damage.

Only one book may be borrowed at a time.

EPPING FOREST:

ITS LITERARY AND
HISTORICAL ASSOCIATIONS

'EPPING FOREST . . . the loveliest forest in the world! Not equal to what it was, but still the loveliest forest in the world, and the pleasantest, especially in summer; for then it is thronged with grand company, and the nightingales, and cuckoos, and Romany chals and chies. As for Romany-chals there is not such a place for them in the whole world as the Forest. Them that wants to see Romany-chals should go to the Forest, especially to the Bald-faced Hind on the hill above Fairlop, on the day of Fairlop Fair. It is their trysting place, as you would say, and there they musters from all parts of England, and there they whoops, dances, and plays; keeping some order, nevertheless, because the Rye of all the Romans is in the house, seated behind the door.'

GEORGE BORROW, *Romano Lavo-Lil.*

'To make a thing real you must make it local.'
G. K. CHESTERTON.

EPPING FOREST

ITS LITERARY
AND HISTORICAL
ASSOCIATIONS

By

WILLIAM ADDISON

LONDON: J. M. DENT & SONS LTD.

BOOK
PRODUCTION
WAR ECONOMY
STANDARD

PREFACE

First it was the Forest of Essex, a stretch of waste and woodland covering the greater part of the county. Then the Royal Forest of Waltham, where kings had their palaces and hunting lodges. Two great abbeys, one at Barking and one at Waltham, stood on its borders. Before the Dissolution most of it belonged to the monks, but when Waltham's fame declined, and its energies were diverted from piety to gunpowder, Epping gave its name to what remained of the unfenced woodlands.

The splendours of the Royal Forest faded. Its area was reduced, and what was left of it became the haunt of deer-stealers and highwaymen. Its villagers, who had formerly lived in dread of the law, now lived in dread of those who broke the law. All who had to pass through it rode quickly, so that they could be home by nightfall.

In the nineteenth century it was threatened with complete destruction; but axes were swung for freedom, and the Forest was saved. It became the People's Forest for ever.

Such facts as these appear in every history of Waltham or Epping Forest. With the natural scene, they form the unchanging background, and they have their place in the following pages, where another story is told. The Forest has had its poets as well as its princes. Few of its historians have made even passing references to the remarkable record of literary associations found in this small corner of Essex. We are frequently reminded that William Morris was born at Walthamstow, and that 'The King's Head' at Chigwell is the Maypole Inn of *Barnaby Rudge*. Most districts have one or two such associations to offer; few are so rich in them as Epping Forest. The most interesting are collected in these pages, so that those whose chief delight is in books may find themselves in the company of old friends while rambling through the open Forest.

To avoid the confusion of using two names, the region covered has been called the Forest throughout, instead of first Waltham Forest and then Epping Forest. Roughly, this region is the stretch of broken, hilly ground bounded by the Lea on the west, from Roydon to Bow Bridge, by the high road from Stratford to Romford on the south, and by a less clearly defined enclosing line—with which some liberties have been taken—on the east and north.

A complete list of authorities consulted in writing this book would fill several pages, but the following recent sources are gratefully acknowledged: numerous articles in *The Essex Review* and *The Essex Naturalist*; the publications of the Walthamstow Antiquarian Society; *Companion into Essex*, by Herbert W. Tomkins; *Knole and the Sackvilles*, by V. Sackville-West; *William Byrd* by E. H. Fellowes; *John Clare*, by J. W. and Anne Tibble; *Elizabeth Fry*, by Janet Whitney; *Octavia Hill*, by E. Moberly Bell; *The Taylors of Ongar*, by Doris Mary Armitage; *Tennyson*, by the Hon. Harold Nicolson; *Trollope: a Commentary*, by Michael Sadleir; *Let There Be Sculpture*, by Jacob Epstein. Other sources have been acknowledged in the text. The Oxford University Press and the poet's family are thanked for permission to quote the poem by Gerard Manley Hopkins at the end of the book.

Finally, I wish to thank all who have helped me to collect my material (though it would be impossible to name them all here), especially Mr. Percy Thompson for his generous help with illustrations, and my friends, Miss E. M. Chisholm, Mr. Aubrey Finch, and Mr. Sidney Gresty, for reading the book in manuscript and rescuing me from many errors and indiscretions. The mistakes that remain are due to my own ignorance or carelessness.

W. A.

LOUGHTON.
Easter, 1945.

CONTENTS

CONTENTS ix

ILLUSTRATIONS

(Placed together at the end of the book)

The sixteen modern photographs are by Musto of Leytonstone

CHAPTER I

Forest legends—The founding of Waltham Abbey—The naming of
  Havering-atte-Bower—The blind beggar of Bethnal Green

THE past has life in the Forest. Nowhere is it easier to imagine
the long pageant of history than against this unchanging scene
of heath and woodland, with a herd of frightened deer leaping
into cover. Time is no longer fenced into patterns and periods.
When the north wind tears through the beeches we can believe
ourselves witnessing those long carousals that followed days of
hard hunting in feudal times, when rude ballads were chanted
in these high glades. Ancient earthworks remain, the work of
rough hands that broke this Essex clay so many centuries ago.
In the Forest, part of a lost world lingers on into our later
civilization.

As we gaze upwards, a green vault of shifting leaves and sway-
ing branches fascinates us, and in the glancing lights and moving
shadows of the long aisles strange old legends seem credible
enough. The disbelief of our scientific and industrial world is
dumb. The deer, those wild and nervous creatures that man
has never tamed, grazing silent in a clearing, symbolize this
fabulous world of distant centuries.

The most famous of these old legends tells how Waltham
Abbey, on the western edge of the Forest, came to be founded.
It is read in the *Liber de Inventione Sanctae Crucis Nostrae,*
written by a canon of the abbey about the reign of Henry I.

At Montacute, in Somersetshire, the legend relates, lived a
smith who was sexton to the village church. One night this
worthy man was told in a dream that he must go to the priest
next morning, and beg him to call all the people of the parish
together for prayer, exhortation, and fasting. At the end of this
preparation, priest and people must go in procession to the top of
a nearby hill, where the men must dig until they found a treasure
that had been hidden in the earth for ages.

But the smith was afraid of the ridicule of his neighbours, and
kept his dream to himself.

On the following night it came to him a second time, solemnly
repeating the message. When the smith awoke he lay on his
bed thinking.

I

'If I should tell,' he asked, 'who would listen to me? I should only be laughed at for my pains.'

So he got up and went about his business. But his mind was not easy, and his wife noticed his troubled look.

'What ails you?' she asked.

When the smith told her the story of his dream she, poor woman, was even more afraid of ridicule than her husband was, and begged him to tell no one, not even the priest, about his strange experience. So the second day went by, and on the third night the dream came to him yet again, warning him so solemnly against continued silence that he went to the priest next morning and confessed everything.

The priest knew that his sexton was an honest man and no fool, and believed that the message had come from God. He called his parishioners together for prayer in the village church, and after a solemn service led them to the top of the hill, the people singing litanies as they walked. When they reached the place revealed in the dream, they began to dig, and after going to a depth of forty cubits found a huge stone with a fissure through the middle. On removing part of the stone they found a crucifix of black flint, with a smaller crucifix under the right arm, and under the left arm a bell of ancient workmanship, such as were seen round the necks of cattle. They found also a copy of the Gospels.

Not knowing what to do with these sacred things, they placed a tent over the hole until Tovi, lord of the manor of Montacute, and standard-bearer to King Canute, could be brought to inspect the treasure. When he arrived he ordered the villagers to move it to the parish church, while he called together the priests and monks of the neighbourhood to discuss with them what should be done. After prayer and thought it was agreed that the smaller crucifix should be placed in the village church. The larger one was placed with the book and the bell in a wagon, because it had been revealed that this larger crucifix must be set up wherever twelve red oxen and twelve white cows, harnessed to the wagon, should carry it.

Tovi, proud of the discovered treasure, prayed that the beasts might be guided to one of his many dwellings in different parts of the country, promising that if his prayer was granted he would endow the servants of the Holy Cross with the revenues of the town that received it. The wagon, however, could not be moved.

All the strength of the oxen and cows, aided by the efforts of the bystanders, could not drag it out of its rut. At last Tovi thought of the hunting lodge he had begun to build in the Forest of Essex, and immediately the wagon plunged forward at such a speed that those who saw it declared that the wagon appeared to drive the oxen, and not the oxen to draw the wagon, until it came to rest finally at Waltham, or Weald-ham, which means 'forest dwelling.'

It is said that on the day appointed for the erection of the cross, a workman attempted to drive a nail into the right arm, in order to fasten to it the jewelled ornaments given by Tovi. When the nail pierced the stone, a stream of blood ran from it, which was kept in the consecrated house built near the cross.

Glitha, Tovi's wife, presented a splendid golden and jewelled crown. A circlet, which she wore in common with all the noble-women of her day, was fixed to the image on the cross. Bracelets and other jewels were set at the foot, along with a stone which sent out rays of light to guide wayfarers at night.

Tovi made a foundation for two priests and other clergy, and presented gifts of gold and silver. His own homestead he kept, leaving it at his death to his son Athelstan, a man of weak character, who so neglected his patrimony that the Waltham property was taken away from him by Edward the Confessor, and presented to Harold.

According to tradition, Harold was cured of paralysis by the Holy Cross at Waltham, and to show his gratitude built a magnificent church near it. This church is said to have been the finest in the kingdom until the king's abbey at Westminster was completed a few years later. It was to this church that Harold came on his way to fight the Normans. A strange tale is told of this occasion. Harold prostrated himself in the form of a cross before the altar. As he did so the image, which before that time looked upwards, bowed its head as a sign that the future held no promise. The chronicler, writing in the twelfth century, says that he had this story from old Turkil, the sacrist, who was by the altar at the time.

There are conflicting accounts of what happened to the body of Harold after he had been killed by a bowman's arrow at Hastings. One says that he was buried at Waltham, another that William refused to give up the body, and had it buried on the seashore; yet another, that Harold escaped death on the field of battle, to live the remainder of his days as a monk. The most probable story appears to be that he was buried first on the cliffs above Hastings, and afterwards moved to Waltham. Robert of Gloucester says that Harold's mother begged William to give her the body of her son, and that it was carried with great honour to Waltham, where it was buried, 'in the holy rode Chyrche, that he let him self rere.'

Harold's church at Waltham was built by the Norman builders brought to England by Edward the Confessor, who was present at the consecration in 1060. In Edward, the Saxon line returned to the throne, but he was a monk rather than a king. Before being called to rule England he had lived among French monks, and his heart remained with them. It is one of the ironies of our history that Edward won the reputation, to which no king was less entitled, of being a great legislator. In Westminster Abbey our kings have sworn to observe the laws of Edward the Confessor, though so far as we know he never made any laws. If he had thought more about such matters the Conqueror might never have set foot on English soil.

Edward reigned from 1042 to 1066, and during this time he made the palace at Havering-atte-Bower, on the south-eastern fringe of the Forest, his favourite retreat. From his wooded acres he could look across the Essex marshes to the Kentish hills, with little to distract his pious soliloquies except the nightingales. A legend relates how this famous palace got its name. The name Bower needs no explanation, but according to our Forest legend the first part of the name came in a curious way.

Edward was present at the consecration of the church dedicated to St. John the Evangelist. During the procession, an old man disguised as a beggar walked up to him, begging for alms. Edward had no money on his person, so he drew from his finger a ring, which he gave to the old man, who then disappeared.

Some years later, two English pilgrims were travelling through the Holy Land. They had lost their way and were feeling bewildered when they saw a glorious company in white, with a brilliant light shining about them. Behind the two pilgrims stood a man of great age, who asked who they were and where they had come from. When the pilgrims told him they came from England he led them into a fine city. There he set them before a table richly furnished with all kinds of delicacies, inviting them to eat, and afterwards to sleep.

The following morning the old man set them on their way, and as they were about to leave him he stood in their path, blessed them, and told them that he was John the Evangelist, adding:

'Say ye unto Edward, your king, that I greet him well by the token that he gave me, this ring, with his own hands, at the hallowing of my church; which ring ye shall deliver him again, and say ye to him that he dispose his goods, for within six months he shall be in the joy of heaven with me, where he shall have his reward for his chastity and good living.'

The two pilgrims returned to England, and found the king at his bower in the Forest. There they handed to him the ring and the old man's message, saying: 'HAVE RING,' from which came the name Havering-atte-Bower. Robert of Gloucester tells us that soon afterwards the king fell sick, distributed his wealth to the poor, and prepared himself for death.

This legend was a favourite study with artists during the Middle Ages. It was represented in bas-relief, on tapestry, and on glass. At Westminster Abbey it is represented in one of the east windows of the presbytery, where the glass is probably fifteenth century, and carved on the stone screen of Edward the Confessor's Chapel, where Edward was buried. It was painted on the east window of the south aisle of Romford church, and is seen again on the Elizabethan seal of the Liberty of Havering-atte-Bower. What was believed to be the actual ring was preserved for centuries in Westminster Abbey, and those who touched it were supposed to be cured of falling sickness.

A third legend of the Forest is connected with one of the many noble families that had country seats on its border. The de Montforts held the manors of Leyton and Kelvedon, as well as those of Marks Hall at Coggeshall, Purleigh, Goldhanger, and Totham.

One of this family left two sons, of whom the elder became a monk, so the younger inherited the patrimony. This younger son, Robert, had to flee to Jerusalem to escape the indignation of the king, Henry I, whom he had offended. His lands were taken from him and given to Henry de Essex, the traitor who cast away the royal standard in Wales during the reign of Henry II, leaving the king's life in danger.

After this treacherous act, Robert de Montfort reappeared and challenged Henry de Essex to single combat, which was fought in a meadow near Reading Abbey before the king and Queen Eleanor.

When Henry de Essex went down in the fight the king intervened on his behalf. His life was spared; but the rest of his days were spent as a monk in Reading Abbey, his lands being forfeited.

In the reign of Henry III, the de Montfort name was made famous by the great Simon de Montfort, who fell at the battle of Evesham. His son, Henry de Montfort, was with him, and was wounded along with his father, but not killed. This Henry de Montfort was found on the day following the battle by a noble lady, who nursed him, and later became his wife. But he remained blind for the rest of his life, and was obliged to live in hiding for fear of his enemies. He lived at Bethnal Green, where he was known as the Blind Beggar.

The Blind Beggar of Bethnal Green and his wife had a daughter so beautiful that her poor garments were never noticed, though she was despised by her neighbours on account of her father's mean condition. Wearying of her dull life, she left home to go in search of better fortune, and a ballad was written about her which says:

> She went till she came to Stratford-le-Bow,
> Then knew she not whither, nor which way to go,
> With tears she lamented her hard destiny,
> So sad and so heavy was pretty Bessee.
>
> She kept on her journey until it was day,
> And went unto Romford along the highway,
> Where at the Queen's Arms entertainèd was she,
> So fair and well favoured was pretty Bessee.
>
> .   .   .   .   .   .
>
> The young men of Romford in her had their joy,
> She showed herself courteous, and modestly coy,
> And at her commandment still would they be,
> So fair and so comely was pretty Bessee.'

The ballad relates that when the young men of Romford discovered that she was the daughter of a blind beggar they forsook her—all except a young knight who loved her for her beauty and asked her hand in marriage.

At the wedding of the young knight and the beggar's daughter, the guests were surprised to see a minstrel enter the room, who began to play upon his lute and tell the story of his life. It was the bride's father, and the young knight discovered that he had married, not the daughter of a despised beggar, but the heiress of the de Montforts, a descendant of princes.

CHAPTER II

LITTLE of the character of the old Forest remains to-day in
Barking, Ilford, or West Ham. Villages that were once silvan
have now scarcely a tree or patch of green turf to cheer the eye.
For centuries they bordered the Forest, and were familiar to
kings and nobles. When the Conqueror came he made Barking
his headquarters while the Tower of London was being built—
Barking, with its famous abbey, founded in 666, in days when the
preaching of Bishop Cedd was slowly bringing light to the demon-
haunted folk of the Essex marshes. In its early days it was a
double monastery—two establishments, one for monks and one
for nuns, with no communication except through the abbess, who
ruled both. Three queens were abbesses of Barking, and other
kings besides the Conqueror were entertained there, cooks and
pudding-wives preparing barons of beef and haunches of venison
for magnificent feasting. And Barking did not neglect its
other offices. The poor and sick were cared for by the nuns,
whose good works were known across all the wild heaths of
the Forest.

Travellers through the Forest in the Middle Ages would turn
aside to pray at the shrine of the Virgin Mary and St. Thomas of
Canterbury on Ilford Hill, where a hospital was founded for a
prior, a master, two priests, and thirteen poor lepers. This
hospital was endowed with a hundred and twenty acres of Forest
land, in addition to a mill at Ilford and tithes at Warley and
Barking. When King David of Scotland came to Barking to
visit his sister, Queen Maud, the abbess, he found her washing
the feet of the lepers in this hospital at Ilford.

Barking was the richest nunnery in England. At one inventory
its treasures included 3,586 ounces of silver, a jewel of 65 ounces,
along with other jewels and vestments of cloth of gold and tissue.
The founder was St. Erkenwald, Bishop of London, who founded
it at the express desire of his sister Ethelburga, who became the
first abbess. About 1390 a poem was written describing a
miracle wrought by St. Erkenwald in St. Paul's. A coffin was

found in the cathedral, containing a body in a king's robes. At the time, the poem states:

> The Primate and his prelacie was partyd fro home,
> In Essex was Ser Erkenwolde an abbay to visite.

When the saint returned to London he bent over the body and addressed it. The body replied that he was a heathen who wished to embrace the Christian faith, so the saint baptized him, and the body immediately crumbled to dust.

On the upper floor of the Fire-Bell Gate at Barking Abbey was the Chapel of the Holy Rood. By the east window is a late twelfth- or early thirteenth-century rood in stone, with figures of the Virgin and St. John.

Both the abbess of Barking and the abbot of Waltham were privileged to hunt hares and foxes in the Forest, and each year they received in addition generous grants of venison. Richard II, we find, allowed the abbots of Waltham three bucks each winter and three does each summer. The Bishop of London, and also the Dean and Chapter of St. Paul's, had the right to hunt when passing through the Forest, which was a famous hunting ground even before the Conquest. But its greatest fame came with the Tudors. By a charter of King John, confirmed by Edward IV, its area had been reduced. The Tudors restored it.

The courts of the Tudors hunted and hawked from Havering-atte-Bower, and from the palace at Chigwell, which stood at the foot of what is now Palmerston Road, Buckhurst Hill, and which appears to have been built solely for use as a royal hunting lodge. The name of this old palace was Langfords. A house bearing the same name now stands on or near the site, though every trace of the original Langfords has disappeared. A third hunting lodge was Pimp Hall, below Friday Hill, Chingford.

Henry VIII hunted till the last years of his life, and we have many records of payments to persons in the Forest for services in connection with his entertainment. In 1543, for instance, a certain George Maxey was paid thirty pounds for work at the 'Great Stonedeings,' the building now known as Queen Elizabeth's Hunting Lodge, Chingford, and for laying out the king's 'new park at Fayremeade,' where the Epping Hunt continued to meet hundreds of years after Henry's park had become waste again.

Between Queen Elizabeth's Hunting Lodge and Fairmead slopes

the Forest is level ground. Green glades branch out in all directions from Grimston's Oak, named after a cricketer, which stands behind Connaught Water. Between them are groves of oak and hornbeam, with dense undergrowth of bramble, hawthorn, and blackthorn, which stars its branches with frail white blossoms in April, making a brave show against the leafless gloom of the unawakened Forest. All this was part of Henry's park.

We require little imagination to make the Tudor scene real again. Swinging out of a hornbeam thicket on a crisp October morning we can fancy we hear the old song:

> The hunt is up, the hunt is up,
>   And it is well-nigh day;
> And Harry our king is gone hunting,
>   To bring the deer to bay.

Even in the East End reminders of Henry remain. A story goes that Anne Boleyn had been betrothed to a young nobleman who died young. Ten months after his death the king desired to marry her, but Anne begged to be allowed to complete the customary year of mourning for her lover. Henry granted her request, and to amuse her built a brick tower, still called Anne Boleyn's Castle, in Green Street, East Ham, from which she had a fine view of the Thames from Greenwich to below Gravesend.

Henry and Anne were familiar figures in the Forest while Anne enjoyed the king's favour. On the day of her death, Henry, it is said, rode out into the Forest and breakfasted under a great tree. There are several versions of the story. Harrison Ainsworth is responsible for one which transfers the incident to Windsor Forest, apparently without any justification in fact. The oldest accounts say that it was to Waltham Forest he came. He wanted to be out of London, but near enough to hear the Tower gun fired. The king's party sat quietly under a tree waiting. At last the gun was heard, and Henry exclaimed:

'The day's work is done. Uncouple the hounds, and let us follow the sport.'

The incident is related in a ballad which says:

> King Henry stood in Waltham Wood
>   One morning in merry May time.

After the gun had been heard it continues:

> And why so jovial grew his Grace,
>   That erst was sad and sullen?
> With that boom from the Tower had fallen
>   The head of fair Anne Bullen.

It ends:

> Gaily the king for Greenwich rides,
>   Each moment makes his glee more;
> He thinks: 'To-morrow I 'm betrothed
>   At last to young Jane Seymour.'

> The sunshine falls, the wild bird calls,
>   Across the slopes of Epping;
> From grove to glade, through light and shade,
>   The troops of deer are stepping.

The tree under which Henry sat was probably at High Beach or Beech, the spelling of which is hotly contested. There is no definite authority for either. It is simply a local name for this part of the manor of Sewardstone. Beech appears to be the more popular spelling now, inevitably, perhaps, in view of the fine beeches found there. Edward North Buxton, the author of *Epping Forest*, stood out for Beach, or bank, and this spelling is used throughout the present book. Both spellings are appropriate.

Henry was a frequent visitor to Waltham Abbey. 'Waltham Bells told no tales when the King came there,' said old Thomas Fuller. On one occasion Henry visited the abbey alone, disguised as one of his own guard. Dinner was on the table, and the king was invited to sit down with the abbot. His appetite was so good after hunting that his host, who did not recognize him, exclaimed: 'Well fare thy heart, and here 's a cup of sack to the health of thy master. I would give a hundred pounds could I feed so heartily on beef as thou dost; but my poor queasy stomach can hardly digest the breast of a chicken.'

A few days later the good abbot of Waltham was carried off to London and locked in the Tower. There he was fed on bread and water, demanding in vain to know what crime he had committed. After several days of this mean diet a loin of beef was set before him. The abbot made short work of it, and, just as he finished, the king walked in to demand his hundred pounds. We can imagine the twinkle in Henry's baleful eyes as he did so. It is only fair to add that the story is also claimed for an abbot of Reading.

It was a conversation in the Romeland, near the abbey, which facilitated Henry's divorce from his first wife, Catherine, and, incidentally, of course, led to something much more important. Thomas Cranmer, than a young fellow of Jesus College, Cambridge, was living at Waltham to escape the plague. He was acting as tutor to the sons of Mr. Cressy, whose wife was related to Cranmer. The topic of the day was the legality of Henry's marriage. Cranmer, representing the new and progressive learning, in conversation with Gardiner, Bishop of Winchester, who represented those of the old learning who only desired to be free from Rome, and Edward Fox, afterwards Bishop of Hereford, advocated that instead of waiting month after month, and perhaps year after year, for the pope's decision, it would be better to have this question of the legality of a man's marriage with his brother's widow referred to the learned divines and universities. When Edward Fox reported this opinion to the king, Henry, with an oath, exclaimed that the Cambridge fellow 'had the right sow by the ear.'

This incongruous association of a king's passion with a religious reformation produced some strange comments. The poet Gray suggested that Henry saw the gospel light first dawn in Anne Boleyn's eyes, but whatever light Henry saw in those eyes we may be sure had little to do with the gospel. That sturdy chronicler, William Cobbett, saw the matter rather differently, but he was inclined to blame Anne.

'I could have excused her,' he writes, 'if there had been no marrying in the case; but hypocrisy, always bad, becomes detestable when it resorts to religious ceremony as its mask. She, no more than Cranmer, seems, to her last moments, to have remembered her sins against her lawful queen.' In writing of Foxe's *Book of Martyrs*, which comes into our story presently, Cobbett says it 'ought to be called "The Book of *Liars*,"' for it says that 'Cranmer, the recanter and re-recanter, held out his offending hand in the flames, and cried out, "that hand, that hand!" If he had cried out *Catherine! Catherine!* I should have thought better of him; but it is clear that the whole story is a lie, invented by the protestants, and particularly by the sectarians, to white-wash the character of this perfidious hypocrite and double apostate, who, if bigotry had something to do in bringing him to the stake, certainly deserved his fate, if any offences committed by man can deserve so horrible a punishment.'

We are able to look at these old disputes more soberly now, and we know that both gain and loss came from the Reformation. The old abbeys in their prime had provided most of the light there was in the dark centuries. In the Middle Ages the hymns of monks and lay brothers, under the influence of the liturgical chant, were the main stream of lyrical expression. The tendency of early English poetry was against melody, which springs most naturally from emotion. The narratives intoned to entertain hunters and warriors had little music. The new melody came from Christian sources:

> Merrily sang the monks of Ely,
> When Cnut King rowed thereby;
> Row, knights, near the land,
> And hear we these monkes sing.'

The monks of Waltham, we may believe, sang no less merrily, for the early hymns had something of the folk-song about them.

It is, however, to secular poetry we turn for reflections of common life. The description of an ale-house wife, by John Skelton, Henry VIII's tutor, gives an insight into the character of the times:

> She breweth nappy ale
> And maketh thereof post sale
> To travellers, tynkers,
> To sweters, to swynkers,
> And all good ale drinkers . . .
> Instead of coyne and money
> Some bring her a conny,
> And some a pot of honny,
> Some a salt, and some a spone,
> Some of their hose, and some theyr shone.

Amongst her customers came Margery Mylkeducke:

> Her kyrtell she did uptucke
> An ynche above her knee
> Her legges that you might see . . .
> And yet she brought her fees,
> A cantell of Essex cheese
> Was well a fote thycke,
> Full of maggotes quycke.

What a joy it is to meet the word 'nappy'—foamy! Ale with a head on it! And 'cantle,' meaning slice, a word which Charles Lamb appears to have been the last to use. A cantell of Essex cheese would, no doubt, be welcome in exchange for ale in the Forest inns. The most usual payment in the Forest for larger debts was in swine. We find even daughters' dowries made, and masses paid for, in swine. There was an almost inexhaustible supply of acorns, and for a long time the value of an oak was reckoned by the number of swine that could lie under its branches. W. C. Waller, in his *Loughton in Essex*, has many instances of curious methods of payment. He tells us of one 'John, son of Roger le Pyrle, who, at Michaelmas and Easter, paid to Richard de Munfichet for his land in Loughton the sum of sixpence, with three hens and a cock on St. Stephen's day in every year.'

Brindwoods, a farm at Chingford, was held from the rector by a quaint act of homage. The tenant, usually a huntsman, his wife, man- and maidservant, were required to go to the rectory, the tenant carrying a hawk on his wrist, his manservant leading a greyhound in a slip, both for the use of the rector that day. The rector gave a chicken for the hawk, a peck of oats for the tenant's horse, and a loaf of bread for his greyhound. After dining with the rector's household, the tenant blew three blasts upon his horn and paid twelve pence. But the most romantic rents in the Forest were those of the two manor houses, Chambers, Epping, and Bedfords, Havering-atte-Bower, both held by fealty and rent of one red rose.

Not all the songs the monks sang came from the inspiration of the liturgical chant. By Henry VIII's time, at all events, they had their ribald moods. There was a great deal of scandal about the association of the monks of Waltham with the nuns of Cheshunt. Fuller tells us that Sir Henry Colt of Nether Hall, Roydon, played a little practical joke on these weaker brethren to the great amusement of the king.

One evening the deer trackers reported that a party of monks from the abbey were on their way to the nunnery. Sir Henry was with the king at the time, and begged to be excused, promising His Majesty much diversion upon his return. He rode down to the nunnery and had the deer nets spread along the road outside, laying his men in ambush. When the monks came out the keepers made a great clamour with their lanterns, driving the monks into the nets. 'A Coltish trick,' comments Fuller. The next morning the monks were carried before the king, who swore that he had seen sweeter, but never fatter, venison.

This reference to Sir Henry Colt reminds us that in 1505 Sir Thomas More married Jane Colt of Nether Hall, Roydon. Roper, More's son-in-law, says that More 'resorted to the house of one Mr. Colt, a gentleman in Essex that had oft invited him thither, having three daughters whose honest conversation and virtuous education provoked him there to especially set his affection.'

More, we are told, preferred a younger sister of the lady he married, but took the older one because he felt she would be distressed if she were passed over. Some years later, Erasmus, who was in England at the time of the marriage, published an

account of the philosopher's romance which is so like the story of
Milton's first marriage that it is worth recalling. More, in spite
of what Roper says about virtuous education, desired a bride who
was quite undeveloped in mind, so that he could educate her
himself. Jane Colt appeared suitable. As soon as she and Sir
Thomas were married the process of education was begun. Jane
had been brought up in a household where learning had no
value, so she proved a dull pupil. Her husband bored her with
his witty conversation, his clever friends frightened her. Whenever More tried to encourage her she burst into tears, sometimes
throwing herself to the ground, and beating her head against the
floor. She longed for her home on the edge of the green Forest.

Completely at a loss with her, More suggested a visit to her
parents, hoping they would instruct her in wifely duties. Jane
was glad enough to return to Roydon, to the old, free life of the
country. But More followed later and explained his difficulties
to her father, who replied that the remedy was in the husband's
hands, to make himself clear adding: 'I have given her to you
and she is yours. If she doesn't obey you, use your rights and
beat her into a better frame of mind.'

Colt then spoke to his daughter, with the result that a reconciliation followed, and Erasmus adds, we hope truly, that 'in this
happy state of mind she continued until her death.'

More was the greatest figure on the Catholic side of the controversy over Henry's divorce. In protesting against the Act of
Supremacy, which made Henry the supreme head of the English
Church, he declared: 'There are things which no Parliament can
do. No Parliament can make a law that God shall not be God.'

If there are points of similarity between the marriages of More
and Milton, the similarity does not extend to their characters.
In temperament no two men could differ more than the bland
and tolerant philosopher and the stern and tyrannical poet, even
if Milton was really much less stern than he is usually represented.

Thomas More and Jane Colt did not enjoy each other's society
for long. Jane died in 1511, after only six years of the 'happy
state of mind' observed by Erasmus. Within a month her
virtuous and distinguished husband married Alice Middleton, a
widow with one daughter, and the second wife appears to have
been very different in character from the first. Lady Alice was
a proud, ambitious woman. If More succeeded in instructing his

first wife in the Christian virtues of gentleness and humility, with his second he had to be constantly fortified with them himself.

Those were times when few men had the courage of More to express their opinions frankly. We wonder, for instance, what old John Stonard of Loughton Hall thought about the changes in Henry's reign. Stonard's name appears several times in the accounts of the privy purse during these years. Once his wife's name appears, against a payment for twenty shillings, 'in reward,' probably for hospitality to the king, who may have ridden over from his pleasure house at Waltham, or from his hunting lodge at Chigwell. Waller tells us that when John Stonard wished to lease additional lands from the Crown, he wrote to Thomas Cromwell: 'I shall do my best to further the King's pleasure and yours.' But how genuine this sentiment was we do not know. John Stonard had formerly been the tenant of the abbots of Waltham. We know he had been a faithful member of the old church. In his will, which was made before the Dissolution, he left the abbot his 'best ambling nag.'

Memorials to this grand old yeoman may still be seen at Loughton. His son became involved in the Pilgrimage of Grace, and under threat of death was compelled to pay a fine of one hundred pounds.

Old Loughton Hall has gone. Nether Hall is now a ruin: a gaunt mass of broken towers and twisted chimneys, surrounded by a moat. Nettles and docks grow among the ruins. Henry's reign saw many changes in English life. Queens and ministers passed in and out of favour. But Thomas Cranmer continued to hold his position in the king's regard, from the time when he first attracted attention at Waltham Abbey to the last scene when Henry lay dying, affirming his faith in God, with his hand in the archbishop's. At the king's death, Cranmer was one of the executors of his will, and a member of the regency appointed to govern during the minority of Edward VI. Mary sent him to the Tower, though he had often saved her from her father's anger. His character will always remain a problem; but nothing can cancel the great debt we owe him for the Book of Common Prayer.

CHAPTER III

Mary Tudor at Copt Hall—John Foxe at Waltham Abbey—Foxe's family

BEFORE Queen Victoria, Edward VI was the only English sovereign whose diary was available to us. In it we read of disputes arising from the Princess Mary's religion. Her home at the time of these disputes was Copt Hall, an old house on the crest of a hill between Waltham and Epping.

Copt Hall has been rebuilt twice. The first hall, built in the thirteenth century by Richard FitzAucher, whose family long held the office of Forester, and the second, built by Sir Thomas Henneage in Elizabeth's reign, stood on the same site. The present hall, built between 1753 and 1757, stands a little to the east of the old site. Sir Thomas Henneage's Copt Hall was said to be the finest house in Essex. It was built in the form of a quadrangle, surrounding a court, and included a gallery fifty-six yards long, which was blown down in a gale at the end of 1639. The beautiful 'Ferdinand and Isabella' window, considered by authorities to be one of the finest stained glass windows in England, now the east window at St. Margaret's, Westminster, was formerly at Copt Hall. This famous window, which has such an entrancing depth of colour, especially in the blue, took five years to make. It was originally intended that it should be a present to Henry VII, in honour of the marriage of Prince Arthur with Catherine of Aragon. But by the time the window was finished both Henry VII and Prince Arthur were dead. When it arrived in this country from Holland, where it was made, Henry VIII sent it to Waltham Abbey, and it remained there until the Dissolution. It was then removed to New Hall, Boreham. It was preserved by General Monk through the Civil War, and came back into the Forest to Copt Hall some time during the eighteenth century, when it was purchased by Mr. Conyers. Mr. John Conyers, the son of the purchaser, sold it in 1758 to the churchwardens of St. Margaret's for four hundred guineas. Even then its fate was uncertain. Other officials of St. Margaret's were offended by what they considered its popish character, and tried to get it removed. Fortunately they did not succeed, and the window remains at St. Margaret's.

There are many points in the history of this famous window that do not appear to have been cleared up. It is not certain whether it was to be a present from Ferdinand and Isabella or from the Dutch States-General. It has even been stated that the window was set up at Copt Hall immediately after the Dissolution —a likely story, but one not proved.

Before the Dissolution, Copt Hall belonged to Waltham Abbey, and was used by the abbots as a place of retirement. Robert Fuller, the last of them, presented the hall to Henry VIII in the hope of being allowed to keep the abbey and its revenues for himself and his monks. Needless to say, he was disappointed, though he and other officials at the abbey received large surrender pensions, and the servants one year's wages when they left.

It is interesting to find fourth on the list of lay pensioners the name of Thomas Tallis, the organist at the time of the Dissolution, who will be referred to later. The abbey estates were bought by Sir Anthony Denny, one of the king's favourites, who appears in Shakespeare's *King Henry VIII*. A small endowment was left for the support of the parish priest, so small that Thomas Fuller, the Church historian, says he 'must have kept more fasting days than ever were put in the Roman Calendar.'

The deed of surrender was countersigned by Sir William Petre as royal commissioner, and we meet this knight again in an entertaining account, found in the records of the Privy Council, of a visit to Mary at Copt Hall by Sir William Petre, Lord Chancellor Rich, and Sir Anthony Wingfield. Three members of Mary's household had been summoned to London to receive certain expressions of the king's displeasure, which they were commanded to communicate to their mistress. On their return, Mary forbade them to mention the matter to her chaplains, and sent them back to the king with a letter, in which she said that her soul was God's, and she would neither change nor dissemble her faith. Edward, after consulting the Privy Council, replied that the practice of celebrating mass must cease. Her servants refused to return to Copt Hall with this message, so it was decided that the three ministers named should bear the king's letter to the princess, and enforce the orders of the Privy Council. They arrived at Copt Hall on the morning of Friday, 28th August 1551.

When the letter was presented, Mary received it upon her knees, but in case the ministers should misinterpret her dutiful attitude, she hastened to inform them that she adopted it for the honour

B

of the king's majesty's hand, with which the letter was signed—
and here she kissed it—and not for the matter which it contained.
'The matter,' said she, 'I take to proceed not from His Majesty,
but from you of the council.'

After saying this, she opened the letter and read it quietly to
herself, pausing at one point and saying aloud:

'Ah! good Mr. Cecil took much pains here.'

In discussing the question of the mass, Mary constantly reminded the three ministers that they had promised the emperor
not to interfere with her religion.   She was at no disadvantage
during the discussion, and found great satisfaction in sarcastically
reminding the three gentlemen of the benefits they had derived
personally from the Dissolution.   At one point she said:

'Though you esteem little the emperor, yet should you show
more favour to me for my father's sake, who made the more part
of you almost of nothing.'

The question of her servants detained in London was discussed.
When Lord Rich offered to supply new servants she quickly told
him that she was capable of engaging her own, having 'years
sufficient for that purpose.'   If any of his servants entered that
house, she said, she would leave it.   When the ministers tried to
pacify her with smooth words, she retorted that she was more
impressed by deeds than words.   She had no recollection of anything in their past that could inspire her with confidence in their
professions of goodwill.

When the princess retired to her room, the three ministers
turned to her chaplains.   They were determined, they said, to
put an end to all ceremonies of the Roman Catholic religion in
that house.   Having made this clear, they were about to leave
when Mary intimated that she would like a word with them from
her window.   They offered to go up to her room; but Mary repeated that she would speak to them from her window, so they
went out into the courtyard.   Would they, she asked, be good
enough to return to her the servant who kept her accounts, for
since he left she had been obliged to keep them herself, and she
had learned 'how many loaves of bread be made of a bushel of
wheat, and I wis my father and my mother never brought me
up with baking and brewing.   And, to be plain with you, I am
weary of my office.'

Finally, she bade them God speed, but not without a last sneer
at them:

'I pray God to send you to do well in your souls and bodies, too —for some of you have but weak bodies.'

With that the three ministers left her, making their way down to Waltham Abbey, which would be the way to take then. The miry bridle-paths of the Forest were infested by thieves and cut-throats, and all three loved life and property too dearly to take undue risks. Lord Rich was later to proclaim Mary queen, after having signed a proclamation for Lady Jane Grey.

The early death of Edward VI caused both Rich and Petre to readjust their political and religious views with disconcerting rapidity. Both had unsavoury records. It was Rich who had betrayed Sir Thomas More to death, putting into his mouth words he had never uttered. To-day, a great monument to Rich's memory may be seen at Felstead. He is depicted in his robe of state, leaning on his elbow. Three scenes from his life are figured on the panels behind him. On the first we have a youth bearing a cross and a document; he is attended by Truth and Wisdom. On the second the Speaker of the House of Commons is attended by Virtue and Justice. On the third the Lord Chancellor is attended by Hope and Charity.

No better account can be given of Sir William Petre. It is reported of him that when the young king's health began to fail he drew up a memorial, under the direction of the king and the Privy Council, limiting the succession to Protestants. But when Edward died it was found that Mary had a powerful party behind her, so Sir William Petre's memorial was shelved. He and his friends joined Mary's party and supported her claim. When Mary drove into London from Wanstead House to be crowned, Sir William's wife attended her. This astute man took good care to become, as important to the new queen as he had been to her father and to her half-brother. So important did he in fact become that the pope, Paul IV, issued a bull confirming his title to all the lands he had acquired at the Dissolution, about which Mary had taunted him at Copt Hall. This bull is believed to be the only one of its kind in England.

When Elizabeth became queen, Sir William again changed his religion to suit the new court. He died in 1572, and a memorial to him may be seen at Ingatestone, where he was buried. It may, however, be said of both Lord Rich and Sir William Petre, that whatever they lacked in moral character, they were men of great ability.

Several martyrs were sought out from the Forest during
Mary's reign, Lord Rich playing a sinister part in the trials.
John Rogers, the first of them, was rector of Chigwell by virtue
of holding the prebend of St. Pancras, to which the Chigwell
living was attached at that time. Chigwell had both a rector
and a vicar, the rector being patron of the vicarage. Under the
assumed name of Thomas Matthew, Rogers compiled a Bible
from Tyndale's and Coverdale's versions, and presented it to
Henry VIII. This was one of the five texts which the translators
responsible for the Authorized Version were enjoined by James I
to consult. Of his end we have a vivid account in the *Book of
Martyrs*. His wife and their eleven children met him on his
way to Smithfield; but their presence did not shake his resolution.
He was burned to death on 4th February 1555.

Foxe's *Book of Martyrs* was the first great prose work in English to show the possibilities of the language for vigorous and
dramatic narrative. The free use of English as an artistic medium
of expression had found its first inspiration in the translations of
the Scriptures. There had been little grace in English prose
before the full tide of biblical translation brought it so miracu-
lously to fullness of power. John Foxe lived at Waltham Abbey
at the height of his fame.

The first English edition of the *Book of Martyrs* appeared in
1563, and we know that Foxe was living at Waltham in 1565.
He had been expelled from Magdalen College, Oxford, for adopting
the principles of the Reformation. Afterwards he had lived as
tutor with noble families before fleeing to the Continent in 1554.
In October 1559 he had returned to England, but we do not know
at what date he came to Waltham. Fuller says he lived there
while preparing his great work, which cannot mean more than
while translating it into English, because the original version had
been written in Latin and published while Foxe was on the Continent. The English translation was begun in 1561. Foxe may
have been living in Waltham at that time, or soon after. However that may be, he was living there when the astonishing fame
that followed the publication of the English edition came
to him.

No work did more for the Protestant cause, though there are
more opinions than one about the value of its effect in inflaming
strong and intolerant passions. In Foxe's pages may be found
an account of the martyrdom on Stratford Green, which twenty

thousand people are said to have witnessed. Stratford Green
was where the municipal college and public library now stand.
In front of St. John's Church, Stratford, is a spire capped with a
martyr's crown. On one side the burning is depicted, on the
other sides the names and dates of the local victims are to
be read.

Two of John Foxe's children were baptized at Waltham Abbey
on 29th January 1565. In the previous year Sir Thomas Henneage had come to reside at Copt Hall, and we know that the
two families were on friendly terms. Lady Henneage frequently
consulted Foxe on spiritual matters. On one occasion she sent
for him during an illness. Foxe told her that while it was always
wise to be prepared for death, she would not die of her present
sickness. Fortunately for his reputation as a prophet she did
recover.

Foxe was a man of determined, vigorous character and great
austerity. When his son Samuel returned from a visit to the
Continent, dressed in continental fashion, his father greeted him
with the question:

'Who are you?'

'Sir,' replied the young man dutifully, 'I am your son Samuel.'

'Oh, my son!' groaned the old man, 'what enemy of thine hath
taught thee so much vanity?'

Foxe would not have his sons near him at his death; he did not
wish them to see his wasted condition, for, as Fuller puts it,
Foxe 'was not nipt in the bud, nor blasted in the blossom, nor
blown down when green, nor gathered when ripe; but even fell
of his own accord, when altogether withered.'

This son, Samuel, Foxe's eldest son, lived in the Forest during
the greater part of his life. In 1587, the year of his father's death,
he entered the service of Sir Thomas Henneage of Copt Hall,
and was given the charge of the palace of Havering-atte-Bower.
In 1591 he was appointed to the clerkship of Epping, and some
time after 1594, the date of one of Elizabeth's visits to Havering,
he settled at Warlies, Upshire, more recently the residence of the
Buxton family, where several of his children were born.

Dr. Thomas Foxe, the eldest son of Samuel, born at Havering
Palace in 1591, married the grand-daughter of Mrs. Honeywood,
whose name comes down to us in biographies of John Foxe himself. An amusing story is told of this lady. She had what we
should call a nervous breakdown, and came to despair of her

spiritual condition. Several clergymen visited her without any helpful effect, one of them being John Foxe. Her fears of endless misery grew stronger as her faith grew weaker, until one day she happened to be bemoaning her fate with a drinking glass in her hand. Overcome by a passion of despair, she threw the glass to the ground violently, exclaiming that she was as surely damned as the glass was broken. It was an effectively dramatic gesture. But the glass failed to break.

This Dr. Thomas Foxe had many connections with Waltham Abbey. Farmer tells us that an estate was left in trust to him for the repair of Waltham Church, in which he was buried. One of his most intimate friends was Fuller's patron, the second Earl of Carlisle, who lived at Waltham Abbey, and is buried in the chancel. And so we might follow the connections of John Foxe's family with the Forest right down to the last century; but we must return to our period.

CHAPTER IV

MANY of the great Elizabethans lived in the Forest, others came as visitors. Roger Ascham, the queen's tutor, who was born two years before Foxe, lived for a time at Walthamstow, which was then a small village. Ascham was probably the best Greek scholar in England, and he was a master of English. Along with Sir John Cheke and Thomas Wilson he set himself against over-elaboration of style, the 'ink-horn' terms and 'aureate' phraseology of the period. In his desire to set the English language free from continental influences he demanded the discipline of the classics in writing, but made a blunder in trying to establish classical versification in a language which cannot employ it naturally.

Ascham had great faith in the value of physical recreation, prescribing the use of the bow as a necessary national exercise. Towards the end of his life he took up cock-fighting. So, although a scholar, Ascham was an open-air man who must have enjoyed life in the king's forest.

He came to Walthamstow on obtaining, through Sir William Petre, a grant from the queen of the lease of Salisbury Hall Farm, at the low rent of twenty pounds a year. In 1559, Mr. Bosworth of Walthamstow tells us in *The Manors of Low Hall and Salisbury Hall, Walthamstow*, he had to mortgage his lease, owing to the circumstances of his wife's father. *The Scholemaster*, which occupied the last five years of his life, was written in the Forest, at the invitation of Sir Richard Sackville, one of whose descendants comes into our story later.

Ascham was never robust. His death in 1568 was the result of applying himself too closely to the composition of a poem intended as a present to the queen on the anniversary of her accession. That, at all events, is the story repeated in biographical sketches, though, if true, it would appear that death in his case was due to highly unnatural causes. When Elizabeth heard of his death, she said: 'I would rather have cast ten thousand pounds into the sea than have lost my Ascham.'

Roger Ascham was not the only royal tutor of the period with Forest associations. A Leyton lady, Lady Margaret Bryan, was

governess to the Princesses Mary and Elizabeth, and to Prince
Edward. Her son, Sir Francis Bryan, shared the king's revels
and sports in the Forest. He was cousin to Anne Boleyn, and
was sent to the pope in an endeavour to persuade him to dissolve
Henry's marriage with Catherine.

Another royal servant was Edward Elrington, of Birch Hall,
Theydon Bois, who was chief butler to Edward VI, Mary, and
Elizabeth.

At Cambridge Ascham was influenced by Sir Thomas Smith,
a Saffron Walden man who settled in the Forest, and rebuilt
Hill Hall, Theydon Mount, near Epping. This fine old hall was
built by Sir Thomas in Renaissance style from a design made by
John of Padua, whom Sir Thomas met during his travels in Italy,
but the design was spoilt when the hall was altered about 1713.
The great entrance hall, fifty-six feet by twenty feet, was added
later again. Theydon Mount estate was acquired by Sir Thomas
when he married as his second wife the widow of Sir John Hamp-
den, and Hill Hall is built in a commanding position, with views
almost as extensive as those from the neighbouring Toot Hill,
one of the finest view-points in, or near, the Forest.

In the church at Theydon Mount may be seen a memorial to
Sir Thomas Smith, and this time we have none of the uncomfort-
able recollections we had in looking at the memorials of Sir
William Petre and Lord Rich. Sir Thomas is represented as a
dignified figure, wearing the mantle of the Garter. Round the
arch under which he lies we read:

'What ye Earth or Sea or Skies conteyne, what Creatures in
them be, My Mynde did seeke to knowe, my Soule the Heavens
continually.'

After walking in the lanes about Theydon Mount, it is pleasant
to sit for a while in the simple little church and reflect upon the
life of this true-hearted English gentleman. It is recorded of him
that he never raised the rents of his tenants, and that he never put
one out of his holding. He never sued any man, nor did any man
sue him. When he died, in 1577, at the age of sixty-five, he was
famous as a philosopher, statesman, mathematician, and historian. He wrote: *Voyage and Entertainment in Russia*; *The
Whole Art of Gunnery*; *The Authority, Form, and Manner of holding Parliaments*, and many other works. The most famous of
his writings is the *De Republica Anglorum; the Maner of Government or Policie of the Realme of England*, which was finished in

1565, though not printed until 1583, six years after his death. It is written in the simple, unadorned language that Ascham admired and copied, but though we can still appreciate the lucid and concise style in which the book is written, it is difficult now to appreciate fully the importance of its arguments to the Elizabethan world. A reprint of *De Republica Anglorum*, edited by F. W. Maitland and L. Alston, was published in 1906.

England had been behind the Continent in political thought until the break from Rome made independent politics necessary. After that break patriotic sentiment became intense. There was great respect for the authority of the Crown in Mary's reign, but the oppression of Protestants made such men as Sir Thomas Smith realize that it had become necessary for someone to try to define a better state ideal. Sir Thomas compared England with other countries, and boldly classed it not with the monarchies, but with the democracies.

As a staunch Protestant himself, he was forced to retire from public affairs during Mary's reign, and thus gained time for reflection. He had travelled extensively, and possessed considerable learning. In spite of the persecution under Mary, he still upheld to the full the popular respect for the Crown, though he felt that the power of the sovereign should be restricted. In considering the Aristotelian forms of government he did not feel that England could conform to any one of them singly. Though he visualized England as essentially a democrary, it was one in which the Crown, the nobility, and the yeomanry should all play their parts and preserve their stations. Free co-operation of all classes for the good of the community was the ideal he kept in mind. Shakespeare had the same idea when he wrote the speech on degree in *Troilus and Cressida*:

> . . . O, when degree is shaked,
> Which is the ladder to all high designs,
> The enterprise is sick! How could communities,
> Degrees in schools, and brotherhoods in cities,
> Peaceful commerce from dividable shores,
> The primogenitive and due of birth,
> Prerogative of age, crowns, sceptres, laurels,
> But by degree stand in authentic place?
> Take but degree away, untune that string,
> And, hark, what discord follows!

Though we cannot claim Shakespeare himself for the Forest, his name appears in its records. A Simon Sakesper was one of the verderers in 1250.

* B

The Smith family trace their descent from the Black Prince, through Roger de Clarendon, his natural son; but Sir Thomas remains the most distinguished member of the family. At Cambridge he established a reputation as a scholar. Later he became provost of Eton, reforming the pronunciation of Greek there. Latimer, Ridley, and Cranmer were all indebted to his learning and sound judgment, while Somerset made use of his statesmanship by sending him abroad as an ambassador. It must have been a severe blow when Mary's accession drove him into retirement. But he occupied himself in rebuilding the hall, and also applied himself to studies which made him the better fitted for the distinguished part he played, both as ambassador to Paris, and as Secretary of State, when Elizabeth became queen.

Sir Thomas's great work on government ran through ten editions in the hundred years following his death. It was translated into Latin, Dutch, and German, and altogether had considerable influence in the development of modern political thought. No doubt his belief in democracy was supported by his personal knowledge of the character of the English yeoman. Such men as John Stonard of Loughton Hall and others of his kind, who would be known to him, were the backbone of the country. Under Mary he had seen many yeomen stand firm when courtiers appeared only anxious to retain their lands and positions, won at the Dissolution. He symbolized his own position in Mary's reign by adopting as his crest a salamander living in the midst of flames.

Sir Thomas formed a plan for the 'colonization' of Northern Ireland, and his only son was killed by a 'wild Irishman' in an attempt to put the plan into operation. The Theydon Mount estate passed to the descendants of his brother George, and continued in their possession for over three hundred years.

Theydon Garnon, the neighbouring parish to Theydon Mount, was the home of Robert Fabyan, the chronicler of the second half of the fifteenth century, who died in 1513. He wrote *New Chronicles of England and France*, a work based on records made by monks. Fabyan's work was quoted by John Richard Green in his *Short History of the English People*.

During Elizabeth's reign interesting political experiments were being made. One of them took form in what is called the 'Liberty of Havering-atte-Bower,' where the tenants and inhabitants were constituted one body corporate and politic to possess the lordship of the 'Liberty.' The steward of the manor and one of the 'discreetest and honestest' tenants or inhabitants were given power to try all felons, trespassers, and persons who committed unlawful acts within the manor. In cases of treason or felony, the reservation was made that the king's leave must be obtained.

No officers of the crown, noblemen, or men of great state might take anything from the tenants, or set up any fences against their will. These tenants and inhabitants of Havering-atte-Bower, and their heirs and successors, were released from any obligation to answer before any justices, judges, or commissioners in any action referring to their land or tenements in the manor, in any court outside it. These privileges were achieved by degrees, until the main points were finally confirmed by James I. One interesting provision was that there should be a hospital for the relief of the poor and sick.

The Liberty probably originated in the desire of sovereigns, who frequently resided there, to have special authority within its boundaries. For this purpose it was separated from the rest of the kingdom. But in the privileges allowed under the Tudors it is interesting to find democratic ideas being developed in a district so deeply rooted in monarchic tradition.

CHAPTER V

The Green Knight, George Gascoigne of Walthamstow

SIR THOMAS SMITH turned to letters in adversity. Normally, literature is a flower that flourishes in freedom, so the liberation of a vast section of the community from feudalism during the Tudor period produced in a single generation an astonishing spate of writing. Playhouses were filled. Actors prospered. The godly saw the Bible and Foxe's *Book of Martyrs* go into every parish. The wealth of the land fell into the hands of landed gentry and merchant adventurers, who directed it into new channels. The whole island was quickened into activity. Men of action were also men of imagination. Enterprise was a summoning bell, and the tide was there to be taken. Material and spiritual interests were not divided as they became later when the wealth gained had to be guarded, and a less creative type came into power. Courtiers were poets, and poets were adventurers. The new nobility tingled with personality.

Against this background we see George Gascoigne of Waltham-stow—the Green Knight, as he chose to style himself—Nicholas Breton, his stepson, and Thomas Lodge of Leyton, who wrote *Rosalynde*, upon which Shakespeare founded *As You Like It*. Gascoigne married the well-to-do widow of William Breton. She was living in Walthamstow at the time, and like Gascoigne himself she was of Yorkshire stock. Nicholas, her son, was only a few years younger than his stepfather. The date of birth is uncertain with both, but they were probably born in the fifteen-forties. The two were good friends. William Breton, Nicholas's father, had owned Dice Quay, near Billingsgate. He had been a prosperous business man. Nicholas cared little for money, but he was ambitious to become a poet like his stepfather.

We can imagine the two sitting together in their garden at Walthamstow, Gascoigne talking of the days when he, as he put it, 'professed arms in the defence of God's truth,' taking care not to disclose that he took to soldiering to escape from his creditors. Like most of the wealthy men of his time, Gascoigne had been a gay dog in his youth, though whenever his friends reminded him of those merry days, he complained that his youthful indiscretions had been exaggerated by slanderous report. Nicholas

28

may have had his own opinion about that. Had not old Sir John Gascoigne disinherited his son? And what of the love poems, those 'lewd lines' of his youth, that he regretted so eloquently? Gascoigne preferred to forget his mistresses after settling with his wife at Walthamstow. But when his friends, Sir Walter Raleigh or Sir Humphrey Gilbert, came down to visit him, or his relative, Sir Martin Frobisher, who owned land at Walthamstow, and came to look over it, Gascoigne liked to entertain them with his account of the siege of Middelburg.

'It was in '72, was it not?' we can imagine we hear one of them asking, 'that you sailed for Holland?'

'Aye,' we hear Gascoigne reply, 'I had received a captain's commission in the army of the Prince of Orange. Well do I remember the crossing. The pilot was drunk, and twenty of the crew were drowned. The prince was ever my good friend.'

That was true. There was the occasion when the poet became involved in an affair with a lady at The Hague, which was occupied at the time by enemy troops. The lady wrote him a letter about a portrait he had given her. This letter fell into the hands of his colonel, who made use of it to persuade the Dutch burghers that Gascoigne was unfaithful to their cause. In explaining the affair in later life, Gascoigne would often avoid reference to the lady, but would complain bitterly about the colonel, whose vindictiveness, he said, caused him privations lasting 'a winter's tide.' The following year the prince had the whole affair laid before him and the poet's honour was vindicated. The prince also gave him passports for visiting the lady.

At the siege of Middelburg Gascoigne had shown great bravery, and the prince had presented him with

> Three hundred guilders good above my pay,
> And bad me bide till his abilitie
> Might better guerdon my fidelitie.

Then there was the story of the attack on the unfinished fort at Valkenburg. Reinforcements had been sent from England to the Spaniards. Gascoigne, serving under Captain Sheffield, had been sent to the fort. Soon after their arrival the attack began. The Spaniards numbered three thousand, the Dutch five hundred. In addition, the fortifications were incomplete and the garrison short of provisions and ammunition. Gascoigne and his companions were forced to retreat to Leyden. They arrived to find the gates of the town closed against them, and were forced to

surrender to the Spaniards who were close behind them, though
they were able to do so upon what were considered to be honourable terms.   After four months' captivity the officers were sent
home to their own countries.

Gascoigne expressed his disillusionment in *The Fruites of Warre*:

> My promise was, and I record it so,
> To write in verse (God wot, though little worth)
> That war seems sweet to such as little know
> What comes thereby, what fruits it bringeth forth:
> Who knows none evil his mind no bad abhors,
> But such as once have felt the scorching fire,
> Will seldom efte to play with flame desire.
>
> Then war is bad; and so it is indeed,
> Yet are three sorts which therein take delight,
> But who they be now hearken and take heed,
> For (as I may) I mean their names to write,
> The first hight *haughty heart*, a man of might,
> The second *greedy mind* most men do call,
> And *miser* (he the mome) comes last of all.

Gascoigne had many tales of adventure to entertain his friends
with when they visited him at Walthamstow.   His wife probably
preferred to talk about the queen's regard for her gallant husband.
There was the occasion when he attended my Lord Leicester at
Kenilworth, assisting in the production of masques and pageants
for the entertainment of Elizabeth.   Gascoigne's contribution
was entitled *Princely Pleasures*, but the queen left before it was
produced, though the players had been ready in their costumes
for two or three days, waiting to be called.   When Her Majesty
announced that she was about to leave, Leicester turned to Gascoigne and begged him to devise something quickly, so that she
might not go without due ceremony.   The poet must often have
told his guests in the Forest how he dressed as Sylvanus, the
god of the woods, and met the queen while she was out hunting.
How he ran alongside her horse, and how, when she called a halt,
fearing the poet might become short of breath, he humbly be-
sought her to continue, declaring that he would rather be Her
Majesty's footman on earth than a god on horseback in heaven.
'Dame Flora' was entreated to make it continually spring for
her, 'with stores of redolent and fragrant flowers,' Ceres to yield
plenty, and Bacchus to send her the first fruits of his vineyards.

Those were splendid memories.   Gascoigne was always an
exuberant rhymer of great metrical dexterity.   No doubt Nicholas Breton would tell his friends how his stepfather once im-

provised poems in five metres given to him by friends riding with him on horseback.

Sitting in the garden at Walthamstow the poet must often have thought about the festivities at Kenilworth, and wished he could talk them over with old Dr. Mulcaster, that fine old scholar from Cumberland, who had just retired to the living at Stanford Rivers after twelve years as headmaster of St. Paul's School. Mulcaster, too, had figured in the Kenilworth festivities. It was of this Dr. Mulcaster that Fuller wrote: 'It may be truly said (and safely for one out of his school) that others have taught as much learning with fewer lashes.'

It was Gascoigne's way at Walthamstow to affect the tone of wise old age. He should have been in the prime of life, but it was probably difficult to believe that there was so little difference in age between Nicholas Breton, who developed slowly, and gives the impression in his work of being younger than his years, and Gascoigne the man of experience.

It was true that Gascoigne had crowded a great deal into his short life, and that, on the whole, he had been disillusioned by adventure. He now preferred honour and respect as a poet. At Walthamstow he spent most of his time preparing his works for the press. They contained, he found, a great deal of embarrassing material he would dearly love to suppress. On the other hand, the best poetry was in the more daring stanzas, so he could not afford to sacrifice them. He would, however, make it clear that he regretted the morals.

Gascoigne had become extremely jealous of his fame, feeling acutely the envy of rivals and the malevolence of critics. In fact, he fretted so much about these things that his health was undermined. His inactivity at Walthamstow caused him to brood too much over his lost youth. Nicholas, always a cheerful companion, could make him feel gay and vigorous again at times; but his most common mood was one of sombre moralizing. The writer of fulsome love poetry in youth now found most pleasure in composing such passages as this:

'The minds of young men, being only trained in knowledge of the arts, and never persuaded in points of moral reformation, become oftentimes so proud and so heady that they are carried away with a vain imagination of their own excellence. . . . For the mind of man is so heavenly a thing, and of such rare excellence, that it always worketh, and cannot be idle. And if with the quickness

of conceit it be tempered by a modest moderation, to have regard
unto virtue and morality, then proveth it both goodly and godly;
whereas if it be headstrong, only led by natural considerations of
causes, it may prove admirable for some passing quality, but
it seldom is seen commendable, or allowed to perfection.'

Gascoigne had reached the stage where the indiscretions of
youth become a grave responsibility. Men did not see in his day
any more than in ours, that when a man begins to take the problem of youth so seriously, he has himself become part of the much
more serious problem of age. However grave a matter youth
may be, it is at worst a sickness from which most men recover.

Among Gascoigne's friends at Walthamstow was Bartholomew
Withypoll. When Bartholomew, 'Mine owne good Bat,' was
about to take a journey to Genoa, Gascoigne gave him some sober
advice. Apparently the youth was given to gaiety, for Gascoigne
advised him to 'jape not over much,' for the fault of japing

> hath run to fast
> Both in thy flesh and fancie too sometime.

He was also advised to say his prayers daily:

> First, euery day beseech thy God on knee
> So to direct thy staggring steppes alway
> That he which euery secrete thought doth see
> May holde thee in, when thou wouldst goe astray:
> And that he deigne to sende thee safe retoure
> And quicke dispatche of that whiche is thy due.

Gascoigne also begged Bartholomew not to return to Walthamstow an Englishman Italianate, decked with newfangled continental fashions. Finally he bade him beware of wine, women,
and wilfulness.

In literary history Gascoigne is entitled to a prominent place.
He wrote what is often claimed to be the first prose comedy in
English, *The Supposes*, from which Shakespeare is said to have
borrowed his underplot for *The Taming of the Shrew*. He wrote
the second English tragedy in blank verse, *Jocasta*. It has been
claimed for him that he wrote the first masque, the first regular
satire, and the first treatize on poetry, *Certayne Notes of Instruc-
tion*, a brief and excellent essay, in which, like his master Ronsard,
he assumes that verse is the condition if not the essence of poetry.

Gascoigne died in 1577. Nicholas Breton continued to think
about him. He remembered the pleasure it had given his step-

father to set up those simple verses at the end of his Close Walk
at Walthamstow:

> If any flower that here is grown,
>   Or any herb, may ease your pain,
> Take and account it as your own,
>   But recompense the like again;
> For some and some is honest play,
> And so my wife taught me to say.
>
> If here to walk you take delight,
>   Why, come, and welcome when you will:
> If I bid you sup here this night,
>   Bid me another time, and still
> Think some and some is honest play,
> For so my wife taught me to say.
>
> Thus, if you sup or dine with me,
>   If you walk here, or sit at ease;
> If you desire the thing you see,
>   Or have the same your mind to please,
> Think some and some is honest play,
> And so my wife taught me to say.

And those other verses for a seat in his garden:

> If thou sitte here to viewe this pleasant garden place,
> Think thus: At last will come a frost, and all these flouers deface
> But if thou sitte at ease to rest thy wearie bones,
> Remember death brings finall rest to all oure greeuous grones:
> So whether for delight, or here thou sitte, for ease,
> Think still upon the latter day, as shalt thou God best please.

BRETON did little writing until after Gascoigne's death, but he was undoubtedly greatly influenced by his stepfather's work. Throughout his formative years Walthamstow, which would have a population of not more than two thousand at the time, was his home, and the Forest became the background to his fancy.

Breton struck the lighter note which became characteristic of the Elizabethan miscellanies, the 'sweet pipings' and 'native wood notes wild' that came before Ben Jonson's polished and classically pointed verses of a few years later. He does not give the impression of having been a scholar; but he had a natural and easy gift of rhyming which Gascoigne must have encouraged him to cultivate. The cast of his mind was less heroic than his stepfather's, but his genuine appreciation of nature was far greater. Small country things delighted him in the way they were later to delight John Clare, with whom he has some affinities. Nature was friendly to Breton. He would creep up to see

> . . . the subtle fox,
> How the villain plies the box;
> After feeding on his prey,
> How he closely sneaks away,
> Through the hedge and down the furrow,
> Till he gets into his burrow;
> Then the bee to gather honey;
> And the little black-hair'd coney
> On a bank for sunny place
> With her forefeet wash her face.

A natural sweetness of temper is reflected in everything that Breton wrote, a perpetual springtime of light-heartedness. The pastoral mood came naturally to him. The graceful tunefulness of his lines suggests a heart at ease. Of his life we know little. In middle age he described himself as 'a certaine odde Diogenes of the world, like a forlorne creature on the earth, throwne lately out of the fortune of his Mistres favour,' but we must not imagine that he was seriously bewailing his lot. He appears to have lost part of the wealth he inherited from his father. At all events, he says in his last book that he has little money himself, so persuades himself that it is a dangerous metal, the ruin of the wicked.

It suited his quiet humour to note the changes of the seasons and the simple circumstances of human life, sometimes registering his impressions without adornment, sometimes enlivening his descriptions with his own capricious fancy. 'Now are the hedges ful of Berries, and the highwayes full of Rogues,' is a characteristic reflection. Again, it is six o'clock, and through his mind run all the circumstances of the hour:

'It is now the sixth houre, the sweet time of the Morning, and the Sunne at every window calls the Sleepers from their beds; the Marygold beginnes to open her leaves, and the Dew on the ground doth sweeten the Ayre: the Faulconers now meet with many a faire flight, and the Hare and the Hounds have made the Huntsman good sport: the Shoppes in the City begin to shew their wares, and the market people have taken their places. The Schollers now have their Fourmes, and whosoever cannot say his Lesson, must presently looke for Absolution: the Forester now is drawing home to his Lodge, and if his Deere be gone, he may draw after cold scent: Now begins the curst Mistresse to put her Girles to their taskes, and a lazy Hylding will doe hurt among good Workers: Now the Mower falles to whetting of his Sythe, and the Beaters of Hempe give a hoh to every blow! The Ale Knight is at his cup ere hee can well see his drinke, and the Begger is as nimble toung'd, as if hee had beene at it all day.'

He liked to let his mind run over the characters he had met, presenting them to us in the soft, mellow light of his quiet style. Returning home from his walk, we can imagine him settling down like his own 'Countryman' to 'a Crust and an Orenge, a Sallad and a cup of Sack . . . then after all, a stretch and a yaune, and a pipe of Tobacco, weare bootes for want of shooes, or else that the garters and the roses are at pawne.'

He would stay for a gossip with a farmer's servant girl, and listen quietly to her tale of troubles, remembering every grievance in order:

'I must serve the olde Woman, I must learne to spinne, to reele, to carde, to knit, to wash buckes, and by hande, brew, bake, make Mault, reape, bind sheaves, weede in the Garden, milke, serve Hogges, make cleane theyr houses; within doores, make beddes, sweepe filthy houses, rubbe dirtie ragges, beate out the olde Coverlets, drawe up olde holes: Then to the kitchin, turne the Spitte, although it was but seldome, for we had not rost meate often: then scoure Pottes, wash Dishes, fetch in Wood, make a fire, scalde milke Pannes, wash the Cherne and butter dishes, wring up a Cheese clout, set everything in good order. And, alas, to all this, was but another maid and I.'

His delight in the domestic life about him finds expression constantly, and his accounts are always animated and graphic. Yet a letter is attributed to Breton which suggests that he endured his share of life's misfortunes, including being 'plagued with an unquiet wife,' and being 'indebted to his heart's grief, and fain would pay and cannot.'

The Elizabethans had conventions of joy and sorrow: but there is a naïve candour about most of Breton's work that usually makes us inclined to believe him. He never soared to any heights; he never sank to any depths; he is often long-winded and he prattles; but he inspires affection and infects us with his own blithe spirit. Who could resist his description of country delights?

'Now for the delight of our Eyes, wee have the May-painting of the Earth, with Flowers of dainty colours and delicate sweets: we have the Berryes, the Cherries, the Pease and the Beanes, the Plums and the Codlings, in the month of June: in July the Peares and the Apples, the Wheat, the Rye, the Barley and the Oates, the beauty of the wide Fields, and the labours with delight and mirth, and merry cheare at the comming home of the harvest cart. We have, againe, in our Woods the Birds singing: in the pastures the Cowe lowing, the Eue bleateing, and the Foale neighing, which with profit and pleasure makes us better musique than an idle note and a worse ditty, though I highly doe commend Musique, when it is in a right key. Againe, we have young Rabbets that in a sunny morning sit washing of their Faces, while as I have heard beyond the Seas there are certaine old Conies that in their Beds sit painting of their faces: wee have besides Tumblers for our Conies, and Greyhounds for our Courses, Hounds for our Chases, Haukes of all kinde for the Field, and the River, and the Wood: so that what can reason conceive, that nature can desire? but for the delight of both the country doth afford us. . . . And having all this, if we serve God withall, what in God's name can we desire to have more?'

Nicholas Breton was a natural accepter, happy to take life as he found it. If he disliked any one, it was the grumbler. One of his most serious efforts is an attack upon those who complained about the Government. It was typical of him to be

satisfied with things, and impatient with reformers; but there
was more in it than that.   His defence of existing institutions was
characteristic of many of his contemporaries too.   We have seen
how loth Sir Thomas Smith was to disturb the order of the State.
Shakespeare was no reformer.   A great reformation had come in
Henry's reign.   Things were going well in Elizabeth's, and there
was a desire to see life settled.   Breton argues, as the Greeks had
argued before him, and the scholastic philosophers after them,
that the State was an organism like the body, with power distributed through various organs which fulfilled mean or noble
purposes by design.   Breton's expression of this idea is eloquent,
if quite unconvincing to those who cannot accept the analogy.
In modern spelling it reads:

'God made all the parts of the body for the soul and with the
soul to serve Him, and all the subjects in a kingdom to serve their
king and with their king to serve Him.   If the head of the body
ache, will not the heart be greatly grieved, and every part feel
his part of the pain of it?   And shall a king in his will be displeased
and the heart of his kingdom (the hearts of his subjects) not have
any feeling of it? . . . Can the labourer, the foot, be wounded,
but the body of the state will feel it, the head be careful, the eye
searchful, and the hand be painful in the cure of it?   And can
the commonwealth, the body, be diseased, but the king, his
council, and every true subject will put to his hand for the
help of it?'

Nicholas Breton was probably in the service of Sir Philip
Sidney.   Amongst his friends he numbered John Florio, the
translator of Montaigne, who must have been a congenial spirit.
To Florio he sent a copy of *A Mad World, my Masters,* inscribed:
'A token of my love, in a little fruit of my labour.'   Francis
Bacon was his learned and honoured friend, and addressing the
Countess of Pembroke he subscribed himself as 'Your Ladyship's
sometime unworthy Poet and now and ever your Beadman,
Nich Breton.'

The link with Sidney is interesting from the Forest point of
view, because Elizabeth saw a pastoral from his pen performed in
her honour at Wanstead when she visited the Earl of Leicester there.
Perceval gives a full account of the occasion in *London's Forest.*

He tells us that as the queen walked in the garden at Wanstead
House, she was accosted by a woman 'attired like an honest man's
wife of the country,' who asked the queen's advice.   The daughter

of this countrywoman had two lovers, one a shepherd, the other a forester. The girl was unable to decide which to favour, liking them equally well. At this point the two lovers were heard quarrelling in the Forest, and appeared on the scene in the company of the undecided young lady. The village schoolmaster was trying to settle their differences, and was treated with scant ceremony for his pains. The queen was appealed to, though with the admission that, beautiful as the maiden was, her beauty was not to be compared with Her Majesty's—'the beautifullest lady these woods have ever received.'

We learn that the forester was a high-spirited youth who would steal venison for his loved one, as well as perform 'prettier services.' But he had a bad temper. The shepherd was less dashing as a lover, but never hurt his lady's feelings. After hearing much song and argument the queen was pleased to pronounce in favour of the shepherd.

That Sidney was bold enough to hint that the forester was given to stealing venison, yet remained a candidate for favour, is interesting, in view of the forest laws. It is, however, the fact that these laws were not administered with any severity during Elizabeth's reign, or indeed under any of the Tudors. The pardon granted to John Potter of Chigwell in December 1541, for hunting and slaying deer in the Forest, is one of many instances of the relative clemency of the Tudors.

Only a turf-covered mound remains now to mark the site of Wanstead House, but a picture of Elizabeth, with the old Wanstead House in the background, is to be seen at Welbeck.

Elizabeth is still remembered in the Forest whenever we pass the old lodge at Chingford. It is believed that the sides of this building were originally open, and that it was a kind of grandstand, from which the royal party might watch the hunt.

No words ever spoken by the queen were more inspiring than those addressed to her soldiers at Tilbury: 'I know I have the body but of a weak and feeble woman, but I have the heart and stomach of a king, and a king of England, too.' They were spoken when the Spaniards threatened England, and we remember that the hundred of Becontree, which includes West Ham, East Ham, Walthamstow, Leyton, and Ilford, is named from the beacon which blazed on Windmill Hill at Woodford, summoning the knights of the Forest to take up arms in their country's defence.

CHAPTER VII

Thomas Lodge at Leyton—The martyrdom on Stratford Green—*Rosalynde* and *As You Like It*—William Byrd at Stondon Place—Thomas Tallis at Waltham Abbey

UNLIKE Breton, Thomas Lodge, our third Elizabethan poet, did not find the world a gay and sunny place. He was born at West Ham in 1558, the son of Sir Thomas Lodge, the Lord Mayor of London whose ships began the carrying of slaves from Africa.

Five years before Lodge was born, the people of West Ham had seen a splendid cavalcade of knights and ladies ride through the village. With this cavalcade was the Princess Elizabeth on her way from London to greet her half-sister Mary at Wanstead House. Mary was about to be proclaimed queen. From Wanstead House Mary entered London amidst scenes of such splendour as only a Tudor could evoke. She reigned five years, and before the end of her reign West Ham had witnessed scenes of another kind. A different procession, a mob of ill-clad, avid people had passed through on their way to the martyrdom on Stratford Green, afterwards called Gallows Green. They had seen eleven men tied to three stakes, and two women, untied, standing with them, burned to death 'with such love to one another, that it made all the lookers-on marvel.' As a boy Lodge must have heard of these things. As a man he may have watched, at the same place, William Kempe, the great comedian and buffoon from Shakespeare's company, trip through Stratford on his nine day's morris dance from London to Norwich. There is little in the Stratford of to-day to remind us of all the comedy, romance, and tragedy of its history. Yet lovers of literature cannot forget how early it was immortalized in Chaucer's lines:

> And Frensh she spak ful fairè and fetisly,
> After the scole of Stratford atte Bowe,
> For Frensh of Paris was to hir unknowe.

Sir Thomas, the poet's father, was a quarrelsome man. In his seventieth year he was found guilty of assault upon a fellow alderman. Twice he went to prison for debt, though he was a member of a wealthy city company. The poet inherited his father's temperament. When his mother died, leaving him property in Essex, the trustee refused to make a conveyance to

39

him because of 'the disorderly kynd of lyffe that he sawe or deemed
to be' his. Both father and son were excessively assertive
individualists.

Like Gascoigne, Lodge had the Elizabethan flair for combining
literature with a life of action. He was both soldier and physician
as well as poet. In the early 1590's he accompanied Thomas
Cavendish to Brazil and the Straits of Magellan. *Rosalynde*
itself, by which he is now remembered, was written at sea, every
page wet with spray. In spite of all he had heard about Catholic
persecution he became a convert to that religion, probably as a
result of his association with the monks of the Jesuit College at
Santos in Brazil.

He settled in Leyton in 1596. In 1600 he took a medical
degree at Avignon, and later a doctorate in medicine at Oxford.
For many years he practised as a doctor in Leyton, finding time
also to write histories and satirical romances, most of them now
forgotten. Like Gascoigne, he repented his love poems, writing
at Leyton *Wit's Miserie, The World's Madnesse*, and *Prosopopeia*,
in which he regretted his 'lewd lines' of other days. Repentance
did not improve his poetry. His love poems remain, his peni-
tential pieties are forgotten.

Towards the end of his life Lodge wrote a treatise on the plague,
and is said to have died a victim of that scourge.

Wild acclamation quickly turned to bleak despair in Mary's
short reign, though the despair can be exaggerated—'Many who
were burnt in Mary's reign drank sack in Elizabeth's.' When
James became king, a similar change was witnessed. It sprang
from a different cause. During the last ten years of Elizabeth's
reign every one was wondering what would happen when she died.
Anarchy and civil war were expected. When James gained the
throne without effective opposition the relief of the people resulted
in delirious demonstrations. Lady Anne Clifford wrote in her
diary:

'About 10 o'clock King James was proclaimed in Cheapside by
all the Council with great joy and triumph. I went to see and
hear. The peaceable coming in of the King was unexpected by
all sorts of people.'

But within a few months the scene changed. Thirty thousand
people, one-eighth of the population, had died of the plague in
London.

The atmosphere of these distressing times is felt in Shakespeare's

King Lear, but little of it is found in Lodge's *Rosalynde*, upon which Shakespeare founded *As You Like It*. *Rosalynde* itself was based on *The Tale of Gamelyn*, a romance of the fourteenth century formerly attributed to Chaucer. The pastoral setting, however, was new to the plot, and so was the love story, which heralds the fiction of later centuries. Pastoral romance, of course, was by no means unfamiliar to the Elizabethans. Sidney's *Arcadia* was, in fact, published in the same year as *Rosalynde*, though it had been written ten years earlier.

These pastorals were entirely conventional and sophisticated. The poets who sang so sweetly of the country rarely lived in it. Greene, one of the most popular of them, died in a London slum. Lodge had no more interest in the country than Greene, though one sentence in *Rosalynde* suggests that he may have ventured into our Forest thickets at some time:

'Take heed, forester; step not too far, the ford may be deep, and you slip over the shoes: I tell thee, flies have their spleen, the ants choler.'

One of the sources of the Elizabethan pastoral was *Diana Enamorada*, by Jorge de Montemayor, which Lodge, with his knowledge of Spanish, would have read. These conventionalized pastorals are not very convincing to the Englishman of to-day, for, as Steele pointed out in a later century, 'The difference of the climate is also to be considered, for what is proper in Arcadia, or even in Italy, may be quite out of place in a colder country.'

In manner Lodge was the child of his age, ornate and fantastic. His flattering speech: 'It is she, O gentle swain, it is she, that saint it is to whom I serve, that goddess at whose shrine I do bend all my devotions; the most fairest of all fairs, the phoenix of all that sex, and the purity of all earthly perfection,' is similar in character to Gascoigne's elaborate and ridiculous compliments to Elizabeth at Kenilworth, and Sidney's at Wanstead.

Rosalynde was the last book of note to employ this convention of language. But it is graceful and can be read to-day without irritation, which cannot be said of Greene's *Menaphon*. The story is told reasonably well, and it has the English love of adventure and respect for woman.

When Shakespeare came to use Lodge's *Rosalynde* for the plot of *As You Like It*, he condensed it and treated it in a most interesting way. The time of action, which runs to several months in the romance, takes ten days in the play. The love plot is given greater prominence, and the features generally become clearer, as though we were seeing through a window that had been cleaned, characters who had been brought nearer. Interesting comparisons can be made, though it has to be remembered that Shakespeare was writing in verse, Lodge in prose. When Alinda pleads before King Torismond, she says:

'Rosalynde and I have been fostered up from our infancies, and nursed under the harbor of our conversing together with such private familiarities, that custom had wrought a union of our nature, and the sympathy of our affections such a secret love, that we have two bodies and one soul.'

Shakespeare's Celia says:

> . . . if she be a traitor,
> Why so am I; we still have slept together,
> Rose at an instant, learn'd, play'd, eat together;
> And whereso'er we went, like Juno's swans,
> Still we went coupled and inseparable.

Lodge lived in the age of the lute, the viol, and the virginal, at the time when music and poetry were wedded, and the union blessed as never before in England, and never since. Poetry was composed for the singing voice. It had variations in pitch as well as in metre, and the repetitions which sometimes appear monotonous to us were full of meaning when presented in different modulations. So often now we find that when poetry is set to music the melody of the poet is sacrificed to the melody of the musician. With the Elizabethans this rarely happened. The words sang themselves into tunes, and the composer's part was a natural and almost inevitable extension of the poet's. Nothing could be more mellifluous than Lodge's

> Love in my bosom like a bee
> Doth suck his sweet,

or:

> Like to the clear in highest sphere
> Where all imperial glory shines.

'There is not any music of instruments whatsoever,' said William Byrd, whom Essex also claims, 'comparable to that which is made of the voices of men.'

Lodge's songs were written for the voices of men.

Byrd was the most popular musician at Elizabeth's court, and he lived at Stondon Place, Stondon Massey, near Ongar, for thirty years, first as tenant and later as owner. In his will he trusted that he might die there and be buried near his wife. We do not know whether he did, in fact, die at Stondon Massey or not, because the parish registers earlier than 1700 have disappeared; but it is at least probable that he did.

Stondon Place was part of the sequestered estates of William Shelley, who had been found guilty of complicity in a 'popish plot.' It passed through two or three hands until, in 1593, William Byrd obtained the lease for three hundred pounds. Two years later this lease was extended to cover the lives of his three children, Christopher, Elizabeth, and Rachel, and after obtaining this second lease he spent large sums of money improving the property. Byrd by this time was a well-to-do man, enjoying a good income from the exclusive privilege, which was his, of printing music and vending music paper, so he could maintain his family in good style.

Nothing of Byrd's Stondon Place remains, and such information as we have about his life in Essex shows him to have been very unpopular in the Stondon neighbourhood. He was a Catholic, and therefore unpopular with the local Protestants in those days of partisan feeling. Though a Catholic, he enjoyed the estate of a fellow Catholic who was imprisoned for his faith, and therefore he was unpopular with the local Catholics who had been friends of William Shelley.

In the Proceedings of the Archdeaconry of Essex, 11th May 1605, we find 'William Birde, Gentleman of the King's Majestie's Chapell, is presented for popish practices.' Again in 1612 the churchwardens at Stondon Massey reported to the archdeacon that 'Wyllyam Byrd, gent., hath been recusant a long tyme, no lesse than XVI. yeares as the churchwardens do think,' and the same year a further complaint was made 'for that he will not pay to the Rate for his land lying in the Parish to the reparation of the Church and bells, which some is XXs.'

When Shelley died in 1597, his widow petitioned the queen for the restoration of the property, on the ground that it had been part of her marriage jointure. Elizabeth so far admitted the justice of Mrs. Shelley's claim as to allow her to draw the rent, but upheld Byrd's right to the use of the property. Mrs. Shelley again tried to gain possession when James came to the throne, but the king stood by Byrd, writing to Mrs. Shelley, on 24th January 1604, a very reasonable letter.

'We lately upon your suit,' wrote the king, 'delivered you your

jointure lands, being our inheritance, which the late queen refused
to do. But you use our said grant contrary to our meaning to
the undoing of our servant, William Bird, Gentleman of our
Chapel. He took leases of your farm and woods of Stondon Place,
in the County of Essex, now parcel of your jointure, from the late
queen for three of his children's lives, paid fines and bestowed great
charges on the house and barns, paid his rent ever since the death
of your husband, and deserved well of you. Yet notwithstanding
you go about to thrust him out of his possessions to his present
undoing having no other house, and to the great danger of his
children's future estate. For staying of which your hard course,
neither your own conscience, nor our benignity towards you,
nor the decrees of our Exchequer Chamber yet in force, nor the
letters of our Privy Council, nor any reasonable composition
offered you by our said servant, move you. Being a woman of
great living and no charge, and having many better houses than
his, we marvel that in those lands which you so lately received
from us, and which are our inheritance, you offer so hard measure
to our servant. Whereupon we require you to permit him to
enjoy the said farm and woods, and give no cause hereafter
for complaint.'

But Mrs. Shelley was a difficult woman to suppress. Four
years later she tried again, advancing grievances against Byrd to
support her claim, one of them being that he had caused her to
spend at least £1,000 in defence of her titles, for which Byrd
could hardly be blamed. This document was sent to Cecil, who
endorsed it:

'27th October 1608.

'This matter hath bene depending in Court and therefore lett
her represent unto the Barons that which she hath there delivered
unto me, who are better acquainted with the whole proceedings
than I am, and will take some leysure to heare her complaint
for I have none.'

The suit dragged on until the old lady's death, after which Byrd
bought the estate outright from her son.

In spite of all the litigation Byrd was drawn into, he does not
appear to have been a quarrelsome man by nature. His fellow
musicians spoke of him with affectionate regard. He was a man
of wide culture. He wrote well in both Latin and English,
concisely, with a clear head and kindly heart. If he had been of a
contentious nature it is hardly likely that one so highly placed

would have escaped persecution for his religion. The grave courtesy of his prefaces was probably true to his character, and that Essex did not esteem him more highly is not to the county's credit. Byrd's family continued to be connected with Stondon Massey for at least twenty-five years after their father's death.

Thomas Tallis, Byrd's master, the father of English church music, was, as we have already seen, organist at Waltham Abbey at the Dissolution. In the Lansdowne collection (No. 763) there is a treatise on music bearing the autograph of Tallis, which was written by John Wylde, precentor of Waltham Abbey about the year 1400. It contains, we are told, all the music known at the time. The work is written on vellum, and consists of 131 folios. Immediately after leaving Waltham, Tallis went to the Chapel Royal, remaining there from 1540 to his death in 1585. Tallis was not, as some local guide-books would have us believe, organist at Waltham for thirty years. The date of his birth is uncertain, but it was probably about 1510, which would make his age thirty at the time the Dissolution affected Waltham, the last of the abbeys to be dissolved.

There used to be a memorial brass to Tallis in Greenwich Church reading:

> Enterred here doth ly a worthy wyght,
>   Who for long tyme in musick bore the bell;
> His name to shew was Thomas Tallis hyght,
>   In honest vertuous lyff he dyd excell.
>
> He serv'd long tyme in chappel with grete prayse,
>   Fower sovereygnes reygnes (a thing not often seene)
> I mean Kyng Henry and prynce Edward's dayes,
>   Quene Mary, and Elizabeth our Quene.
>
> He maryed was, though children he had none,
>   And lyv'd in love full three and thirty yeres
> With loyal spouse, whos name yclept was Jone
>   Who here entomb'd, him company now beares.
>
> As he dyd lyve, so also dyd he dy,
>   In myld and quyet sort, O happy man,
> To God ful oft for mercy did he cry,
>   Wherefore he lyves, let Deth do what he can.

When the English Book of Common Prayer was adopted, musical settings had to be made for the new liturgy. Tallis and Byrd were alive to the need, Tallis writing music for the Litany, the *Te Deum*, the *Magnificat*, the *Nunc dimittis*, and other parts of the English church service. One of his eight tunes in Day's Psalter, *Tallis's Canon*, is still used to Ken's evening hymn.

In 1575 Tallis and Byrd published together a collection of motets and hymns, and later Byrd, by the knowledge he gained from his study of Tallis, achieved his unique place amongst writers of church music. Masterly in technique, original and courteous in mind, for the beauty of his phrasing and the rightness of his notes he remains unsurpassed.

The Elizabethans explored foreign literature as well as foreign lands. Gascoigne and Lodge brought back spoils that permanently enriched our national language. For a time that language, still unaccustomed to finer usages, had difficulty in assimilating the new elements, and Ascham had reason to deplore what was too often merely a varnish on the surface, giving a gloss and polish that had no relation to the substance it covered. But it was all part of the development of our literature. Byrd and Tallis established the English tradition in the music of the church. All these men played distinguished parts in the fashioning of English culture, and the Forest is proud to have sheltered them under its wide branches, itself contributing something towards their influence.

CHAPTER VIII

Ben Jonson and Lady Mary Wroth—Ben Jonson at Loughton Hall—
The Wroths of Loughton—Sir Thomas Roe of Woodford—Forest
families

UNLIKE Gascoigne and Lodge, Ben Jonson had little taste
for repentance, though he had left his riotous youth behind
and was courting the patronage and society of the landed
gentry when he visited Loughton Hall as the guest of Sir
Robert and Lady Mary Wroth. James I was king, but he was
out of London most of the time. London was too full of
plague to be healthy.

The Elizabethan flowering of romance was over, and Ben Jonson had only contempt for its extravagances. He was born and
bred a Catholic. The florid optimism of the new Protestant
England nauseated him. But he delighted to honour his friends,
and none more highly than Lady Wroth, to whom he dedicated
The Alchemist, the most widely known of his comedies. Eric
Linklater says that the two were 'on terms of scarcely qualified
intimacy.'

Lady Wroth was a Sidney. She was a daughter of Robert
Sidney, Earl of Leicester, and the niece of Sir Philip Sidney.
She was also a poet herself, with a pastoral romance entitled
Urania, which was considered rather daring, to her credit. Ben
Jonson was not the only poet to pay homage to Lady Mary.
George Wither addressed an epigram to her as the 'Art's Sweet
Lover,' and Chapman wrote to her a sonnet which was printed
in front of his translation of the Iliad. The ladies of the Sidney
family must have been endowed with rare charms. Lady Wroth
and Lady Rutland, daughter of Sir Philip Sidney, had Ben
Jonson at their command. Lady Dorothy Sidney, Sir Philip's
grand-niece, inspired Waller to songs in which he thought he
had made her as famous as Petrarch made his Laura. *Go,
Lovely Rose* itself may have been one of these, but Lady Dorothy
rejected the poet's suit, and married the Earl of Sutherland. These
beautiful and accomplished ladies rejoiced in poetic favours, but
they had too much wit to wed their poets. Of all the poems
addressed to the Sidney ladies none surpasses William Browne's

epitaph on the Countess of Pembroke, whom Breton also had addressed :

> Underneath this sable herse
> Lies the subject of all verse:
> Sidney's sister, Pembroke's mother:
> Death, ere thou hast slain another,
> Fair and learn'd and good as she,
> Time shall throw a dart at thee.

If Lady Mary Wroth had nothing quite so perfect as that addressed to her, she had verses which declare a warmer attachment. It was to her that Jonson wrote the lines:

> Madam, had all antiquity been lost,
> All history seal'd up, and fables crost,
> That we had left us, nor by time nor place,
> Least mention of a Nymph, a Muse, a Grace,
> But even their names were to be made anew,
> Who could not but create them all from you?
> He that but saw you wear the wheaten hat,
> Would call you more than Ceres, if not that;
> And, drest in shepherd's tire, who would not say
> You were the bright Oenone, Flore, or May?
> If dancing, all would cry the Idalian Queen
> Were leading forth the Graces on the green;
> And, armèd to the Chase, so bare her bow
> Diana alone, so hit, and hunted so.
> There 's none so dull that for your style would ask,
> That saw you put on Pallas' plumèd casque;
> Or, keeping your due state, that would not cry,
> There Juno sate, and yet no peacock by:
> So you are Nature's index, and restore
> I' yourself, all treasure lost of th' age before.

Ben had a sturdy independence of speech. While he could pay compliments in this ingratiating way, he did not hesitate to remind his ladies that his celebration of their virtues would do more for them in the eyes of posterity than the virtues themselves. As we read these lines we can imagine the vivacious and talented Lady Mary, in her wheaten hat, entertaining her famous guest on the lawns in front of Loughton Hall, or strolling with him through the sunny Chigwell meadows, golden with buttercups. Ben we imagine boasting to her about his revels in the London taverns, or about the promising young men of his circle, who were going to cleanse English of all its outlandish impurities—that gay lad, Robin Herrick, for instance. She, in her turn, would have tales of the court. Then there were masques rehearsing. We know that she acted in Ben Jonson's *Masque of Blackness*, which was performed at Whitehall. Perhaps she had put on that particular hat in the hope that it would catch her poet's eye, and give him the idea of inviting her to play Ceres. When she dressed as a shepherdess, that, too, may have been done with design. And she had always been a good horsewoman. Even Sir Robert, who was no poet, must have likened her to Diana, though perhaps he had looked a bit sheepish while paying the compliment. Lady Mary may have thought how Ben would have laughed at her husband's clumsy way of paying compliments. But then Lady Mary could be sure that Sir Robert was sincere, and she could never be sure with poets.

Ben Jonson copied out Lady Mary's songs for her in his beautiful handwriting. When we remember that she had so many poetical miscellanies, published during the closing years of the sixteenth century, to provide her with models, we must acknowledge that Lady Mary showed more fluency than skill as a poet. No doubt the library at Loughton Hall had *The Paradise of Dainty Devices*, the *Gorgeous Gallery of Gallant Inventions*, and the *Handful of Pleasant Delights* to direct her numbers. *Urania* was published in 1621. Part is in prose, part in verse, and the characters are Greek shepherds and shepherdesses. One of its songs occasionally appears in anthologies:

> Dearest, if I by my discerning,
> May maintain in your thoughts my love,
> 　　Let me it still enjoy;
> 　　Nor faith destroy;
> But pity Love where it doth move.
>
> Let no other new Love invite you
> To leave me who so long have serv'd:
> 　　Nor let your power decline,
> 　　But purely shine
> On me who have all truth preserv'd.
>
> Or had you once found my heart straying,
> Then would not I accuse your change,
> 　　But being constant still,
> 　　It needs must kill
> One, whose soule knowes not how to range.
>
> Yet may you Love's sweet smiles recover,
> Since all love is not yet quite lost,
> 　　But tempt not Love too long,
> 　　Lest so great wrong
> Make him thinke he is too much crost.

Lady Mary must have looked forward to her poet's visits. No doubt she could talk charmingly to the Smiths from Hill Hall,

c

to the Hickeses from Leyton, and all those people, and could keep
the conversation going without its ever rising above Sir Robert's
head. But with Ben it must have been different. The local
people were good enough in their way, but, after all, Lady Mary
was a Sidney.

Though the hostess was undoubtedly the chief attraction at
Loughton Hall, the poet did not neglect his host. He wrote a
long poem in his honour, describing all the things the good knight
set most store upon. This poem to Sir Robert Wroth of Loughton
gives an excellent description of the life of a country gentleman
of that day:

> How blest art thou, canst love the country, Wroth,
> Whether by choice, or fate, or both.
> And though so near the city, and the Court,
> Art ta'en with neither's vice nor sport:
> That at great times, art no ambitious guest
> Of sheriff's dinner, or mayor's feast.
> Nor com'st to view the better Cloth-of-State,
> The richer hangings, or Crown-plate;
> Nor throng'st, when masquing is, to have a sight
> Of the short bravery of the night;
> To view the jewels, stuffs, the pains, the wit
> There wasted, some not paid for yet!
> But canst at home, in thy securer rest,
> Live, with unbought provision blest;
> Free from proud porches, or their gilded roofs,
> 'Mongst lowing herds, and solid hoofs:
> Along the curlèd woods, and painted meads,
> Through which a serpent river leads
> To some cool courteous shade, which he calls his,
> And makes sleep softer than it is.
> Or, if thou list the night in watch to break,
> A-bed canst hear the loud stag speak,
> In Spring, oft rousèd for thy Master's sport,
> Who for it makes thy house his Court;
> Or with thy friends, the heart of all the year
> Divid'st, upon the lesser deer:
> In Autumn, at the partridge mak'st a flight,
> And giv'st thy gladder guests the sight;
> And in the Winter, hunt'st the flying hare,
> More for thy exercise, than fare;
> While all that follow, their glad ears apply
> To the full greatness of the cry:
> Or hawking at the river, or the bush,
> Or shooting at the greedy thrush,
> Thou dost with some delight the day out-wear,
> Although the coldest of the year.
> The whilst the several seasons thou hast seen
> Of flowery fields, of copses green,
> The mowèd meadows, with the fleecèd sheep,

And feasts, that either shearers keep;
The ripen'd ears, yet humble in their height,
And furrows laden with their weight;
The apple-harvest, that doth longer last;
The hogs return'd home fat from mast;
The trees cut out in log, and those boughs made
A fire now, that lent a shade.
Thus Pan and Sylvan having had their rites,
Comus puts in for new delights;
And fills thy open hall with mirth and cheer,
As if in Saturn's reign it were;
Apollo's harp, and Hermes' lyre resound,
Nor are the Muses strangers found.
The rout of rural folk come thronging in
(Their rudeness then is thought no sin),
Thy noblest Spouse affords them welcome grace;
And the great heroes of her race
Sit mixt with loss of state, or reverence.
Freedom doth with degree dispense.
The jolly wassail walks the often round,
And in their cups their cares are drown'd:
They think not then, which side the cause shall leese,
Nor how to get the lawyer fees.

Such and no other was that Age of old,
Which boasts to have had the head of Gold.
And such, since thou canst make thine own content,
Strive, Wroth, to live long innocent. . . .

The manor of Loughton was held by the Wroth family for several generations. It had come into the possession of Sir Robert Wroth, of Enfield, the father of the Sir Robert addressed by Jonson, through marriage with the daughter of Francis Stonard. But it was held on lease—first from Waltham Abbey, and after the Dissolution from the Crown—until it was bought by the second Sir Robert, who thus became the first resident lord of the manor. At his death in 1614 he was twenty-three thousand pounds in debt. Several properties were sold to meet the creditors, but Loughton remained untouched.

Sir Robert and Lady Mary had one son, James, who was a child five weeks old when his father died. When this only child died, on 5th July 1616, the Loughton estate passed to John Wroth, brother of Sir Robert, subject to the life interest of Lady Mary, who lived to some time later than 1650, and was therefore a widow for about forty years. In his will Sir Robert also left to his wife 'all her books and furniture of her studdye and closett,' amongst other things, as 'testimony of my entire love and affection towards her, albeyet her sincere love, loyaltie, virtuous conversation, and behavioure towards me, have deserved a farre better recompense.'

The first Sir Robert had been anxious to buy the Loughton manor, partly because he wished to spend a large sum of money on necessary repairs, and partly because he had heard that the Earl of Leicester had his eye on it. Sir Robert the first had asked Sir Michael Hickes of Leyton to use his influence with the queen in the matter, promising to make the hall fit to entertain Her Majesty.

Ben Jonson tells us that James I hunted from Loughton Hall. He was not the only sovereign to be entertained there. As we have already seen, Henry VIII visited John Stonard, probably without ceremony, and Elizabeth visited the hall at least twice: first on 17th July 1561, on her way to Havering—on this occasion she stayed two days—and again in 1578, on her way from Lord Rookwood's house at Abbess Roothing to Lord Leicester's house at Wanstead. She was entertained at Loughton Hall on this second occasion immediately after holding a council at Gaynes Park, near Epping, the residence of Sir William FitzWilliam. James, it is claimed, stayed two nights at Loughton Hall.

Some repairs may have been made before James arrived, for we know that royal commissioners were at Loughton in 1602, and reported the hall in a bad state of repair. On the other hand, James may have thought it cheaper to sell. The purchase, we know, was still undecided when the second Sir Robert took up residence, because we find Lady Mary writing to Queen Anne, the wife of James I, asking her to recommend to the king her husband's request for a new lease. She makes use of a naïve argument in her letter, giving it as an additional reason why the queen should do what she can. Sir Robert, she confides, has promised to add it to her jointure if he can acquire it.

In *Urania* we find a passage that must have been written with Loughton Hall in mind:

'He replied, the place he was in was called the Forest Champion . . . a little way from thence, he told him, was a fair house, where a noble knight and his lady lived within a part of the same forest, which they had enclosed, and made like an orderly civil place, from the other's wildness, and shut themselves within a pale.' The lady in *Urania* is 'a young woman, cheerful and pleasant, the daughter of a great Lord, and sister to as fine a gentleman as was in that kingdom.'

When Sir Robert and Lady Mary did gain full possession of the hall, they rebuilt it in splendid style, employing for the purpose Inigo Jones, whom they must have known well. He devised the stage scenery and decorations for the most elaborate masques of the day. They would know him also through the Earl of Pembroke, by whom he was often employed. From a date on the leaden spouts, the rebuilding of Loughton Hall does not appear to have been completed until 1616, so Sir Robert did not live to see it.

Several interesting letters are preserved from members of the Wroth family, which give us entertaining accounts of life in the Forest in Tudor and Stuart times. There is one from the first Sir Robert of Loughton about 'sertaine lewde fellowes,' sometimes mounted, sometimes on foot, who lurked about the heath near Snaresbrook, which introduces us to the Forest footpads, of whom we shall have much to discover later. In another we find the same Sir Robert expressing his disappointment that the great Cecil did not stay with him at Loughton Hall when His Majesty visited the neighbourhood recently. We become rather fond of Sir Robert as we read these letters from him. He appears to have been a most hospitable soul. We find him inviting Leyton friends, and 'any other good company whomsoever they will bring,' to join him in hunting, and suggesting that the ladies should bring bowls with them. With the letter he sent some apricots, regretting that they were not so 'kindly' as in past years. The delightful part of the invitation is that it is completely open. 'The more the better,' he says. 'You shall be hartylie wellcome and, God willinge, wee wilbe merry, onlye this, that I am more sparing of my flesh than heretofore I have been.' With another letter he sent some 'very good oysters.'

The Wroths were a fine old family; but they have left few memorials behind them, either at Loughton or Durants, their Enfield place. Durants stood on the east side of the high road at Enfield, between Ponder's End and Green Street. It was burnt down in the eighteenth century. Of one of the Enfield Wroths Fuller says:

'Sir Thomas Wroth was of the Bedchamber, and a favourite of King Edward the Sixth, who (as I am informed) at his death passed out of the armes of him, his faithfull servant, into the embraces of Christ, his dearest Saviour. Soon after Sir Thomas found a great change in the English Court, but no alteration, as many did (to their shame), in his own conscience, in the preservation of which he was fain to fly beyond the seas.'

A member of the Wroth family appeared in an action taken in 1705 by the Corporation of London against an Essex constable. The Lord Mayor complained that his foot huntsman was committed to custody by John Wroth, Esq., a justice of the peace, for hunting the city's hounds in the Forest. Wroth, in the first place, appears to have questioned the man's statement that he was the city's huntsman, declaring that 'he was a seaman by his face.' In the second place, it appears that he wished to try the city's right of hunting in the Forest.

Lady Mary was not the only spirited woman of the Wroth family. Elizabeth Wroth, who attended her husband John, one of the verderers of the Forest, in King William's campaigns, was described as 'a woman of martial spirit.'

To-day this distinguished family is practically forgotten. We have a Wroth's Path in Loughton; but few know the history of the name. They left no inscription in church or graveyard, not even their name. Their vault is only distinguishable by the iron railings enclosing it and its lack of inscriptions. A few hatchments connected with them hung in the old deserted church of St. Nicholas; but some of these decayed and had to be taken down. Their name lives on, as Ben prophesied it would, in his own pages. It was an unlooked-for memorial; but a deserved one.

That few of Ben Jonson's readers either know or care who Sir Robert Wroth was does not matter much. He had no extraordinary claims to distinction. He was one of those thousands of English gentlemen who lived their honest lives, managed their estates, repaired the property they had inherited, dispensed hospitality, brought thieves to justice and rewarded virtue, married, and brought up their families to worship God and honour the king. Such have little claim to individual distinction; but they were the men who maintained the state of England in their generations, and stood four-square against any foe who threatened her.

Ben Jonson had other friends in the Forest. We find poems addressed to Sir John Roe, to Sir Thomas Roe, and to William Roe:

> Roe, and my joy to name, thou 'rt now to go
> Countries and climes, manners and men to know.

Thomas Roe was the nephew of John and William, and all had

local connections. Sir William Roe, or Rowe, had estates at Epping. He was godfather at the christening of John Foxe, grandson of the martyrologist, on 9th July 1593. This Sir William belonged to a distinguished family with connections at Walthamstow also. Sir Thomas Roe, Sheriff of London, 1560, purchased the manor of Higham in 1566, and was Lord Mayor of London in 1568. William, who died in 1596, rebuilt the old manor house of Benstedes. He is commemorated by a brass in St. Mary's Church, Walthamstow. Robert Roe, of Leyton, the fourth son of Sir Thomas the first, was the father of the famous traveller, also Sir Thomas. There is a verse epistle to this Sir Thomas in Donne's works, but it is now thought to have been the work of a member of Roe's own family. Sir Thomas, the traveller, could manage verse himself, as we know from his elegy on Lord Harrington.

This famous traveller, whose writings appear in the collection of narratives of travel made by Samuel Purchas, a Thaxted man, was ambassador from James I to the Great Mogul and to the Sultan of Turkey. On returning from the East, he was made Chancellor of the Order of the Garter and a privy councillor. It was he who brought back with him to this country the Alexandrian Codex.

Sir Thomas Roe was a great friend of Sir Walter Raleigh, whom he visited in the Tower. Raleigh had many friends in the Forest. There is a memorial in Waltham Abbey to Sir Edward Denny, who was Sir Walter's cousin.

Roe was the first Englishman to sail the waters of the Amazon, which he explored for some three hundred miles, sailing the first two hundred and rowing the rest. Returning to the mouth of the river, he explored the coast as far as the estuary of the Orinoco in search of gold, but found none and came home in 1611.

In 1614 he entered Parliament, and in 1615 was sent on his mission to the Great Mogul to seek permission to establish trading stations for the East India Company, which had established its first post at Surat in 1612. In 1621 he was sent as ambassador to the court of the Sultan of Turkey, where he laboured for the release of English subjects who had been captured and enslaved by pirates from the shores of North Africa. Seven or eight hundred of these slaves owed their liberation to his determined efforts on their behalf. Perhaps Roe's greatest interest was in his endeavour to bring about a Protestant alliance with the Reformed churches.

When he died in 1644 he was buried in the chancel of the parish church at Woodford. It was said of him: 'Those who knew him well have said that there was nothing wanting in him towards the accomplishment of a scholar, gentleman or courtier, that also as he was learned so was he a great encourager and promoter of learning and learned men.' His collections of coins and of Greek and oriental manuscripts are in the Bodleian.

Our reference to William Roe as godfather to one of John Foxe's grandchildren reminds us that Ben Jonson comes into the Foxe chronicle with the letter from Dr. Thomas Foxe informing his family that Ben had just had an honorary degree conferred on him. Later we have the changes rung again when we find Dr. Thomas Foxe writing to Sir Thomas Roe.

All these little sidelights from one corner of the kingdom, though in themselves of small importance, help to show how close the relationship was between poets and patrons in days when men of letters depended to so great an extent upon the goodwill of the landed gentry, and when the landed gentry thought it a great honour to have a poet at their board. Histories of literature deal for the most part with writers and writing only. That is their purpose. Those who write them have neither time nor space to follow all the little byways that we have explored in this chapter. But even great poets live most of their lives amongst ordinary men and women, and to see them against a small local background, as we are trying to do here, should help us to understand them better.

The Wroths, the Hickeses, the Foxes, and the Roes were all great families; but after several centuries they look shadowy in relation to such a figure as Ben Jonson. Yet unless we can see Ben Jonson in the social circles of his day we cannot see him fully alive. Life is in relationships. To see the great man as he really was, we must see him in association with the lesser men of his age and society.

CHAPTER IX

THE Wroths looked across the Roding valley to Chigwell, where
Samuel Harsnett, later Archbishop of York, was vicar from 1597
to 1605. Harsnett was a man of strong and thoroughly English
character. He was simple, scholarly, and humane, but stubbornly
opposed to newfangled ideas. At a time when Englishmen were
more than normally inclined to let their minds run to excesses,
Harsnett knew where he stood, and right or wrong he stood firm.

The brass to his memory in Chigwell Church is of special
interest. It is the latest in date of the five brasses showing a
bishop of the Church of England dressed in stole, alb, dalmatic,
and cope—the garments ordered by the twenty-fourth canon in
the first prayer book of Edward VI. By his own express wish
he appears as a bishop, not as an archbishop, wearing a mitre
without the ducal coronet, and carrying a pastoral staff. The
inscription translated reads:

'Here lies Samuel Harsnett, formerly vicar of this church:
first, unworthy Bishop of Chichester; then, more unworthy
Bishop of Norwich; and last, most unworthy Archbishop of York,
who died on the twenty-fifth day of May, in the year of Our Lord,
1631. Which same epitaph that most reverend prelate, of his
great humility, ordered in his will to be inscribed to his memory.'

The life-size effigy of Harsnett is surrounded by a border,
with the four evangelists, one in each corner. Near each is a
shield bearing arms. At the top we find Norwich on the right
and York on the left. Below Norwich is Chichester; below York
the Harsnett arms. The bishop's alb is open in front, which is
an unusual feature. It has lace round the top, and over it is the
cope, richly embroidered with flowers. In his right hand the
bishop holds a Bible against his breast, in his left his pastoral staff.

This interesting brass was originally on the floor of the old
chancel. Then it was moved and fixed to a pedestal which stood
against the north wall. In the middle of last century it was
restored to its first position over the grave, to be moved again
when the church was enlarged in 1866, and placed against a pier

of the chancel arch. It is characteristically English to find this high dignitary of the Church, not amid the splendours of York Minster, where we might expect to find him, but in the quiet village church where he had lived as a young clergyman. He is buried close to his wife, showing that simple human affections meant more to him than the pride which so often mars the characters of those of humble birth who rise to high places.

Opposite the church is the grammar school he founded in 1629 with money he had saved for the purpose, and in fulfilment of a 'bond and obligation' laid upon himself 'to praise and magnify the goodness of God, who, from a poor vicar of the parish had called him to so high a dignity in his church.' The bust of Harsnett found in the school was done by a Chigwell lady, Miss Ada Palmer, from the brass in the church. No portrait of him is known to exist.

The management of his school was a matter of great concern to the archbishop. Some of the old ordinances make interesting reading. For instance, the masters are not to hit boys on the head, on pain of a fine of forty shillings for every offence. This ordinance reads:

'I constitute and ordain that the schoolmasters do not exceed in their corrections above the number of three stripes with the rod at any one time; that they strike not any scholar upon the head or the cheek with their fist or the palms of their hands, or with any other thing, upon pain of loss of forty shillings for every such stripe or stroke, to be defaulted by the governors out of their yearly wages: that they do not curse or revile their scholars; that for speaking English in the Latin School, the scholar be corrected with the ferula; and for swearing with the rod,' etc., 'and, above all, that they chastise them severely for three vices, LYING, SWEARING, and FILTHY SPEAKING.'

Another reads: 'I constitute and appoint that the Latin schoolmaster be a graduate of one of the universities, not under seven-and-twenty years of age, a man skilful in the Greek and Latin tongues, a good poet, of a sound religion, neither papist nor puritan, of a grave behaviour, of a sober and honest conversation, no tippler nor haunter of public houses, no puffer of tobacco, and above all that he be apt to teach and strict in his government.' It was laid down that the scholars should be taught the classics, 'no novelties nor conceited modern writers.'

Samuel Harsnett was the son of a Colchester baker. He was

born in June 1560, and baptized in the parish church of St. Botolph, Colchester. At that time the country was full of strife and bickering. The Catholics had recently been disendowed. Their property had been confiscated, and the new church services appeared to them irreverent and meaningless. The Protestants, on the other hand, were still shocked and embittered by the terrible burnings in Mary's reign, which had made Harsnett's own town notorious. In Elizabeth's reign we find unity against external foes; but within the nation bitter disunity and fluctuating passion. At the time of the Reformation Essex had been passionately Catholic; later it became a hotbed of Puritan fanaticism.

That was the atmosphere in which Harsnett spent his boyhood, and as he grew older his eager spirit longed to liberate the people from the harshness and horror produced by partisan feeling. Throughout his life Puritanism was growing, and it has to be said that in resisting it he was accused of harshness himself, especially while he was Bishop of Norwich.

At fifteen Harsnett entered King's College, Cambridge, as a sizar, or servitor. King's had just been purged of its 'popish trash' by Bishop Cox of Ely, and its scholarly, humane provost, Dr. Philip Baker, had fled heartbroken to Louvain. Harsnett was always sensitive to grace and beauty, and it was probably the resentment he felt against the bleak Puritanism of King's that sent him to Pembroke, where Spenser and Gabriel Harvey, the latter another Essex worthy, were then students.

At twenty-four he preached at Paul's Cross, where Latimer had preached the sermons which turned the people of London towards the Reformation. Harsnett, with the ardour of youth and the courage that was to distinguish him, challenged splendidly the growing Calvinism of his day, taking as his text Ezekiel xxxiii. 11: 'As I live, saith the Lord God, I have no pleasure in the death of the wicked; but that the wicked turn from his way and live: turn ye, turn ye from your evil ways; for why will ye die, O house of Israel?' He had seen enough of violence and torture in the Papists, and sadistic cruelty in the Puritans. Like Milton he saw that 'New Presbyter is but old Priest writ large,' and he wanted to guide men towards a more enlightened and more genuinely catholic Christianity.

Harsnett was appointed headmaster of Colchester Grammar School in March 1587; but he resigned after eighteen months and returned to Cambridge. We next hear of him as chaplain

to Richard Bancroft, Bishop of London, by whom he was advanced
rapidly when Bancroft became primate. While bishop's chaplain he was licenser of books for the press, and got into trouble
through passing unread a manuscript life of Henry IV, written
by his friend Sir John Hayward, which was later held to be
treasonable. The most offensive feature was a fulsome dedica-
tion to the Earl of Essex, which was never shown to Harsnett.
Sir John Hayward was sent to the Tower, and Harsnett narrowly
escaped the same fate. The defence he made is not always
considered creditable. Barrett, an Essex historian, considers it
wanting in manliness. 'I am,' pleaded Harsnett, 'only a poor
divine, unacquainted with books and arguments of State.' He
realized that he was guilty of neglecting his duty. There was
little to be said in self-defence, so he relied upon the subtle per-
suasiveness of humility. Barrett appears to think it a calculated
humility; but perhaps we may give Harsnett the benefit of the
doubt. At all events, he used his argument to good effect,
whether consciously or unconsciously. After all, his language was
quite in keeping with contemporary convention. When Donne
was fishing for preferment he referred to himself as 'a clod of
clay,' 'so poor a worm as I am,' and he called his letter 'a rag of
paper.' We must not take these phrases too seriously. In the
sixteenth and seventeenth centuries men could use such terms
about themselves without the slightest loss of self-respect.
Most of these *clods of clay* and *poor worms* and *bleeding pieces of
earth* were anything but humble.

In January 1603 Harsnett was made Archdeacon of Essex,
and in March of the following year his most interesting work
was entered in the Stationers' Register. This was entitled: 'A
declaration of egregious popish impostures to withdraw the hearts
of Her Majesty's subjects from their allegiance, and from the truth
of the Christian religion, professed in England, under the pretence of casting out devils.' This book was written after sitting
on a commission which condemned Darell, the Puritan exorcist.
The subject was evidently to his taste, for when he had finished
with Darell he went on to attack all who claimed to be able to
cast out devils, and belief in witchcraft and superstitious practices generally.

Nearly every one at that time still believed in witchcraft.
Henry VIII may or may not have been sincere when he alleged
that Anne Boleyn had practised black magic against him, but

in 1541 he got his Parliament to pass a statute against witchcraft, which imposed the death penalty without benefit of clergy on all convicted of using invocations to destroy any man's person or goods, of making images of men, angels, devils, or beasts, and so forth. In 1562 this Act was re-enacted in a less horrible form, subjecting those guilty of anything less than murder to nothing worse than a year's imprisonment and four exposures in the pillory.

There were few prosecutions for witchcraft in Elizabeth's reign. Reginald Scott, who commanded a company of the army raised to combat the Armada, strenuously exposed the superstition in *The Discovery of Witchcraft*, arguing like Harsnett that the Roman Church was at the bottom of all these superstitions. When James came to the throne he ordered Scott's book to be burned by the common hangman. James wrote on witchcraft himself, and lived in dread of it all his life.

In the Forest—and Harsnett was vicar of Chigwell when he wrote his book—we can well imagine such superstitions being readily believed. They have hardly died out now. During the present century a Bishop's Stortford barber was asked for a cutting of hair from the nape of the neck of one of his customers. The man who made the request fancied that he had been injured by the person whose hair he wanted, and he intended to put a spell upon his enemy. Hair from the body and nail-parings used to be placed in a bottle filled with water. A curse of sickness would be muttered, and the wish was expected to come true if the bottle burst.

In *Folk Lore*, 1903, a lady relates that when she was staying two miles from Epping, twenty-five years before the time of writing, she witnessed an amusing ceremony. A gaggle of goslings was driven out of a lane by an old women who looked for all the world like 'Mother Goose' herself. She drove them to a piece of common by the roadside, then walked up and down in front of them, extending her arms and bowing this way and that, all the time muttering an incantation. On inquiring of a country girl what the old woman was doing, the writer was informed that it was old Mother Jenkins, who made her living by blessing geese in this way.

Harsnett no doubt heard many tales about less benevolent characters than old Mother Jenkins. Freakish and ill-begotten creatures must have haunted the wastes about his parish. When the Roding was in flood, and a fuddled cottager, returning home late, missed his footing, an evil spirit would be held responsible, or the jack-o'-lantern would·be seen by an old widow standing at her door.   Perhaps a neighbouring landowner of gloomy and unsociable habits was accused of having dealings with the devil.

In Harsnett's day Chigwell would have tales

> Of Bedlam beggars, who, with roaring voices,
> Strike in their numbed and mortified bare arms
> Pins, wooden pricks, nails, sprigs of rosemary;
> And with this horrible object, from low farms,
> Poor pelting villages, sheep-cotes and mills,
> Sometimes with lunatic bans, sometimes with prayers,
> Enforce their charity.

Harsnett's book on witchcraft had been read by Shakespeare before he wrote *King Lear*, and Edgar is made to use names of fiends mentioned in Harsnett's book in a way that makes Shakespeare's indebtedness clear.   Each throws light on the other. It is more than likely that poor half-witted villagers at Chigwell found halters in their pews in Harsnett's little church, and suspected ratsbane in their porridge.   It is also interesting to see again that Shakespeare took his material from authentic English sources at a time when foreign influences were so often preferred.

In the records of witchcraft in Essex we find none of the finer characterizations of superstitious fancy.   No fairies, gnomes, or undines.   No Puck.   None of the aerial flights on broomsticks found in Lancashire.   None of the witches' sabbaths found in Scotland.   Essex witches were poor, ill-favoured old women, usually insane, and full of cold, bad-tempered cunning.   They were suspected of offering sacrifices to the devil.   Often they were said to have his ugly marks upon their bodies.   They worked mischief upon the persons of their neighbours, or put a curse upon their cattle.

With so much superstition to contend with, it is good to find Harsnett something of a sportsman, though the great days of the sporting parson had not yet arrived.   We find that Sir Gawen Harvey, of Marks, bequeathed to him his kennel of beagles— 'all but Nancy, which I give to Henry Mildmaie, of Wanstead.'

In 1605 Harsnett was elected master of Pembroke Hall in succession to Lancelot Andrewes (whom he again succeeded as Bishop of Chichester), and had the honour of entertaining King James on his visit to the university.   His term at Pembroke was not altogether a success.   The Hall got into financial difficulties during his mastership, and Harsnett talked of resigning, but did not do so until the fellows presented to the king an indictment against him, under fifty-seven articles. He was also vice-chancellor of the university, and provoked resentment by objecting to the practice of bestowing honorary degrees upon men with no academic claims. One of his protests is interesting to us because it concerns our next poet, John Donne, one of the 'conceited modern writers' he so disliked.

James had persuaded Donne to enter the Church, and after hearing his protégé preach at Whitehall, he insisted that both universities should confer upon him the degree of doctor of divinity. Harsnett, however, had no use for those 'that sought thus to come in at the window when there was a gate open.' Under threat of a mandate from the king, the vice-chancellor had to yield finally; but we cannot help admiring him for making the stand, especially as James was so free with his honours.

From Chichester Harsnett went to Norwich, where he cannot have expected a very hearty reception, for Norwich was the most Puritan diocese in the kingdom. That he should have been bitterly criticized there is not surprising. He had set himself from the first against the inroads of Puritanism. The clergy of Norwich accused him of ruling with a rod of iron. In 1624 he was charged with popery and extortion; but of these charges he managed to clear himself, and in 1629 he became Archbishop of York. One year later he was made a privy councillor.

Harsnett's health was already declining when he went to York. In 1629 he founded Chigwell Grammar School; two years later he died. He had been a man of great power in the Church of England, rising from that humble beginning as a baker's son in Colchester to become one of the princes of the Church. He had encountered strong opposition. Like Donne he had suffered from the 'doctrine men,' with their 'sour faces, humming against him.' The Calvinists had no cause to love him. He certainly had no love for them. In one of his letters we find him lamenting that the hearts of so many were overseas, and he would their bodies were with their hearts. The doctrine of predestination was a particular abomination to him. He lost no opportunity of resisting it, even when it was preached by a bishop of his own church. The accusations of harshness against Puritans were probably not without foundation. Nonconformists got short shrift from him—he did not foresee the great part they were to play in the genuinely religious life of the community, and he did not know how fine a spirit was being raised for nonconformist freedom of worship not far from him in Essex. John Eliot was unknown then. But in most things Harsnett had a firm grasp of essentials, and in an age of superstition, fanaticism, and pretentious heresy, he upheld liberal doctrines.

The opening sentence of Harsnett's will reads: 'I die in the ancient faith of the true Catholic and Apostolic Church, renouncing from my heart all modern papal superstitions and all novelties of Geneva not accordant with the maxims of the Primitive renowned Church.' His library he bequeathed to Colchester, and the well-used and annotated volumes bear evidence of the learning, piety, and catholic judgment of a fine churchman. He left an annuity of six pounds thirteen shillings and fourpence for the maintenance of poor persons living in the almshouse at Chigwell, and twenty-four twopenny loaves for distribution to the poor. He also left fourteen pounds a year for maintaining a footpath five miles long from Abridge towards London. These bequests show how real was his affection for his old parish.

In the neighbouring parish of Lambourne lies another distinguished churchman, Dr. Thomas Winniffe, Dean of St. Paul's and Bishop of Lincoln. Thomas Winniffe became rector of Willingale Doe on 5th May 1608, and on 15th June of the same year rector of Lambourne. In 1631 he succeeded John Donne as Dean of St. Paul's.

When Bishop Williams was translated from Lincoln to York, Winniffe was nominated for Lincoln as one likely to find favour with Parliament, on the grounds of his alleged Puritan tendencies. Parliament, however, was not certain. Francis Rowe moved that Winniffe's consecration should be postponed until a settled Government and religion had been established. But, in spite of opposition, he was consecrated Bishop of Lincoln in February 1642. In the following November the revenues of his see were taken from him when all 'Bishop lands' were vested in trustees for the benefit of the Commonwealth. Winniffe then retired to his living at Lambourne, where he occupied part of his time by giving help to Brian Walton in the preparation of the Polyglot Bible. He died in 1654, in his seventy-eighth year.

The inscription on his monument of black marble at Lambourne surprises us with the information that 'From his attractive countenance, the polish of his style, the allurements of his social intercourse, he might have been taken for a charmer of the other sex.' It does add 'in the family circle,' and we find as we read on that the writer of the inscription was only expressing his surprise that Dr. Winniffe remained a bachelor all his life.

When Lambourne church was closed by the Parliamentarians, Winniffe celebrated holy communion regularly at Lambourne Hall, formerly a monastery, which is said to have been connected with the church by an underground passage.

CHAPTER X

Donne and holy Mr. Herbert—John Donne at Abury Hatch—George
Herbert at Woodford

THE next group of poets discovered in the Forest are very different
from the three Elizabethans, Gascoigne, Breton, and Lodge.
The Elizabethans reached the pitch of poetry inevitably because
the air was electric with discovery and creation. Poetry required of them only an accepting participation in the spirit of the
age. The poets of the seventeenth century were faced by a
problem. The new science of Copernicus and Galileo, and the
new philosophy of Bacon, clashed with the old and harmonious
metaphysic. John Donne grasped the new situation with the
greatest degree of imaginative insight:

> The new philosophy calls all in doubt,
> The element of fire is quite put out;
> The sun is lost and the earth, and no man's wit
> Can well direct him where to look for it.
> And freely men confess that this world's spent,
> When in the planets and the firmament
> They seek so many new; they see that this
> Is crumbled out again to his atomies.

The spirit of doubt had come into men's minds with new force.
Even Milton had the doubt that made it appear necessary for
someone to justify the ways of God to man, and such confidence
in the supreme power of the human intellect that he had the pre-
sumption to think himself capable of doing it.

John Donne and Samuel Harsnett, who died in the same year,
were within a few miles of each other during the last winter of
their lives. With two dignitaries of the Church of such eminence
as the Archbishop of York and the Dean of St. Paul's moving
amongst the great families between Chigwell and Ilford, the story
of how the archbishop had opposed the conferring of a doctorate
upon the dean must have been whispered about the Forest, so
that each might be kept out of conversation in the other's presence. The dean was not a man to be rebuffed, and neither was
the archbishop. But perhaps neither cared much about the
social life of the neighbourhood during those last months. Both
were failing.

Donne came to Abury Hatch, near Ilford, with his aged mother, to visit his eldest daughter, Constance, who had married as her second husband Samuel Harvey, an alderman of the city of London. Mrs. Harvey had previously been the second wife of Edward Alleyn, the actor and founder of Dulwich College, who was thirty-eight years her senior. Edward Alleyn, with Philip Henslowe, the father of Alleyn's first wife, had held the curious office of 'Master of the royal bears, bulls, and mastiff dogs.' James would sometimes amuse himself by requesting Alleyn, 'King of the Bears,' to test the courage of the English mastiffs by setting them against the Tower lions.

Scholars sometimes speculate why Walton, who must have known, does not tell us in his life of Donne that Constance had been married to Edward Alleyn. It is a rather significant omission which may be further evidence of the disrepute in which actors were held in those days. There may have been another reason. From a letter preserved at Dulwich it appears that Donne had attempted to cheat Alleyn out of his wife's dowry.

In Donne's day Abury Hatch, or Aldborough Hatch, consisted of only a few scattered dwellings. It was in the parish of Barking, three miles from the church. When a church was built there twenty years later than Donne's visit, in response to a petition that 'one acre of ground, in some convenient place near the petitioners' dwellings, should be assigned within the Forest of Waltham, whereon to build a house for a meeting place, and that twenty timber trees should be also set out of the Forest towards the building,' Edward Keightley, a relative of Donne's, became minister. Keightley was ejected by Cromwell's 'tryers,' but continued to preach in his own house.

We cannot claim with certainty that any of Donne's poems were written in the Forest, or that it influenced him in any way. He was too old for that. Walton says that the *Hymn to God, my God, in my Sickness*, was written in 1630; but this is almost certainly a mistake. It was probably composed in an earlier illness. Donne was a fevered and fretted man when he came out into the Forest to seek new strength. The new strength did not come, and he remained under his daughter's thatch throughout the following winter. Donne himself had little hope of recovery. 'As soon look for roses at this time of the year as for increase of strength,' he said. And writing to his friend, Mrs. Cockayne, in the January:

'I am afraid that death will play with me so long, as he will forget to kill me, and suffer me to live in a languishing and useless age, a life, that is rather a forgetting that I am dead, than of living.'

He was able to get out a little when the weather was not 'spitefully foul.' In January he even ventured up to London to see about some little seals he was having made, to give to his friends as tokens of affection. He had also to arrange about the future of a diamond necklace that had been deposited with him for safe custody.

There is little to tell of this part of his life. We know that for the first time in twenty years he was unable to preach at Christmas, but that he preached again on the first Friday in Lent, 1631, leaving the Forest a few days earlier. He made his will at Abury Hatch, leaving to Dr. Winniffe, who succeeded him at the deanery, the famous picture called 'The Skeleton,' which has been handed down from dean to dean. He is believed to have worked on his sermons, revising them for the press, though they were not printed until nine years after his death.

While Donne was at Ilford, a report that he was dead circulated in London, and he wrote to a friend:

'This advantage you and my other friends have by my frequent Fevers, that I am so much the oftner at the gates of Heaven; and this advantage by the solitude and close imprisonment that they reduce me to after, that I am so much the oftner at my prayers, in which I shall never leave out your happiness; and I doubt not among his other blessings, God will add some one to you for my prayers. A man would almost be content to dye (if there were no other benefit in death) to hear of so much sorrow, and so much good testimony from good men as I (God be blessed for it) did upon the report of my death; yet I perceive it went not through all; for one writ to me that some (and he said of my friends) conceived I was not so ill as I pretended, but withdrew myself to live at ease, discharged of preaching. It is an unfriendly, and God knows an ill-grounded interpretation; for I have always been sorrier when I could not preach, than any could be they could not hear me. It hath been my desire, and God may be pleased to grant it, that I might dye in the Pulpit; if not that, yet that I might take my death in the Pulpit, that is, dye the sooner by occasion of those labours. Sir, I hope to see you presently after Candlemas, about which time will fall my Lent Sermon at Court, except my Lord Chamberlain believe me to be dead, and so leave me out of the Roll; but as long as I live, and am not speechless, I would not willingly decline that service. I have better leisure to write, than you to read; yet I would not willingly oppress you with too much Letter. God so bless you and your Son as I wish to,

Your poor friend and servant in Christ Jesus,

J. Donne.'

Before the end of the month he was appointed to preach, as he had hoped he would be, and prepared for the occasion. When his friends saw him in London they were shocked by his wasted appearance and doubted his fitness for the pulpit. Donne was not to be dissuaded; though Izaak Walton says that when he appeared: 'Many of them thought he presented himself, not to preach mortification by a living voice, but mortality by a decayed body, and a dying face. And doubtless, many did secretly ask that question in Ezekiel: "Do these bones live? or, can that soul organize that tongue, to speak so long time as the sand in that glass will move towards its centre, and measure out an hour of this dying man's unspent life?" Doubtless it cannot.'

The dean's text on this occasion was 'To God the Lord belong the issues from death.' The sermon was printed in 1633 as *Death's Duel, or a Consolation to the Soule against the Dying Life and Living Death of the Body.*

As soon as Donne was back in London his old physician, Dr. Foxe, visited him, and recommended cordials and a milk diet for twenty days. By this means he considered health might be restored. Donne refused to try the experiment at first; but when the doctor persisted he yielded sufficiently to keep to milk for ten days. Not another day would he endure it. He told the doctor 'he had drunk it more to satisfy him, than to recover his health; and, that he would not drink it ten days longer, upon the best moral assurance of having twenty years added to his life.'

It was Dr. Foxe who persuaded Donne to have a monument made, and he must have been amused to find his appeal to vanity so much more successful than his appeal to forbearance had been. The rest of the story is well known. Walton tells us:

'A Monument being resolved upon, Dr. Donne sent for a Carver to make for him in wood the figure of an Urn, giving him

directions for the compass and height of it; and to bring with it
a board of the just height of his body. "These being got: then
without delay a choice Painter was got to be in readiness to draw
his Picture, which was taken as followeth.—Several Charcole-
fires being first made in his large Study, he brought with him into
that place his winding-sheet in his hand, and, having put off all
his cloaths, had this sheet put on him, and so tyed with knots at
his head and feet, and his hands so placed, as dead bodies are
usually fitted to be shrowded and put into their Coffin, or
grave. Upon this Urn he thus stood with his eyes shut, and
with so much of the sheet turned aside as might shew his lean,
pale, and death-like face, which was purposely turned towards the
East, from whence he expected the second coming of his and our
Saviour Jesus." In this posture he was drawn at his just height;
and when the Picture was fully finished, he caused it to be set
by his bedside, where it continued, and became his hourly object
till his death.'

This friendly man, Dr. Foxe, was the youngest son of the
martyrologist. After leaving Cambridge he lived for a time in
the household of Archbishop Whitgift. Later he went abroad
to study medicine. He saw military service with the Earl of
Southampton in Ireland and the Netherlands, and after being
interned as a prisoner of war returned to England, establishing
himself as a doctor at Amen Corner. When he died in 1642 two
monuments were erected to his memory: one in St. Paul's, where
he was buried, and a bust in the Harveian Museum. He had
contributed generously to Donne's memorial.

What looked like being another Forest association is the verse
letter already referred to, usually printed with Donne's poems,
alleged to be from the poet to Sir Thomas Roe; but this is now
thought to have been from the traveller's brother, Sir John Roe.
A definite link with the Forest in Donne's work is in the six
sonnets dedicated to the Earl of Doncaster. This title is not
quite correct. James Hay, whom the poet addressed, was Vis-
count Doncaster, who became Earl of Carlisle in 1617. He was
one of those who came to England with James I, and he owed his
advancement more to the king's favour than to his own merits,
though he was employed on several important missions. In
1619 Donne accompanied him to Germany, and it was on this
occasion that *A Hymn to Christ at the Author's last going into
Germany* was written.

Hay married a daughter of Lord Denny as his first wife. His second wife was Lucy Percy, Strafford's Lady Carlisle, the heroine of Browning's play, and the subject of flattering addresses by Herrick. The second Earl of Carlisle and his lady come into our story with Thomas Fuller. Though Lucy Percy lived until 1660, she was not the subject of the Fuller story. The first Earl of Carlisle died in 1636, so it was the second earl, who died in 1660, that Fuller knew at Waltham.

It was through Hay that Donne's merits became known to James. In fact, we may say that Donne's career as a churchman ended on the eastern edge of the Forest and began on the western. Of the beginning we have the dramatic story of Somerset posting a messenger to Donne, begging him to come immediately to Theobalds. One of the clerks of the council had died that night, and Somerset hoped to obtain the appointment for the poet. When Donne arrived, Somerset walked with him in the palace gardens.

'Mr. Donne,' he said, 'to testify the reality of my affection, and my purpose to prefer you, stay in this garden till I go up to the king, and bring you word that you are clerk of the council. Doubt not my doing this, for I know the king loves you, and know the king will not deny me.'

Somerset then left the poet and went up to the king. He had been a bold man to prophesy the king's will, and met with a rebuff.

'I know Mr. Donne is a learned man,' said the king, 'he has the abilities of a learned divine; and will prove a powerful preacher, and my desire is to prefer him in that way, and in that way I will deny you nothing for him.'

James then persuaded Donne to prepare himself for the Church. Less than ten years later—in November 1621—Donne was again commanded to wait upon the king. James was at dinner. Turning to Donne in his most gracious manner he said:

'Dr. Donne, I have invited you to dinner; and though you sit not down with me, yet I will carve to you of a dish that I know you love well; for, knowing you love London, I do therefore make you Dean of St. Paul's; and when I have dined, then do you take your beloved dish home to your study, say grace then to yourself, and much good may it do you.'

In his youth Donne had the reputation of being 'a great visitor of ladies, a great frequenter of plays, a great writer of conceited verses.' The court was the background of most of the best poets of the Stuart period, and it was at court that Donne found his most appreciative audience.

Our second poet of the age, George Herbert, was both a courtier and Donne's intimate friend. But though both were poets, parsons, and courtiers, their lives and characters were widely different. Donne was bred a Catholic. 'I had my first breeding and conversation,' he says, 'with men of a suppressed and afflicted religion, accustomed to the despite of death and hungry of an imagined martyrdom.' The influence of his Catholic youth remained with him. While Donne's poetry was complex in the extreme, Herbert's at his best was simple:

> Sweet day, so cool, so calm, so bright—
> The bridal of the earth and sky;
> The dew shall weep thy fall to-night;
> For thou must die.

Herbert's mother, Lady Magdalen Herbert, was Donne's great friend for many years—one of Donne's published sermons was in commemoration of her—so our best metaphysical poet and our best devotional poet were intimately bound to each other.

George Herbert came into the Forest in 1629. He remained twelve months, but left before Donne arrived. We have no record of any meeting between them in the Forest itself, though we may be certain that they would meet in London during that year. Herbert came to Woodford to stay with his younger brother, Sir Henry Herbert, who, like the poet and Lord Herbert of Cherbury, was a scholar and a man of distinction. Sir Henry was a gentleman of the king's privy chamber and Master of the Revels.

All the Herberts were high-spirited. The poet's devotional work must not deceive us about his character. In his youth he was a dandy. Born into a noble family, with all the advantages of birth, brains, and good looks, the university and court were his to command. At Cambridge he was Public Orator and a distinguished and popular figure. Fuller says of him that as Public Orator he performed his duties 'with as becoming and grave a gaiety as any had ever before or since his time.' Of himself Herbert says:

> Such starres I counted mine; both heaven and earth
> Pay'd me my wages in a world of mirth.

His greatest hopes lay in the favour of King James, so when that king died, Herbert, to his extreme disappointment, found that the stars of which he had boasted were darkened from his sky. Life appeared to have lost all purpose for him. For twelve months he was prostrate with mortification. Marriage brought a measure of recovery and made it necessary for him to consider his career again. This time he turned to the Church. But it was a second breakdown in 1629 that brought him to Woodford.

We may claim that Herbert spent the crucial twelve months of his life in the Forest, conquering his proud spirit, with the result that he became one of the saintliest characters the Church has had since the Reformation. 'Though the Iniquity of the late Times,' he wrote, 'have made Clergy-men meanly valued, and the sacred name of Priest contemptible; yet I will labour to make it honourable . . . by making Humility lovely in the eyes of all men.'

We do not know whether Herbert met Harsnett in the Forest. Both were strongly opposed to Puritanism, and it was in the year Herbert came to Woodford that Harsnett wrote his letter to Lord President Conway complaining that the Church was infested with the men of Dan and Bethel, and wishing their bodies were overseas with their hearts. It was also the year Harsnett founded Chigwell Grammar School.

Herbert was seized, says Walton, with a sharp 'Quotidian Ague,' and hoped the Forest air would cure it. He was his own physician, and he believed that he greatly assisted nature by 'forbearing drink, and not eating any meat, no not mutton, nor a hen, or pigeon, unless they were salted.' By this diet, as he believed, the ague left him; but he contracted 'a disposition to Rheums, and other weaknesses, and a supposed Consumption,' so he had to move again in search of health, leaving the Forest for Wiltshire.

There was a division between the material and spiritual world in Herbert's poetry that is not altogether healthy in any one, and certainly not in a poet. His spiritual aspirations came with the decay of his material hopes. They came as an escape from the actual when the worldly hopes he had set his heart upon turned to ashes. Death began to attract him in a way that did not make for vigorous poetry. In his religious musings he is too fond of dwelling upon Christ's death, without carrying his vision through to its Easter triumph.

The Temple was written during his last years, between the time he was at Woodford and his death in 1633. Donne's influence is marked, but Herbert had long been familiar with the classics,

and their fineness and precision are everywhere in his work.
His physical frame would never have been equal to the ardours
of Donne's passion. Nor was that his temper now. He had
come through his conflict a milder man:

> And now in age I bud again,
> After so many deaths I live and write;
> I once more smell the dew and rain
> And relish versing.

He had settled down to cultivating

> The pliant mind, whose gentle measure
> Complies and suits with all estates.

In person Herbert was tall and slight, carrying himself very
erect. In everything he was a gentleman, modest in manner,
courteous in speech, a man of the most engaging presence. He
was inducted into the living of Bemerton on 26th April 1630,
and he told his friend, Mr. Woodnot, that he was at peace:
'I now look back upon my aspiring thoughts, and think my self
more happy than if I had attain'd what then I so ambitiously
thirsted for; And, I can now behold the Court with an impartial
Eye, and see plainly, that it is made up of Fraud, and Titles, and
Flattery, and many other such empty, imaginary painted Pleasures: Pleasures, that are so empty, as not to satisfy when they
are enjoy'd; but in God and His service, is a fulness of all joy
and pleasure, and no satiety.'

The attractiveness of Herbert's personal and daily saintliness
was in its simplicity. It did not separate him from his fellow
men, nor did it banish mirth in his personal life. His chief recreation was music. He would compose tunes for his verses, which
he would then sing to the accompaniment of his lute. Twice
a week he would walk into Salisbury from Bemerton to worship
in the cathedral, and before returning would 'sing and play his
part' with a private musical society that met there. These walks
were a great delight to him, as well as to those who joined him
on the way, for he was fond of friendly conversation, and made
contacts easily. For twelve months this good man lived in the
Forest, where many must have known and loved him.

CHAPTER XI

Francis Quarles of Romford—Elizabeth of Bohemia—John Quarles of Romford

FRANCIS QUARLES, a poet who resembled Herbert in many ways, was born at Stewards, Romford, in 1592. Stewards, which stood where Romford Hall was built later, had been acquired by the poet's father in 1588, with an estate of about 320 acres, including the ground now covered by the Western, Eastern, and Victoria Roads, with the streets branching off them. But while George Herbert might have had something of the Elizabethan spirit of adventure in his youth, if his physical frame had been capable of sustaining it, there can never have been much of it in Francis Quarles. He was a quiet, studious man, rising at three to get to his books, the husband of one devoted wife, and the father of eighteen children. His character has never been portrayed in a way to rouse much enthusiasm, though he had his mildly attractive traits. He, too, was fond of music, and while studying law at Lincoln's Inn sold his gown to buy a lute case.

Normally, Quarles was far too serious; but we approach his solemn *Emblems* now much as we approach old epitaphs, amused by their quaint moralizing. Read in this spirit he can still delight us. When Lamb approached him from one angle he wrote: 'What wretched stuff are the *Divine Fancies* of Quarles! Religion appears to him no longer valuable than it furnishes matters for quibbles and riddles; he turns God's grace into wantonness.' When he approached him from another angle he wrote: 'Quarles and Holy Mr. Herbert, as Izaak Walton calls him; the two best, if not only, of our devotional poets.' Fuller, as usual, hits him off perfectly when he says: 'He had drank of Jordan instead of Helicon, and slept on Mount Olivet for his Parnassus.'

Similar influences went to the making of the minds of Herbert and Quarles. They were nearly of an age, and were at Cambridge together. They were later products of the Elizabethan period, with the craftsmanship learned from the Elizabethans combined with something of the matured scholarship of the great divines whose lives were written by Walton, in whom the Catholic and Protestant elements were, for a few short years, so happily blended. Quarles and Herbert were part of the new movement creating the English Church, and while the creative inspiration was there it was possible for morality to be illumined by poetry.

Quarles was an ardent Royalist. He wrote as if kings were divine beings, mysteriously endowed with more than human wisdom and virtue. The adulation given by so many cavalier poets to their mistresses was given by him to his sovereign:

> Foure Maryes are eterniz'd for their worth;
> Our Saviour found out three, our Charles the fourth.

It is small wonder that the heads of the earlier Stuarts were turned by the flattery they received, for this fulsome praise was not peculiar to Quarles. To most poets of the day the king was seen not as a person but as the highest point in the divinely ordered system of the State. In France we find Bossuet supporting Louis XIV and justifying the divine right of kings with similar extravagances. Under Charles II this kind of thing disappeared. Flatterers were only laughed at for their pains. Later, the Dutch phlegm of William was hardly conducive to adulation.

Quarles came of good family. His ancestors were settled in Northamptonshire before coming to Essex, but must have lived in Romford before taking possession of Stewards, for we read in Archdeacon Hale's *Precedents* that in 1587, 'at the request of Mrs. Quarles, they did bury a maide servant of Mrs. Quarles, without any ceremony, and not according to the communion booke, upon Thursday, being the Vth of June, as we remember Mrs. Quarles did command him to throw earth upon her, and he demanded who should bury her. Mr. Leeche standing by, answered, all we here present, who then threw earth upon her and covered her.'

James Quarles, the poet's father, who had held important offices under Elizabeth, died when the poet was seven, and was buried with heraldic honours in the family vault. His wife died when the poet was thirteen. By his father's will, Francis received an annuity of fifty pounds a year, the family estates going to his brother Robert.

After Cambridge and Lincoln's Inn, Quarles received an appointment that should have cured him of dullness for life. He became cup-bearer to Elizabeth of Bohemia, and remained in her service four years, accompanying her to Heidelberg. If no man is a hero to his valet, perhaps no woman is a queen to her cup-bearer. Whatever the explanation, here we have a poet in the service of the most beautiful woman of the age, and so little

affected that he was able to leave her service, and become secretary
to an archbishop. What strange defect was here? It was
Elizabeth of Bohemia who inspired those lines:

> You meaner beauties of the night,
>   That poorly satisfy our eyes
> More by your number than your light,
>   You common people of the skies;
>   What are you when the moon shall rise?

But Wotton, not Quarles, wrote them. It was Sir Henry Wotton,
Provost of Eton, who addressed her as 'Most Resplendent Queen,'
and who confessed—before he became provost—'I cannot but
fall into some passionate questions with my own heart. Shall I
die without seeing again my Royal Mistress myself?' A gallant
professor of our own day, Sir Arthur Quiller-Couch, wrote of her:
'There are a certain few women in history who in life fascinated
the souls out of men, for good or evil, and still fascinate the
imagination of mankind, though themselves have been dust for
centuries. Helen of Troy is one, of course, and Cleopatra another. These two were wanton and light of love; but virtue, or
the lack of it, skills not. Joan of Arc is a third, a maid and a
saint above saints; and Catherine of Siena, another saint, is a
fourth; and a fifth is Mary Queen of Scots, who was what you
will—except a saint. But of her grand-daughter, Elizabeth of
Bohemia—wayward, lovely, extravagant, unfortunate, adorable,
and peerless—what shall I say? . . . scarce ever a man came in
range of her but he knelt her sworn knight.'

Instead of winning a place among the immortals by celebrating
in verse the beauty of his incomparable mistress, Quarles became
famous as the author of *Divine Emblems*. His works were
voluminous; but this was the most widely read. These books of
emblems, made up of quaint emblematic pictures illustrating
verses on religious subjects, had a considerable vogue. Quarles
is said to have written his collection at Finchingfield. Edward
Benlowes of Brent Hall, Finchingfield, famous as a poet in his
own day, though almost forgotten now, was Quarles's dearest
friend, and the two were enjoying each other's society when the
'emblems' were written. Benlowes was referred to by Fuller
as a 'religious and learned gentleman.' He was a good friend to
Fuller, and to other writers of the day as well as to Quarles.
Pope gave him a place in *The Dunciad* as 'propitious still to block-
heads.' Miss Fell Smith, whose love for Quarles shines through so

many of her charming essays on old Essex, says: 'Close to this old
manor and farm-house [Brent Hall] lies a wooded knoll overlooking a sloping dell, through which the little river Pant winds;
it is blue with hyacinths in Springtime, and thrills to the songs of
nightingales in early Summer; the tall trees crowning the knoll
are an interception to the level sky-line as seen from many miles
around, and the lonely lane that winds through these woods
seldom re-echoes to the sound of wheels.   Here in the deep and
murmuring solitude of the country the Royalist poet is said to
have wandered in pious musings, and here composed his *Emblems*.'

Miss Fell Smith also discloses that the 'Address to the Reader'
which introduces the *Shepherd's Oracles* by Quarles, though
signed by the printer, has been held to be written by Izaak
Walton.   The style is certainly the Angler's:

'He in a Summer's morning about that hour when the great
eye of Heaven first opens itself to give light to us mortals, walking
a gentle pace towards a Brook whose springhead was not far
distant from his peaceful habitation, fitted with angle, lines and
flyes, flyes proper to that season, it being the fruitful month of
May, intending with all diligence to beguile the timourous trout
with which the watery element abounded, observed a more than
common concourse of shepherds all bending their unwearied steps
towards a pleasant meadow where was a large arbour whose walls
were made of the yielding willow and smooth beech boughs,
covered over with sycamore leaves and honeysuckles.'

The friendship between Quarles and Benlowes was a beautiful
thing.   'The fountain of our love was poetry,' says the lesser
poet, 'religion was its close connecting tie.'

After leaving the service of the archbishop, Quarles joined
Charles I at Oxford, and suffered with his fellow Royalists when
the Parliamentarians gained power.   His estate and manuscripts
were seized; the manuscripts were destroyed, and his death in
1644 was hastened as a result.   For the last five years of his life
he held the post of chronologer to the City of London.

The unpopularity of Quarles with the Parliamentarians eclipsed
his fame, along with that of so many others.   It is noteworthy
that in spite of the God-fearing boasts of the Parliamentarians
the best poetry—and much of it religious—was produced by the
Royalists, with one or two famous exceptions.   Fuller commented
that had Quarles been living in Plato's commonwealth instead of
Cromwell's, he would not only have been allowed to live, but have

been advanced. But perhaps the worthy doctor had forgotten on this occasion that neither Plato nor any other great planner could ever find a high place for the disturbing element of poetry.

The sceptical age of Pope could not be expected to take much interest in devotional verse. If the course of history had been different Quarles might have had more readers than can be found for him to-day. His epigrams are not without point, as a few examples will show:

ON THE BOOK OF COMMON PRAYER

The Booke of Common-Prayer excels the rest;
For Pray'rs that are most common are the best.

ON THE WORLD

The World's an Inne; and I her guest,
I eate, I drinke, I take my rest;
My Hostesse Nature, do's deny me
Nothing, wherewith she can supply me:
Where having stay'd awhile, I pay
Her lavish Bills, and goe my way.

His best religious verse has a quiet tenderness:

Close now thine eyes, and rest secure;
Thy soul is safe enough; thy body sure;
 He that loves thee, He that keeps
And guards thee, never slumbers, never sleeps.
The smiling Conscience in a sleeping breast
 Has only peace, has only rest:
 The music and the mirth of kings
Are all but very discords, when she sings:
 Then close thine eyes and rest secure;
No sleep so sweet as thine, no rest so sure.

Francis Quarles passed on much of his talent to his son, John Quarles, who was born at Romford, and bore arms for the king at Oxford when he was only eighteen. When the king's cause declined John, like his father, suffered impoverishment. Little is definitely known about him: he is believed to have travelled abroad as a tutor, and to have died of the plague in 1665. The Stewards estate was in the Quarles family for nearly a century. No part of the old mansion now remains. When Romford Hall was built the name was transferred to a farmhouse on the estate.

CHAPTER XII

Hunting and hawking—King James—Juliana Berners—Bishop Hall at Waltham Abbey

WE recall with pride these many associations of kings and poets with the Forest; but those were hard days for the common people. Heavy fines were being imposed upon squire and peasant alike. The sporting proclivities of every person dwelling in the Forest came under review. In 1630 a census was made of the dogs. For having a crossbow in his house Thomas Williamson of Loughton was fined ten shillings, a large sum for a poor man to pay out of his small earnings in the seventeenth century. About this time, too, representations were made concerning ancient rights, such as those of pasturage, which were being threatened. The law had a long memory. Men were fined for offences committed ten or fifteen years earlier, in days when the king had not turned to these harsh laws as an easy means of revenue.

The old Swainmote, the terror of forest dwellers, was practically in abeyance under the Tudors. They had claimed their ancient rights of vert and venison; but had recognized the villager's rights of pasturage, which were enjoyed at all seasons except during the winter heyning, when the scanty herbage had to be left for the exclusive use of the deer, and the midsummer fence-month, when the does and fawns were not to be disturbed. Swine were allowed to roam the Forest during the time of pannage, which lasted from 14th September to 18th November, when they fed on the fallen beechmast and acorns. There had always been some restrictions of the pasturage. Deer are proud animals; they refuse to pasture along with sheep. They object even more strongly to goats, so the pasturing of goats was always a grave offence. The sensitive nostrils of the deer could not endure them. They tainted the pasture and the vert, or 'greenhue,' to use an old English word.

James was not long in discovering the uses of the laws in his new kingdom. An old writer says: 'I do boldly say that a man in his reign might with more safety have killed another than a rascal

80

deer.' This, of course, was not out of any tenderness to the deer. James was a remorseless hunter of the Forest animals, both from his hunting lodge at Hainault and from his palace at Theobalds, though, curiously enough, he was also very fond of all dumb creatures that could be tamed. He liked to have them about him looking fat and well cared for. He had the keenest interest in every kind of living creature, from the silkworms which he imported and tended in gardens in the Minories, to the white gerfalcons he got from Iceland. He was as excited as a child about the flying squirrels in his menagerie in St. James's Park, and about the live sables that his Muscovite ambassador had brought him. But his greatest joy was in a white fawn which he had sent to Theobalds. A nurse was hired for it, and the Earl of Shrewsbury wrote to Miles Whytakers of Waltham:

'The king's majesty hath commissioned me to send this rare beast, a white hind calf, unto you, together with a woman, his nurse, that hath kept it, and bred it up. His majesty would have you see it be kept in every respect as this good woman doth desire, and that the woman may be lodged and boarded by you, until his majesty come to Theobald's on Monday next, and then you shall know further of his pleasure. What account his majesty maketh of this fine beast you may guess, and no man can suppose it to be more rare than it is, therefore I know that your care of it will be accordingly.'

Theobalds was the favourite residence of James, partly because he loved the Forest, and partly because he feared the plague. The famous plague year was 1665, and we shall have Defoe's account of it later; but the plague also raged with great virulence several times in James's reign, so he always felt safer in the clear air of the country. One of the king's hobbies at Theobalds was of lasting benefit to us. He took great interest in Myddelton's New River scheme, assisting it with a loan. In a poem by William Vallens, entitled *A Tale of Two Swannes*, we have a description of Waltham Abbey as it was at the beginning of James's reign:

> Down all along through Waltham street they passe,
> And wonder at the ruines of the Abbay
> Late supprest, the walles, the walkes, the monuments,
> And everything that there is to be seene.

At great length and with precise detail Vallens describes the 'locke' on the river, with its 'double doores of wood,' and its 'cesterne

D

all of planke,' both of which would be novelties to most people at that time.

Besides supporting work on the New River, it is probable that James made possible the road from Loughton to Epping by way of Golding's Hill. The old main road from Loughton to Epping had gone round by Theydon Bois. Before the seventeenth century Loughton was usually reached by road from the Roding side, and not until modern methods of road-making were devised did it become possible to get heavy wagons up Golding's Hill and Buckhurst Hill during bad weather. The cart track from Thornwood to the Qngar road is a portion of the old London highway, which continued through Coopersale to Abridge, and the villages on the Forest side were reached from this road. Another road ran from Harlow over Rye Hill to Epping Upland and Waltham Abbey. Some traffic had gone through Epping since Henry VIII's reign, when an enterprising Epping mercer, John Baker, left a sum of money out of the rental of Stonards Farm, Theydon Garnon, for the upkeep of a stump road from the corner of Thornwood Common to Epping. This was continued to reach the old road by way of Ivy Chimneys. For more than two hundred years this bequest relieved the Epping inhabitants of their road expenses. But John Baker's road did not continue through the heart of the Forest.

In 1611 a portion of Crown land was offered for sale, and it is thought that this was to allow sufficient land to be purchased to make a road to Epping over Golding's Hill. We know that a new aisle was added to Epping church in 1622, so it appears that the prosperity of Epping as a market town was being established by this time.

In 1628 Sir Robert Heath described the Forest as having 'a very fertile and fruitfull soyle, and being full of most pleasant and delightful playnes and lawnes, most useful and commodious for hunting and chasing of the game of redd and falowe deare.' It was Sir Robert Heath who said that it had been 'alwaies especiallie and above all theire other fforests, prized and esteemed by the Kinges Majestie and his said noble progenitors, the Kinges and Quenes of this Realme of England, as well for his and theire own pleasure disport and recreation from those pressing cares for the publique weale and safetie which are inseparablie incident to theire kinglie office, as for the interteynment of foreyne Princes and Embassadors, thereby to show unto them the honor and magnificence of the Kings and Queenes of this Realme.'

The royal hunters were fairly generous with Forest venison. In 1639 Charles I presented a buck from Woodford Walk to the French ambassador; one from Epping Walk to the Venetian ambassador; one from Chingford Walk to the States ambassador; one from Walthamstow Walk to the Duke of Florence's agent; two from Hainault to the King of Spain's agent; two from Loughton Walk and New Lodge Walk to the Queen and Crown of Sweden's agent. In the schedule of Christmas venison for 1640 a hind from Loughton Walk is mentioned.

But the Stuarts were unpopular in the Forest itself, and not without reason. They tried to extend its area by gaining possession of the lands of neighbouring landowners, sometimes by purchase and sometimes by disputing rights of ownership. Sir Fulke Greville, poet, friend of Sidney and ancestor of Earls of Warwick, resisted the attempts of James to gain his property. On 28th April 1617 he wrote: 'Sir Fulke Greville . . . refuses his Majesty's offer of buying his house and land for more than its value; but he is old and will soon be out of the way.'

That all the pageantry and splendour of the royal Forest should have been attended by so much hardship for the common people is a dark cloud shadowing the revels. The least infraction of the law might lead to heavy fines or physical mutilation. Boundaries were arbitrarily adjusted to suit a prince's pleasure. But there was a hard brilliance about it all, and now that the cloud has passed we can lie in the shade of a leafy covert and think only of the wild gaiety. Perhaps a timid deer will dart in front of us, adding to the romance of the mood, and we are glad that it is only in fancy that we hear the deep, bell-like cry of the staghounds and the excited shouting of the foresters.

There was also that still more aristocratic sport of hawking, in which a man's rank might be recognized by the hawk he bore on his wrist. The gerfalcon was the right of a king; the falcon-gentle of a prince; the falcon of the rock belonged to a duke; the peregrine falcon to an earl; the goshawk to a yeoman, and so on. Before the dissolution of the monasteries the rank of the priests who hawked could be recognized similarly. The ordinary priest was permitted a sparrow-hawk; the clergy of higher rank

claimed more splendid birds, and their pride in them was satirized
in the lines:

> Into the church there comes another sot,
> Without devotion strutting up and down,
> For to be seen, and shew his braided coat;
> Upon his fist sits sparrow-hawk or falcon.

Both leathern and silken straps were fixed to the legs of the
hawk, to train it in short flights and bring it back to hand.　Thus
Othello says of his wife:

> If I do prove her haggard,
> Though that her jesses were my dear heart-strings,
> I'd whistle her off, and let her down the wind,
> To prey at fortune.

It is interesting to discover that in the fourteenth century the
manor of North Weald, near Epping, was held by Edmund
Plantagenet by the yearly gift of a sparrow-hawk to his brother,
Edward II.　A flight of hawks would be a familiar sight in the
Forest.　A bell was attached to the leg of each bird.　These
bells varied in tone, so that a merry, jangling sound was produced.
We may imagine knights and their ladies riding out from Loughton, Woodford, and Walthamstow on a sharp morning, richly
apparelled, with ruff and farthingale, bearing their hawks with
them.　No pleasure in life delighted King James more than this
sport of hawking.

When Essex men think of hawking and hunting, they remember
that it was Juliana Berners of Berners Roothing who wrote the
first English treatise on the subject.　The lady Juliana became
prioress of Sopewell nunnery, near St. Albans, in the middle of
the fifteenth century.　She was beautiful, scholarly, and expert
in manly exercises.　The first edition of her treatise on hawking
was printed at St. Albans in 1481, and was therefore one of the
earliest printed books in the English language.　She wrote also a
book on heraldry, in which she refers to 'the kyngs of the right
lyne of Mary, of whom that gentilman Jhesus was borne, very
God and man; after his manhode kynge of the land of Jude and
of Jues, gentilman of his modre Mary, prince of cote armure.'
Her aristocratic temper made her better fitted to write on sport
than on divinity.　Her works were highly esteemed by those
'gentyll and noble men' to whom they were addressed.　She

made it clear that she did not wish them to fall into the hands of idle and vulgar persons who might destroy the dignity of her favourite sports. No doubt King James knew the prioress's treatise well.

James did many crazy things at Theobalds, where he had his fools and fiddlers, some of whom addressed him as 'old wife,' others as 'Your Sowship,' and where the ladies of the court were wont to roll about in a state of intoxication on festive occasions. While these things suited his humour, oaths were never off his lips, some of which, perhaps, he had learned from the 'mighty-mouthed' Ben Jonson. When these vulgar pleasures began to pall he would indulge in a bout of repentance, translate the psalms, write works of piety, and invite bishops to his board with as much pleasure as he had previously shown to buffoons.

It was in such a mood that he invited Joseph Hall, incumbent of Waltham Abbey from 1605 to 1627, afterwards famous as Bishop Hall, to preach to him.

Hall reintroduces the stupid question of our first English satire, writing:

> I first adventure, follow me who list,
> And be the second English satirist.

Hall's satires appeared in 1597–8; Donne's—and Donne was one of Hall's friends—in 1593; Gascoigne's *Steele Glasse* in 1576, and so on. Whichever claim is allowed, we see that in the Forest we had close associations with the beginnings of satire in England. Whatever may be said in general about Hall's claims as satirist, it is conceded that he was the first Englishman to take Juvenal as a model. He turned the Roman form into a most effective means of holding up to ridicule the antique affectations of Spenser and the extravagances of Marlowe's 'Turkish Tamberlaine.' His work interestingly foreshadows the satirical literary criticisms of Pope in the eighteenth century. Some of his satires deal with weaknesses in human nature that we are still far from having overcome. We have the story of the drivelling old man Lollio, for instance, who toiled night and day to give his son a good education. The son entered the inns of court, and acquired means to cultivate the fashionable vices of his day. He became too proud to recognize his father's acquaintances. It is a familiar, and perhaps a dull story; but the twist of irony comes at the end, when the young man returns to his old home, and is admired by the simple rustics for what they consider to be his fine manners. Thus the old man has his reward, and dies happy to have produced this entirely worthless son.

Hall preached before James several times. We can imagine how he must have been tempted to satirize his royal patron. Perhaps he did so and had the good sense to keep it secret, for the Scottish Solomon might have been even more effective as a subject than the Turkish Tamberlaine. Hall was quickly advanced in the Church through gaining the king's ear; but he suffered much at the hands of the Puritans, though he was himself accused by Laud of having Puritan leanings. His house at Norwich was plundered, his cathedral despoiled, his estate sequestered, and he was reduced to poverty. Before Norwich he was Bishop of Exeter, with Robert Herrick as a country parson in his diocese. Herrick addressed to Hall one of his quaintest and most delightful poems. Within a few weeks of becoming Bishop of Norwich, Hall was sent to the Tower with twelve other prelates for protesting against the passing of laws by Parliament during their enforced absence from the House.

Hall's story is an interesting one. As a youth he had a strong desire for a university training, but his father, who had a large family, could not see how it could be afforded. We read that the father was just about to sign a bond that would have deprived Joseph of his education, and have robbed the Church of a distinguished scholar, when a relative arrived at the home of the Halls. This relative had just passed through Cambridge, and brought glowing accounts of the life there. After some persuasion the father decided to make the necessary sacrifices.

Perhaps it was this and other apparently fortuitous circumstances in his life that gave Hall his unusually strong belief in the intervention of God in the common affairs of daily life. He had many other occasions to offer as evidence of what he held so firmly. For instance, at the end of his university period a promising appointment was vacant at Tiverton grammar school, for which Hall was urged to apply. He had a personal leaning towards parish life, believing that his gifts lay in that direction, but so far yielded to persuasion as to see the Lord Chief Justice, who had the Tiverton appointment. While he was in the street, someone plucked at his sleeve and handed him a letter. He broke the seal and opened it. It was an offer of the living at Halstead.

Again, there was the story of his marriage. One Whitsunday morning, Hall and a clerical neighbour left Halstead church after a wedding, on their way to join the wedding guests. At the door of the house they were visiting stood a 'comely, modest gentlewoman.'

'Who is that?' asked Hall.

'She is one,' replied his neighbour, 'whom I have bespoken for your wife.'

He added a glowing account of her virtues, and how her parents were already willing to welcome him as a son-in-law. To the ingenuous young clergyman this was again the hand of God, though cynics might be inclined to believe that the Almighty's hand had been guided by the parents, and possibly by the young lady, who obviously presented herself so engagingly at the door. However that might be, the union was a happy one and lasted for more than forty-eight years. His last book, entitled *Songs in the Night*, was written on the occasion of his wife's death.

Hall enjoyed life at Waltham. He spoke with appreciation of its ample revenues—which may have been another convincing illustration of divine intervention. Essex men have not been backward in invoking the aid of the Almighty in their private affairs. There is a curious prayer in an old Essex diary: 'O Lord, thou knowest that I have nine houses in the city of London, and likewise that I have recently purchased an estate in fee-simple in the county of Essex. Lord, I beseech Thee to preserve the two counties of Essex and Middlesex from fire and earthquakes.' In Hall's day, the living at Waltham was worth a hundred pounds a year, with certain accommodations, which was a reasonably adequate sum at that time.

While at Waltham, he attended the embassy of the Earl of Carlisle to France, accompanied King James to Scotland, and was sent with other English divines to the Synod of Dort in 1619, but had to return from Holland on account of ill health.

Hall certainly possessed a vivid imagination, and was particularly successful in bringing the Gospel narratives to life. A number of these were published under the title of *Contemplations*. They remained popular for several generations. His satires retain some interest on account of their references to contemporary customs and manners. For instance, he tells us that at that time it was usual for tenants to send New Year gifts

to their landlords, and that the most favoured gift was a capon.
Of his verse at its best, this is a fair example:

THE TRENCHER CHAPLAIN

A gentle squire would gladly entertain
Into his house some trencher-chapelain;
Some willing man that might instruct his sons,
And that would stand to good conditions.
First, that he lie upon the truckle-bed,
Whiles his young master lieth o'er his head.
Second, that he do, on no default,
Ever presume to sit above the salt.
Third, that he never change his trencher twice.
Fourth, that he use all common courtesies;
Sit bare at meals, and one half rise and wait.
Last, that he never his young master beat,
But he must ask his mother to define
How many jerks she would his breech should line.
All these observed, he could contented be
To give five marks and winter livery.

Perhaps he is remembered best now for his defence of episcopacy,
which so roused the anger of Milton. At the end of his life he
settled in the modest living at Higham, near Norwich, dying
there in 1656, aged eighty-two.

CHAPTER XIII

Honest Izaak—Izaak Walton and the river Lea—Walton and Fuller at
Waltham Abbey—Nightingales and gipsies

OUR next well-remembered visitor came out from London for
milder sport than hunting and hawking. As the times were,
perhaps we may say for milder sport than preaching, too. We
must now move out of the Forest itself, and take our ease in the
sunny pastures that bank the river Lea, which still marks the
western boundary of the Forest. We are invited to breathe
God's good air in the company of honest Izaak Walton.

We may be inclined to think of him as an angler rather than as
a writer. That is how he would have us think of him, though he
was, in fact, as fine an artist with a sentence as we shall meet
in these pages. John Buchan pointed out that in Walton's copy
of Eusebius there are three attempts to make the beautiful
sentence on Donne's hymns in the *Life of Herbert*: 'These hymns
are now lost to us; but doubtless they were such as they two now
sing in heaven.' Many such sentences must have been turned
this way and that by the Angler as he sat on the banks that
separate Essex from Hertfordshire.

Walton's *Lives* have been described as obituary poems. They
are less widely read than *The Compleat Angler*, but must be
amongst the most treasured possessions of those who have them.
While engaged on them, Walton stepped over to Waltham Abbey
to see Thomas Fuller, to whom he was 'my worthily respected
friend,' and we have a delightful account of their meeting. Both
were given to mingling mirth with graver matters. Did not
Walton say: 'If thou be a severe, sour-complexioned man, then
I here disallow thee to be a competent judge'?

Fuller's *Church History* had just been published, and Walton
came in search of information for his own *Life of Richard Hooker*.
These two genial spirits discussed together the new work.

'What do you think of it?' asked Fuller.

'I think,' replied Walton, 'that it should be acceptable to all
tempers, because there are *shades* in it for the warm, and *sunshine*
for those of a cold constitution. With youthful readers, the
facetious parts will be profitable to make the serious more

*D   89

palatable, while reverend old readers will fancy themselves in a
flower garden, or one full of evergreens.'

'And why not the Church history so decked?' asked Fuller,
'as well as the Church itself at a most Holy Season, or the Taber-
nacle of old at the Feast of Boughs?'

'That was but *for a season*,' Walton objected. 'In *your* Feast
of Boughs, we are so overshadowed that the parson is more seen
than his congregation; who may wander till they are lost in the
labyrinth.'

'Oh,' said Fuller, 'the very *children* of our Israel may find their
way out of *this* wilderness.'

'True,' returned Walton, 'as indeed they have here such a
Moses to conduct them.'

It was all good-humoured badinage; but at the same time
Izaak had put his finger on Fuller's weak point, and was too
honest not to chuckle a little at having found it.

There are few records of Walton crossing the Lea into Essex,
though Waltham is named in the following:

'My friend Coridon and I will go up the water towards Ware';
to which Piscator replies: 'And my scholar and I will go down
towards Waltham.' Piscator is said to have taken his scholar to
an inn which stood at Cook's Ferry, where a bridge now stands,
linking Chingford to Edmonton. 'The Thatched House' at
Hoddesdon, named on the first page of *The Compleat Angler*, no
longer stands. Perhaps all these friendly inns, with lavender in
the windows and ballads hanging on the walls, with their comely
and civil hostesses, were never as trim and inviting in their own
villages as they are in the Angler's pages. But while the pages
remain we have no cause for complaint on that score.

Some of our Forest inns had been visited a few years earlier
by John Taylor, the Water Poet—'The White Hart' at Abridge
and 'The Cock' at Epping, for instances. But how real Walton's
inns are! We do not seem to be reading about them, but to be
entering them and seeing their white sheets smelling of lavender.
Through the open window we hear the milkmaid singing in the
meadow, and feel a cool breeze blowing up to us from the river.
We see the fish leap, the flies dart above the water, the cowslip
bank and sweet-smelling honeysuckle hedge. Few writers have
had the same power of making the country scene real to us in this
completely convincing way.

It is not a pleasant experience to see a black cloud sail out into a clear sky on a summer afternoon, and when the rain comes down to seek what uncertain shelter an unlopped hedge affords. Huddling there we are less inclined to be aware of the earth about us than of the sky above. But to Walton all occasions were occasions of new and pleasant sensation, and a rain shower was no exception. Under his hedge he watched the rain, which 'falls so gently upon the teeming earth, and gives yet a sweeter smell to the lovely flowers that adorn these verdant meadows.' While sheltering he looked towards a beech-tree, under which he had sat on a previous occasion, and listened to 'the birds in the adjoining grove' that 'seemed to have a friendly contention with an echo, whose dead voice seemed to live in a hollow tree, near to the brow of that primrose hill.'

Charles Lamb might well say: 'It might sweeten a man's temper at any time to read *The Compleat Angler.*' This is not the artificial pastoral of Elizabethan fancy, but the veritable soil and substance of England.

The hunter offers to bear the angler company as far as Theobalds, and there leave him, to turn up to the house of a friend who mews a hawk for him.

Montaigne is quoted, another who, like Walton, and unlike many others in these pages, did not feel his free spirit overburdened by accusing conscience. We are sometimes inclined to think that the break-up of the old monastic system brought in a secular age, and to forget that Raleigh was a theologian as well as a discoverer and poet, and that sermons were as great a part of the literary life of both the sixteenth and seventeenth century as songs. With this in mind, it is interesting to see how much of the medieval sense of sin did persist. The seventeenth century is the age of the great metaphysicals; but the mind enjoyed greater freedom in its flights, and men like Walton are found, who were free from the more superstitious aspects of the old theology.

It would be strange if we were to have an account of the Forest in literature, and find no place for the nightingales. None of the more famous poems to the nightingale was actually written in an Epping glade; but no poet has paid more eloquent tribute to that most celebrated bird than Walton when he wrote:

'But the nightingale, another of my airy creatures, breathes such sweet loud music out of her little instrumental throat, that it might make mankind to think miracles are not ceased. He that at midnight, when the very labourer sleeps securely, should hear, as I have very often, the clear airs, the sweet descants, the natural rising and falling, the doubling and re-doubling of her voice, might well be lifted above earth, and say, "Lord, what music hast Thou provided for the Saints in Heaven, when Thou affordest bad men such music on Earth?"'

We go to him also for a glimpse of the gipsies who made the Forest their haunt through so many centuries:

'On the other side of this very hedge sat a gang of gipsies, and near to them sat a gang of beggars. The gipsies were then to divide all the money that had been got that week, either by stealing linen or poultry, or by fortune-telling, or legerdemain, or indeed by any other sleights and secrets belonging to their mysterious government.' We read how they wrangled over the last shilling, but were too wise to go to law, 'and did therefore choose their choice friends, Rook and Shark, and our late English Gusman, to be their arbitrators and umpires; and so they left this honeysuckle hedge, and went to tell fortunes, and cheat, and get more money and lodging in the next village.' The beggars were then heard quarrelling about a cloak, with voices so loud that one could not tell what another said: 'but, at last, one beggar craved audience, and told them that old father Clause, whom Ben Jonson, in his *Beggar's Bush*, created king of their corporation, was to lodge at an ale-house called "Catch-her-by-the-way" not far from Waltham Cross, in the high road towards London,' and they agreed to refer the matter to him.

We cannot avoid smiling when, on the fifth day, we find Piscator and Venator enjoying 'the cool shade' of a 'sweet honeysuckle hedge' only a mile from Tottenham High Cross. But we forget the incongruity as Piscator begs his friend to consider how many reasons there are for thankfulness, and how good it is to reflect on them, for 'God has two dwellings, one in heaven, and the other in a meek and thankful heart.'

Izaak was a wise moralist. He believed there was more promise in leading men to love the good than in bidding them hate the evil, for by praising the worthy he had faith that they would be drawn away from the unworthy.

In the first chapter of the *Angler*, when Piscator fears his discourse may seem tedious, he gives it 'a sweet conclusion' by quoting George Herbert's poem *Providence*.

Such is the varied company we may keep in these

> . . . lofty woods, the forests wide and long,
>   Adorned with leaves and branches fresh and green,
> In whose cool bowers the birds, with many a song,
>   Do welcome with their choir the summer's queen;
> The meadows fair, where Flora's gift among
>   Are intermixt, with verdant grass between;
> The silver-scaled fish that softly swim
> Within the sweet brook's crystal watery stream.

CHAPTER XIV

John Eliot, the Apostle of the Indians—Essex and New England—Charles I at Barking

MOST of our Forest personalities have been associated with at least one other, passing on, as it were, a handshake from generation to generation, or shall we say with lives entwined like the woodbine on one of Izaak Walton's hedges? But before looking in upon the great Thomas Fuller, we step aside to notice one who had no place in the high circles in which most of our famous men so far have moved. He is John Eliot, the Apostle of the Indians in North America, who is believed to have been born at Nazeing, though Charles Lamb's Widford, six miles away, claims him on the ground of his baptism there.

Eliot was born in 1604. He was educated at Cambridge, and went from there to a post as usher in the Rev. Thomas Hooker's school at Little Baddow. Hooker was a Puritan. He had been curate and lecturer at Chelmsford, and as dissent was strong in Essex at this time his school was flourishing when Eliot joined it. This success, however, was brief. Puritans were under severe disabilities, and when Hooker was summoned before Laud to answer for his views he felt obliged to flee to Holland. Eliot, already converted to Hooker's principles, decided to join the company of Essex men who planned to emigrate to America. Over half the Pilgrim Fathers, who had left the country twelve years earlier, had been drawn from Essex, Suffolk, and Hertfordshire. Eliot may have had friends or relations among them. The company he joined was known as the Braintree Company, and sometimes 'Mr. Hooker's Company.' Though Thomas Hooker was not one of their number, most of them had been members of his flock.

Eliot settled in Boston for a year while he looked round for a field in which to labour. The Indians settled round Massachusetts Bay attracted his sympathy, and he resolved to dedicate his life to their service. At first he found them hostile, but he held his course, studied their language and customs, and built the first English church at Natick in 1660. In this church he preached to the Indians in their own language, slowly gaining their confidence.

94

It was Eliot's zeal that induced the Long Parliament, in 1649, to set up a corporation for propagating the gospel in New England. The Hon. Robert Boyle, one of the founders of the Royal Society, was governor of this corporation, and in 1675 Eliot wrote him an interesting letter describing his trials.   He had much to contend with in his endeavour to gain the confidence of the frightened Indians.   We find him trying to help three hundred and fifty poor souls in one place.   They had been put on a bleak, bare island, where they suffered hunger and cold.   Often there was neither food nor fuel to be had.   Clothing was scant, and nothing would induce the Indians to work or help themselves effectively. Their apathy was pitiable.   Food was supposed to be supplied to them by the governing body; but the difficulties of getting it across were great.

Eliot describes how he had visited Pawtucket, where the poor Wamesit Indians had fled to the woods in terror and were half starved.   A young fool had ridden into their settlement, called them out of their homes, shot at them, apparently for no reason, killing one and wounding five.   With difficulty Eliot regained their confidence, persuaded them to return, and got them settled again.

In another place he found that more than a hundred had been carried away captive, for what purpose he could not discover. Another company of his converts had fled to the Unkas, and he set out in an endeavour to trace them.   Such were the labours of this fine old missionary, who lived amongst these unhappy people, ministering to them with simple, Christian understanding and affection to the great age of eighty-six.   His name is too little known in this country; but in New England it is still held in reverence.   Baxter said of him: 'There was no man on earth whom I honoured above him.'

John Eliot translated the Bible into the language of the Massachusetts Indians, his version being the first edition of the Scriptures to be printed in America.   It appeared at Cambridge (Mass.) in 1663.   In addition to his Bible, he translated Baxter's *Call to the Unconverted* for them.   Of this book only one copy is now known to exist, and this was sold a few years ago for £6,800.

We hear of Eliot in the neighbourhood of the Merrimac River from Thoreau, in his *Week on the Concord and Merrimac Rivers*, where he quotes Gookin's *Historical Collections of the Indians in New England* thus: Wamesit, 'being an ancient and capital seat of Indians, they come to fish; and this good man [Eliot] takes this opportunity to spread the net of the gospel, to fish for their souls. . . .'

In addition to his translations, which included a psalter, he produced an Indian grammar. He was also the author of a number of original religious works; *The Christian Commonwealth* was one of the titles. In 1665 he founded an Indian college. At his death he had lived sixty years in America, every single one of which had been packed full of the grandest service for the Indian people at a time when they looked like being driven out of existence.

Thomas Shepard, who shared with Eliot the distinction of being one of the first in the mission field, was another Essex man. A sturdy independence of mind has always characterized men of the eastern counties. It was a Dunmow man, Robert Fitz-Walter, who led the barons against King John. The Rev. Stephen Marshall, vicar of Finchingfield, played no small part in the rebellion against Charles I. So it is not surprising to find the map of New England marked with so many Essex place-names.

Roger Williams, one of the most resourceful of those who went out to seek freedom of worship, a man who figures prominently in American history, was chaplain for a time to the Masham family at High Laver, where John Locke lived later. Williams became a minister of Salem, preaching a great many radical doctrines as well as the gospel, amongst them the necessity for the separation of Church from State. He was driven out for his views, and travelled across the snows to Rhode Island. In 1636 he founded Providence as a place where complete religious toleration might be enjoyed. Roger Williams obtained a charter granting self-government to the towns of Rhode Island, giving them special status as an independent commonwealth.

Thomas Hooker eventually joined his friends in New England, and became a leader in the western churches—at least in one section of them, for we find that though in theory these heroic men were advocates of toleration, in practice they were not very good at living with each other. The persecution of the Quakers later, by the sons of these advocates of toleration, makes sad reading.

In England the Puritans continued to gain strength. In the Forest we find that Harsnett's memory was no longer honoured at Chigwell. His old parishioners were pleading with Parliament for their high church minister to be removed. Many of the Forest parishes had the same story to tell. The way was being prepared for Cromwell, though Charles I was not without his loyal supporters in west Essex. John Aylet, of Magdalen Laver, for instance, spent seven hundred pounds a year in the service of the king. He raised a troop of horse at his own charge and was in numerous engagements during the Civil War. He was at Colchester during the siege, where he was sentenced to be shot, but escaped disguised as a lady. Later he purchased his life from Parliament for four hundred and sixty pounds, and at the Restoration went to live at White Roothing, close to his old estate.

A little light relief from these serious matters is provided by the story of Charles I playing bowls with Mr. Shute at Barking Hall. The two played for high stakes, and on one occasion when the game had gone against the king, Mr. Shute said:

'And may it please Your Majesty, one thousand-pound rubber more, perhaps luck may return.'

'No, Shute,' replied the king, laying his hand on his friend's shoulder. 'Thou hast won the day, and much good may it do thee, but I must remember I have a wife and children.'

CHAPTER XV

Worthy Doctor Fuller—Thomas Fuller at Waltham Abbey—The effect
of the Commonwealth on the Forest—Waltham worthies—The Anabaptists at Waltham—George Fox and his Quakers—Fuller and
Saltmarsh—Fuller and the examiners

WALTHAM Abbey has reason to be proud of its distinguished
incumbents. Joseph Hall was a remarkable man; but one of the
Church's greatest sons was to follow him. The Civil War gave
the abbey ten years of the life of Thomas Fuller, surely designed
by nature for the deanery of St. Paul's. During Fuller's day the
influence of the London pulpit was at its zenith. Fuller himself
says that those who held the helm in the pulpit could steer the
hearts of the people whichever way they pleased. Parliament,
therefore, lost no time in ejecting the loyal preachers, and sub-
stituting those 'silver trumpets of the sanctuary,' who, as Fuller
says, put the wrong end into their mouths and sounded not
religion but rebellion.

Fuller's attitude towards both sides was conciliatory. To
large and fashionable congregations at the Savoy he constantly
preached peace. But passions were aflame, and after a time it
became clear that they must take their course. When Fuller
was required to take the Parliamentary oath he fled from London
to join the king at Oxford. There he was welcomed until his
sermons proved that his opinions were unchanged. The Royalists
accused him of being lukewarm in their cause; but there is a great
difference, as Fuller pointed out, between being lukewarm and
being moderate. The man was not lukewarm who could fear-
lessly condemn the Puritans, on the one hand, for preaching
rebellion instead of religion, and the Royalists, on the other hand,
whose 'heaven upon earth was to see the day that they might
subdue and be revenged of the Roundheads,' and both for being
'so wicked and wilful as to deny many good men (though misled)
engaged on both sides.' Fuller's counsel remained one of moderation throughout, though his loyalty to the king was unquestionable.

One man there was on the Royalist side whose character and
intelligence the good doctor could appreciate fully. This was
Sir Ralph Hopton, whom Fuller joined as chaplain, travelling
with him through the west country, with 'little list or leisure to
write, fearing to be made a history, and shifting daily for my

safety.' If these marches did not leave him much leisure for writing, they did provide him with material for use later. He collected information from the churches he visited, from country houses, often with useful libraries, from local gossips, and from every available source for his history of the Church and his collection of Worthies. Some of the acquaintances made in this way became lasting friends, for not the least remarkable thing about Fuller was the correspondence he maintained all his life.

Fuller had the great gift of being able to suffer fools gladly, and a temperament that enabled him to consort with all classes and conditions. Perhaps there is no surer mark of a great soul. He could walk with kings without losing the common touch. An anonymous writer says: 'Nor did the good Doctor ever refuse to light his Candle in investigating Truth from the meanest person's discovery. He would endure contentedly an hour's or more impertinence from any aged Church-officer, or other superannuated people for the gleaning of two lines to his purpose. And though his spirit was quick and nimble, and all the faculties of his mind ready and answerable to that activity of dispatch, yet in these inquests he would stay and attend those *circular* rambles till they came to a *poynt*; so resolute was he bent to the sifting out of abstruse Antiquity. Nor did he ever dismisse any such feeble Adjutators or Helpers (as he pleased to style them) without giving them money and chearful thanks besides.'

Fuller is not widely read to-day, largely because there is no popular edition of his works, but he has never lacked discriminating readers. Coleridge said of him that 'Next to Shakespeare, I am not certain whether Thomas Fuller, beyond all other writers, does not excite in me the sense and emotion of the marvellous: the degree in which any given faculty or combination of faculties is possessed and manifested, so far surpassing what one would have thought possible in a single mind, as to give one's admiration the flavour and quality of wonder! . . . Fuller was incomparably the most *sensible*, the *least* prejudiced, great man of an age that boasted a galaxy of great men. He is a very voluminous writer, and yet in all his numerous volumes on so many different subjects, it is scarcely too much to say, that you will hardly find a page in which some one sentence out of every three does not deserve to be quoted for itself, as motto or as maxim. *God bless thee*, dear old man!'

The praise is obviously excessive; but its very extravagance shows how much Fuller can excite his reader to enthusiasm both for himself and for his subjects. This 'jovial monk' was an impressive figure. He was of handsome proportions, with a ruddy complexion that matched his geniality of temperament, though sparing and temperate in his diet, allowing himself only two meals a day—he believed that the vapours from an overburdened stomach clouded the brain. He slept little, and took little exercise apart from his parish work, which was done on horseback. He was, we are told, grave and dignified in manner, with a stateliness of walk that attracted attention, though he dressed carelessly and had no affectations of speech or manner. Of the great personalities of our own day, the one most closely akin to him was G. K. Chesterton.

Perhaps the devout might complain that Fuller was too much at ease in Zion. Others will be of his own persuasion on that point. Let us be at ease with him ourselves. We look over his shoulder to find him considering the life of St. Hildegarde, and pondering upon her resourcefulness in performing miracles. At first he is impressed. But, bless me, he thinks, this is carrying things too far. 'I must confess,' he writes, 'at my first reading of them, my belief digested some, but surfeited on the rest: for she made no more to cast out a devil, than a barber to draw a tooth, and with less pain to the patient.' He looks puzzled for a few moments; but the smile is broadening on his face. 'However,' he concludes, 'Hildegardis was a gracious virgin, and God might perform some great wonders by her hand.'

Who could resist such a style as this? 'Dear fine silly old angel,' Lamb called him. But then Lamb, like Fuller, could never resist a good story. Fuller is incorrigible in this respect, and how good it is to meet with such a man in the Cromwellian period! 'Forgive me, reader,' he says, after indulging his humour a little, 'though I would not write these things they are so absurd, I cannot but write them they *are* so absurd!' He was a character, and everything he wrote was coloured by his own originality. It was coloured also by his kindliness. His wit was mingled with quiet humour, and with a sense of form and comeliness. Wits are rarely loved as Fuller was. To his own generation he was good Tom Fuller.

The date of Fuller's arrival at Waltham Abbey cannot be ascertained accurately. Neither the registers nor the churchwardens' accounts disclose it, but it was probably towards the end of 1648. One of the engraved maps in *A Pisgah Sight of Palestine* is dated 'apud Waltham, 1649.' He came by the patronage of the Earl of Carlisle, who had the gift of the abbey living. The earl had been on the king's side when war broke out; he had been wounded at Newbury in 1643, and had changed sides the following year, compounding for his estate.

There can be little doubt that Fuller was glad to have a settled living again, and Waltham was not without its attractions. The earl supplemented the income for his benefit by making him his personal chaplain. Several gentlemen of means and culture were already living in the parish; others came who may have been attracted by his presence. The church itself, with its long and interesting history, delighted him. The crypt he described as the fairest that ever he saw. He had long been familiar with Foxe's *Book of Martyrs,* and he believed that it had been written at Waltham. That the author had lived in the little town, worshipping in his own church, must have been a pleasant reflection. 'When I consider,' he wrote, 'how many worthy works which had their first being within the bounds of this our Parish, I may justly be ashamed that my weak endeavours should be born in the same place.' Bishop Hall was still an inspiring memory. 'I must pay the tribute of my gratitude to his memory,' writes Fuller, 'as building on his foundation, beholding myself as his great grandchild in that place, three degrees from him in succession, but oh! how many from him in ability! His little catechism hath done great good in that populous parish; and I could wish that ordinance more generally used all over England.'

So great a lover of antiquities must have been pained to see the marks of vandalism which Cromwell's men had left behind them. The stained glass representation of Harold in the church had been destroyed. The Eleanor Cross, a short distance away, had suffered rough treatment. Other damage had been done.

The abbey itself Fuller describes as 'a structure of Gothish building, rather large than neat, firm than fair. Very dark (the design of those days to raise devotion), save that it was helped again with artificial lights; and is observed by artists to stand the most exactly east and west of any in England. The great pillars thereof are wreathed with indentings, which vacuities if formerly filled up with brass (as some confidently report) added much to the beauty of the building. But it matters not so much their taking away the brass from the pillars, had they but left the lead on the roof, which is but meanly tiled at this day.'

To his great work, *The Church History of Britain*, Fuller appended a history of Waltham Abbey, compiled from a folio volume of four hundred and thirty-six pages left by Robert Fuller, the last abbot, who handed over Copt Hall to Henry VIII, and to whom John Stonard of Loughton Hall left his best ambling nag. This *Waltham Leidger Book* was then in the possession of the Earl of Carlisle. Thomas's irrepressible and whimsical humour enlivens the old abbot's pages. For instance, after the Dissolution the great tower, which held 'five great tunable bells,' was considered unsafe and pulled down. In the churchwardens' accounts for 1556 we find an entry 'for coles to undermine a piece of the steeple, which stood after the first fall, two shillings.' These bells were hung for some years in a timber frame at the south-east end of the churchyard. They remained there until the new tower was completed; but the building funds were inadequate and the bells had to be sold to raise the necessary money. Fuller added this information to his namesake's account, remarking characteristically that Waltham, which formerly had 'steeple-less bells, now had a bell-less steeple.' He did, however, get bells for his 'steeple,' and in his time those bells used to chime every four hours. The great bell rang out at 4 a.m. to rouse the apprentices. Each ringing had some similar association for the parish. The parson was fond of his bells, and of bells everywhere. Does he not refer to England in one place as 'the ringing island'?

Of the Forest he writes: 'Fourteen years since, one might have seen whole herds of red and fallow deer. But these late licentious years have been such a Nimrod—such an hunter—that all at this present are destroyed, though I could wish this were the worst effect which our woful wars have produced.'

The division of the river Lea could not escape remark by one so much attracted by the curious. This stream, he noted 'not only parteth Hertfordshire from Essex, but also seven times parteth from itself, whose septemfluous stream in coming to the town is crossed again with so many bridges.' 'The air of the town,' he informs us, 'is condemned by many for over-moist and aguish, caused by the depressed scituation thereof; in confutation of which censure we produce the many aged persons in our town (above threescore and ten, since my coming hither, above threescore-and-ten years of age), so that it seems we are sufficiently healthful, if sufficiently thankful for the same.   Sure I am, what is wanting in good air in the *town*, is supplied in the *parish*, wherein as many pleasant hills and prospects are as any place in England doth afford.'

But the abbey and the roads about his parish were in a neglected state when Fuller came to live at Waltham.   In 1641 Charles I was entertained there by the Earl of Carlisle, who petitioned the king to grant a small toll on cattle coming over the bridge, the money to be used for repairs to the highways and the church.   The king graciously granted this request, provided it was done with 'the privity and consent of a great prelate (not so safe to be named as easy to be guessed).'   The prelate was Laud, of course.   When this proud man was informed that the earl had applied to the king before mentioning the matter to himself, he vetoed the plan.   The Civil War would not have improved either the roads or the church.   It was the movements of troops at this time that completely ruined such roads as there were, so that a Turnpike Act came to be passed while Fuller was at Waltham.

If the fabric was in need of restoration not in Fuller's power to provide, a more important service he could and did perform. The old abbey church was filled Sunday after Sunday to hear the great man preach.   Most of his parishioners were poor herdsmen tending the cattle pastured in the rich grass country of the Lea valley.   Others found employment at the powder factory, which was already established, though privately owned then. The charcoal used in the manufacture of the gunpowder came from the willows growing in the marshes.   The nearness of this now famous factory was not an unmixed blessing.   'It is questionable whether the making of gunpowder be more profitable or more dangerous,' he wrote, 'the mills in my parish having been five times blown up within seven years; but, blessed be God! without the loss of any one man's life.'

When Fuller came to Waltham Abbey the second Earl of Middlesex lived at Copt Hall.   The first earl, who had been Lord Treasurer to James I, had died in 1644, leaving behind him an exceptionally fine library.   The second earl died seven years after his father, and was succeeded by his younger brother, Lionel, who appears to have had a great affection for Fuller. When the earl saw how much Fuller missed his own books, which

had been taken away from him by the Parliamentarians, he
presented to him all that remained of his father's library. In
acknowledging the gift, Fuller says: 'Thanks be to your Honour,
who have bestowed on me (the treasure of a Lord-Treasurer)
what remained of your father's library: your father, who was the
greatest honourer and disgracer of Students, bred in learning:
honourer—giving due respect to all men of merit; disgracer—who
by his mere natural parts and experience acquired that perfection
of invention, expression and judgment, to which those who make
learning their sole study do never arrive.' The books had evidently been neglected since the old earl died, for Fuller had to
dry and dust them and 'rout those moths which would quarter
therein.'

In the *Appeal of Injured Innocence* we have a pleasant glimpse
of Fuller at Copt Hall. He tells us that he was walking in the
park there one Sunday, thinking over his sermon, when the third
son of the Earl of Dorset, 'a child in coats,' ran up to him.
Fuller hesitated when the child asked if he might join him on his
walk. He was afraid he might lose his young friend while con-
centrating on his sermon, and said so. 'Then you must lose
yourself first,' replied the child, 'for *I* will go with *you*.'

Fuller relates the story to draw a moral. 'This rule I always
observe,' he smilingly confesses, 'when meddling with matters
of law: because I myself am a child therein, I will ever go with a
man in that faculty, such as is most eminent in his profession,
so that if he lose me, he shall first lose himself.'

This Earl of Dorset was Richard Sackville, fifth earl, who
obtained the Copt Hall estate by marrying Frances, daughter of
the first Earl of Middlesex, ultimately heiress to Lionel, her
brother, the third earl. The child in the story was Lionel
Sackville.

Of other well-known residents in Fuller's parish we have the
names of Dr. Hamey, a prominent physician of the day, and
Matthew Gilly, to whom Fuller wrote: 'Solomon saith, "and there
is a friend that is nearer than a brother." Now, though I have
read many writers on the text, your practice is the best comment.'
Gilly was buried at Waltham in 1662. Others were Edward
Palmer, a fellow of Trinity College, Cambridge, an eminent
Greek scholar, and Samuel Mico, a London alderman. At
Cheshunt, the next parish, he counted Sir Thomas Dacres and
William Robinson amongst his friends. Near Ponders End there

was Sir Henry Wroth, while many contemporary representatives of famous Forest families were patrons of his works, Lady Eleanor Roe, the widow of the famous traveller, being one.

Three years after coming to Waltham Fuller married his second wife, a member of the Roper family. No record of the marriage has come to light in Waltham or elsewhere, but records remain of births and tragic deaths that must have saddened the early years of the marriage. The first son, James, was baptized at Waltham on 27th December 1652. Eighteen months later he was buried. On 17th November 1653 a daughter, Anne, was born. She also died, and was buried on 19th April 1655. A few days later, 7th May, a second son was born. We know little of this child, but, at all events, he did not die in infancy. In 1661 he was mentioned as being 'six years old, a very hopeful youth.'

Fuller's life at Waltham was not easy; but nothing could ever cloud his genial mind for long. Besides his domestic troubles, there were the Anabaptists, who were already established in his parish. They gave him a good deal of trouble, but his references to them are only further evidence of his kindly and enlightened spirit. Their views he considered errors, but 'not such as intrencheth on Salvation (because not denying, but deferring baptism), and only on the out-limbs (not vitals) of religion, wherein a latitude may and must be allowed to dissenting brethren.' The Anabaptists had accused him of moroseness in his behaviour towards them. He publicly replied to the charge: 'This I do promise, and God giving me grace I will perform it. Suppose there be one hundred paces between me and them in point of affection, I will go ninety-nine of them on condition they will stir the one odd pace, to give them an amicable meeting.'

The Anabaptists were probably in considerable force. One of their number, Colonel Packer, who, according to George Fox, the Quaker, had a 'light, chaffy mind,' lived in part of Theobalds, the old palace, and set up a meeting there. Fox had come into contact—one dare not say conflict in referring to the Quaker——with Packer. 'He and the Ranters,' wrote Fox, 'bowed and scraped to one another very much; for it was the manner of the Ranters to be exceedingly complimental. . . . They were exceedingly high, and railed against Friends and truth, and threatened to apprehend me with their warrants if ever I came there.' After this challenge, we may be sure that Fox would soon be moved by 'the Lord God' to go down to Theobalds! And so it proved:

'Then I went to Waltham hard by him, and had a meeting there; but the people were very rude, and gathered about the house, and broke the windows. Whereupon I went out to them, with the Bible in my hand, and desired them to come in; and told them, I would show them scripture both for our principles and practices. And when I had done so, I showed them also, that their teachers were in the steps of such as the prophets, and Christ, and the Apostles cried against.'

Shortly after Fox's visit the parson's lot was further complicated by the establishment of a Quaker meeting in the town, in a lane leading off the Sewardstone road, called Quaker's Lane. Fuller's tolerance appears to have been strained to breaking point by this new sect of dissenters. Ministers, he complained, were regarded by them as 'Cains and Balaams, and Dogs and Devils.' He did not conceal his dislike for the Quakers when he came to write his history of the Church. He was, no doubt, driven by experience to the conclusions he reached about them. We can only feel that he would have written differently about them if he had been living now; but then they, on their side, would have shown more courtesy towards him. Fuller's strictures on the excesses of the early Quakers were not by any means without foundation.

It was easy to understand divisions in the Church, he felt: 'The reason is because none know either perfectly or equally in this life.' Differences must be recognized, and, above all, he says, we must beware of 'opprobrious language,' which will 'widen the wound between us to make it worse than it is.'

Fuller would find Essex Puritan in its sympathies, siding with Parliament against the king. Most of the clergy were on the same side as the people, some carrying their zeal to ridiculous lengths. The vicar of Leyton of the day preached in the parish church clad in a soldier's buff coat and girt with a trooper's sword. He was moved by his particular 'Lord' to declare to the people that all were blessed that died in the cause of Parliament, 'and other such stuff.' Amongst all this fanaticism and bigotry, Fuller's humane and sweet sanity is as refreshing as a spring morning. Religious or party labels had no effect on him. Always he dealt with the man, and discussed the problems of the day from the human angle. He had the strength of one who has his own in-

tegrity, untouched by outward events, his still centre, or what
Montaigne, who has many affinities with Fuller, would call his
'back shop.'

This spiritual detachment from the world exposed him to
savage attacks from ministers whose minds were less tempered
than his own.   One of these was the Rev. John Saltmarsh, who
was minister at Ilford for a time.   He was a man of note in his
day, a preacher 'full of poetical raptures, and highly conceited
of himself and parts,' says Wood.   Fuller, always magnanimous
towards his clerical opponents, described him more generously
as 'of a fine and active fancy, no contemptible poet, and a good
preacher.'   When Saltmarsh attacked Fuller in *Examinations*,
he confessed that his work was hurriedly prepared, in fact 'but
the thoughts of an afternoon.'   No doubt he would have defended
this haste by pleading the urgency of defending the flock from
the wolf, Fuller.   The reply was delightful.   'You have,' wrote
the good doctor, 'almost converted me to be of your opinion
that some extraordinary light is peculiarly conferred upon men
in this age: seeing what cost me many days to make, you, in
fewer hours, could make void and confute.'   He knew that
Saltmarsh's friends would resent this flippancy.   He could not
help it, but added in exculpation of his acknowledged weakness
that 'some mirth in this sad time doth well.'

To the prevailing fervour for reformation he replied, that so
far as he could see no better way could be found than for each man
to reform himself: 'which is a race long enough for the best
breathed private Christians, though they start in their youth and
run till their old age. . . . At the last day of judgment, when
God shall arraign men and say, "Thou art a drunkard, thou art
an adulterer, thou art an oppressor," it will be but a poor plea
for them to say, "Yea, Lord; but I have been a public Reformer
of Church and State!"'

Saltmarsh was invited to reply; but did not do so, alleging as
his reason for leaving the field that he had heard it rumoured
that Fuller was dead.   Fuller, however, was to outlive his showy
opponent in the flesh as well as in fame, and to give Saltmarsh a
place in his *Worthies*.   Unlike Pope, who made a gallery of a
very different kind in his *Dunciad* for those who had offended
him, Fuller's generosity and courtesy were unbounded.   He
recorded that Saltmarsh had heard that he was dead and thanked
fame, 'for so good a lie,' adding: 'See how Providence hath

crossed it: the dead (reported) man is still living; the then living man dead. And seeing I survive to go over his grave, I will tread the more gently on the mould thereof.'

Saltmarsh is forgotten; but a greater than either Saltmarsh or Fuller in point of genius, Milton himself, crossed Fuller's path. They had been at Cambridge together; Milton had attacked Hall; in almost everything they differed. When Milton's pamphlet, *Of Reformation touching Church Discipline in England*, appeared, Fuller was the first critic of consequence to notice it, though much of it shocked him. Milton's biographer, Masson, said of Fuller: 'There was not a better soul breathing, and certainly not a more quiet and kindly clergyman, than Thomas Fuller.'

He certainly knew how to handle the Puritans. When he came before Cromwell's 'tryers' he not only retained his own freedom to preach, he also gained the restoration of his living for a neighbour. Fuller had a phenomenal memory—one of the most remarkable of which we have record. With it he was able to astonish the Ecclesiastical Board, and seeing their amazement he proceeded to entertain them with the feats he could perform. By this means he was able to coax them into a good humour. When the right moment came he slipped in his plea:

'Your Worships have thought fit to sequester an honest, poor, but Cavalier parson, my neighbour, from his living, and committed him to prison; he has a great charge of children, and his circumstances are but indifferent; if you please to release him out of prison and restore him to his living, I will never forget the kindness while I live.' The board were in so good a humour by this time that they granted the request at once.

In another examination he was being tried on a delicate point of doctrine. Again his humour triumphed. 'Sir,' he said, 'You may observe that I am a pretty corpulent man, and I am to go through a passage that is very strait: I beg you would be so good as to give me a shove and help me through.' Would not Chesterton have said just the same? But on at least one occasion Fuller's wit got him into trouble. He read some witty verses on a scold to his patron, the second Earl of Carlisle. The earl laughed and asked for a copy of them. 'What need of that, my lord?' replied Fuller, 'you have the original.' The remark is said to have cost him the earl's favour. Perhaps it was indiscreetly passed on to the lady herself, who was Margaret, the third daughter of Francis, Earl of Bedford. At all events, he never regained the friendship of his patron, and the offence he had given may have been his chief reason for leaving Waltham Abbey in 1658.

The Forest never harboured a wiser counsellor. 'Fuller's instinct is infallible,' wrote Leslie Stephen. Coleridge was right in saying that rarely had such a combination of faculties been found in one mind. To learning he brought charity, to wisdom wit, and the dullest chapters of Church history were enlivened by his gaiety, his good sense, and his tolerant humour. In every situation he was the same genial and kindly commentator. Whenever the air became too heavily charged with controversy or passion he would lighten it with a jest. Principles he had and held; but theories, either political or theological, do not appear to have troubled him much. They were at best mere speculations.

Fuller's niece became the grandmother of John and Charles Wesley—an interesting family development.

God rest his soul! He was a merry man.

THE Commonwealth put an end to all the gaiety and splendour of the royal forests. Most of the deer disappeared from them, so that they had to be restocked at the Restoration, when we find a number of English noblemen presenting to Charles II three hundred head of deer, which were divided between Windsor, Waltham, and Enfield. The Forest's former proud state, however, was never restored. 'Its green retreat' had ceased to be 'At once the Monarch's and the Muse's seat.' It came to be regarded principally as a nursery for timber. That was certainly how Pepys regarded it. We read of his coming out to see the trees 'a-hewing,' and afterwards going to Ilford, where he measured the tables and other objects in the room while dinner was being prepared, until he was able to gauge the width of timber accurately at a glance.

All the timber cut from the Forest was taken to Barking, where there was a slide into the Creek. From Barking it was transported on rafts to the dockyards at Deptford and Woolwich. Pepys suspected cheating in supply, and also slackness in delivery. In 1663 he tells us that he sought an order for speeding up the transport of timber, which was 'much wanted for the repair of ships.' No doubt some of this timber found its way to the bakers in what is now the East End of London. Bakers are said to have abounded in this district on account of the great supply of fuel at hand in the Forest.

The Forest timber continued to be used for the Royal Navy up to about 1725, by which time all the best tall trees had been cut down.

Pepys had many Forest associations, principally with his friends the Battens, who lived at Walthamstow. Another friend, Sir John Minnes, lived at The Meads, Loughton, and a story has been passed down through successive owners of this interesting old house that Pepys stayed a night there. The story appears to lack written confirmation. He certainly stayed overnight at Epping, where he played a game of cards, and had a merry talk with the 'plain bold maid of the house' before retiring to bed for

the night.   The following morning he had red herrings for breakfast while his boot-heel was being repaired.   He informs us that
the boy cobbler left the hole as big as he found it.   Riding forward
to London he found only one good path, which he kept, he noted,
as if he were riding through a 'kennel,' or gutter, all the way.

If Pepys had called upon Sir John Minnes on this occasion he
would probably have mentioned the visit in his *Diary*, which
throws no light on the local story.   The country residence of Sir
John mentioned in the *Diary* was near Epsom.

Such references as there are to Sir John Minnes can hardly be
considered favourable.   When this old vice-admiral was appointed
Comptroller of the Navy, Pepys thought he seemed 'in good fair
condition,' and was glad to welcome him to the office.   But he
soon changed his mind, though Sir John had his uses.   He could
tell a good story at dinner, even if all his stories were not believed.
Sometimes he was 'pretty well fuddled,' Pepys thought; at other
times Pepys could only hope that what he heard was untrue, for
if the king's Navy was in the hands of such men as Sir John
described, it was a wonder our plight was not worse than it
actually was.   Again, Pepys was glad to see Sir John Minnes
elected a Master of Trinity House.   Sir William Batten had
contended for the honour, and Pepys was glad to see him passed
over because Lady Batten was already giving herself airs enough.

It was with Sir John Minnes and Sir William and Lady Batten
that Pepys went by coach to Bethnal Green, where he found 'the
greatest quantity of strawberries I ever saw, and good,' in the
garden of the house built by the blind beggar referred to in
the first chapter.   At least it was claimed that the blind beggar
had built the house; but Pepys inquired further and was told that
some of the outhouses were all he had built.

It must have been a disconcerting experience for these lusty old
seamen in their cups to find the diarist's eye suddenly turned on
them.   A pretty wench could do what she liked with him; but
he never lost his head to a man.   Sir John Minnes might have
held his tongue more carefully if he had known the opinion his
friend had formed of him.   Pepys agreed with Sir William
Coventry that it would have been better for the country if the
king had given Sir John Minnes £100,000 than had him as con-
troller, for he did more harm by his dotage and folly than all the
rest by their knavery.

After Sir John Minnes and Pepys had spent a mirthful evening

with Mr. Evelyn, Pepys visited Ruckholt Manor, Leyton, also called
Rookwood, the residence of Sir William Hickes, by whom
Charles II was entertained after hunting in the Forest.   The visit
was paid in the company of Sir William and Lady Batten.
Ruckholt was afterwards described by Pepys as 'a good seat,
with a fair grove of trees by it, and the remains of a good garden;
but so let to run to ruine, both house and everything in and about
it, so ill furnished and miserably looked after, I never did see in
all my life.   Not so much as a latch to his dining-room door;
which saved him nothing, for the wind blowing into the room
for want thereof, flung down a great bow pott, that stood upon
the side-table, and that fell upon some Venice glasses, and did
him a crown's worth of hurt.   He did give us the meanest dinner
(of beef, shoulder, and umbles of venison which he takes away
from the keeper of the Forest, and a few pigeons, and all in the
meanest manner) that ever I did see, to the basest degree.   I was
only pleased at a very fine picture of the Queene-Mother, when
she was young, by Vandike; a very good picture, and a lovely face.'

As Sir William was Ranger of the Forest, no doubt Pepys
thought the dinner had cost him little.   Sir William Hickes was
son and heir of the Sir Michael Hickes we met as a correspondent
of the Wroths of Loughton Hall.   He was created a baronet in
1619, and died in 1680 at the age of eighty-four.   During the
Civil War he suffered for his loyalty to Charles I.   His son,
William, was knighted by Charles II at Ruckholt Manor once
when he came to hunt in the Forest, so there were two Sir Williams,
father and son, at the same time.

The mansion criticized by Pepys was bought by Sir Michael
Hickes from the Parvis family, and remained in the Hickes family
until it was sold in 1720 to Benjamin Collier, who sold it to Earl
Tylney.   It was taken down in 1757.

But the more familiar Forest references are to Sir William
Batten, a commissioner of the Navy, and in 1661 elected member
of Parliament for Rochester, who lived at Walthamstow with
his charming wife and his black servant, Mingo.   According to
Pepys, Sir William lived like a prince, but when he died his family
found that little provision had been made for them.

On 29th May 1661, the king's birthday, Pepys says: 'Rose
early, and put six spoons and a porringer of silver in my pocket
to give away to-day.   Sir W. Pen and I took coach, and (the
weather and way being foule) went to Walthamstow; and being

come there heard Mr. Radcliffe, my former school fellow at Paul's (who is yet a merry boy), preach upon "Nay, let him take all, since my Lord the King is returned," &c. He read all, and his sermon very simple. Back to dinner at Sir William Batten's; and then, after a walk in the fine gardens, we went to Mrs. Browne's, where Sir W. Pen and I were godfathers, and Mrs. Jordan and Shipman godmothers to her boy. And there, before and after the christening, we were with the woman above in her chamber; but whether we carried ourselves well or ill, I know not; but I was directed by young Mrs. Batten. One passage of a lady that eate wafers with her dog did a little displease me. I did give the midwife 10s. and the nurse 5s. and the maid of the house 2s. But for as much I expected to give the name to the childe, but did not, (it being called John,) I forbore then to give my plate.'

There is another amusing reference to Sir William Batten under the date 4th June 1664: 'Mr. Coventry discoursing this noon about Sir W. Batten (what a sad fellow he is!) told me how the King told him the other day how Sir W. Batten, being in the ship with him and Prince Rupert when they expected to fight with Warwicke, did walk up and down sweating with a napkin under his throat to dry up his sweat: and that Prince Rupert being a most jealous man, and particularly of Batten, do walk up and down swearing bloodily to the King, that Batten had a mind to betray them to-day, and that the napkin was a signal: "but, by God," says he, "if things go ill, the first thing I will do is to shoot him."'

There was good reason for this lack of confidence in Batten. During the Civil War he had been on the side of Parliament, and had bombarded Bridlington while the queen was staying there. Her Majesty, we are told, took refuge in a ditch in her night attire. But though Batten was the only Englishman to fire cannon balls at his queen, he was never entirely trusted by the Parliamentarians, most of whom were Independents, while Batten was a Presbyterian. Under the Commonwealth, Batten rose to be vice-admiral, but after a dispute he was relieved of his command, and, to his great indignation, saw a soldier, Colonel Ramsborough, put in his place. He immediately took possession of the *Constant Warwick*, one of the best of the Parliament ships, and several others that were in the Thames at the time, and sailed across to Holland. This formed the nucleus of the fleet subsequently commanded by Prince Rupert.

E

Batten was knighted for the service, but Bridlington was never forgiven. When the king's defeat was assured, Sir William again changed sides, so neither side was ever sure of him.

Few of the entries in the *Diary* concerning Sir William are entirely to his credit, but we are pleased to read that after the Great Fire he sent carts from the country for relief work. Pepys himself was able to get his possessions to a safe place in this way.

In merrier mood, Pepys is found at Sir William's enjoying a bottle or two of wine made from grapes grown at Walthamstow. Only three months later we read that Sir William's body was carried from London, 'with a hundred or two coaches, to Waltham-stow, and there buried.'

Sir William Pen (as Pepys spells the name), Comptroller of the Navy, another distinguished Forest worthy, is mentioned as frequently as Batten, and often in company with him. Sir William Pen consulted Pepys about the education of his son, later to become famous as the founder of Pennsylvania. This famous Quaker was at Chigwell School for a time as a boy. When the father consulted Pepys about him he had lately come from Oxford, and Pepys was asked to recommend a Cambridge college. He named Magdalene. Sir William Pen is described as a conceited man, who always presented his best side in public, and gained popularity by his pretence of sanctity. Three years after the first appearance of William Pen junior in the *Diary*, he appears again in an un-Quaker-like note on his return from France. It reads: 'Mr. Pen, Sir William's son, is come back from France, and come to visit my wife. A most modish person grown, she says a fine gentleman.'

There was talk of Sir William Pen buying Wanstead House, which had succeeded Copt Hall as the finest house in the Forest. At the time it belonged to Sir Robert Brookes. Pepys was surprised, knowing the knight's means were not equal to the upkeep of such a place, and told his friend how foolish such a purchase would be. Sir William knew he could not fool Pepys, so he stammered out something about intending to pull down the present house and build a smaller one on the site, 'and I know not what fooleries. But I will never believe he ever intended to buy it, for my part, though he troubled Mr. Gauden to go and look upon it, and advise him in it.' Wanstead House was a coveted possession. Probably the ambitious knight wished his friends to believe that he was sufficiently wealthy to live there. He knew he could not deceive the astute Samuel, so produced the rebuilding scheme to parry his inquiries. Pepys had no difficulty in seeing that the whole idea was a piece of nonsense.

Unfortunately, the Wroth family are not mentioned in the *Diary*. Pepys was only interested in Forest timber and Forest personalities known to him in connection with his work at the Admiralty; but at the time the *Diary* was being written an interesting thing happened in Forest history, and we should have been glad of a local Pepys to give us more information about the popular reaction to it. Sir Henry Wroth of Loughton Hall, in 1666, was granted a licence to enclose fifteen hundred acres of Forest land. The enclosure was never made; Fisher conjectures that this was on account of local opposition.

At Lambourne lived another famous naval man, Sir Edward Hughes. He was responsible for making the greater part of the road from Lambourne End to Vicarage Lane, Chigwell.

CHAPTER XVII

Old Strype of Leyton

WHAT a wonderful record we should have had if John Strype of Leyton had been another Pepys, or even a Woodeford or Cole! Some have believed that he did keep a diary. If he did it has never come to light. Strype was vicar of Leyton for sixty-eight years, though he was never actually inducted in the whole of his long ministerial life. He lived to the age of ninety-four, and was buried in the chancel of Leyton Church, where his gravestone is now concealed by the new flooring.

Strype was probably of Germanic descent. He was a weak, delicate boy, and all his life lived very carefully. The amount of work he accomplished is astonishing. He wrote the lives of all the famous divines of the Reformation period, including, of course, Cranmer's. In the Forest he found a subject in Sir Thomas Smith of Theydon Mount: *The Life of the Learned Sir Thomas Smith, principal Secretary of State to Edward VI and Elizabeth, wherein are discovered many singular matters relating to the state of learning, the reformation of religion, and the transactions of the kingdom during this time.* Theydon Bois, the next parish to Theydon Mount, had been Strype's first curacy, though he remained there for a short time only.

As a writer the old man was tedious in the extreme, copying into his books anything and everything he came across relating to his period, apparently without the least idea of the relative value of each piece of information. His lack of comment sometimes makes us wonder how much he understood of what he transcribed so painstakingly. But he copied his old documents so faithfully and so accurately that scholars still consult his works instead of looking up the originals, knowing how trustworthy he was. He had, however, one weakness. He collected autographs of the great, and he could not resist the temptation to snip off these signatures from the famous documents that came into his hands.

Strype's work is valuable enough, and must not be disparaged, however dull it appears. It is only when we remember what a wonderful period he lived through, and how long his life was, that we wish he had paid a little more attention to what was going on about him. He was born in Petticoat Lane, at that time a fashionable quarter, in 1643, so his life began in the great struggle between King and Parliament. His family had left the continent to seek refuge from religious persecution. In England they helped to found the Spitalfields silk industry, which reminds us of that pathetic epitaph:

> Here lies the body of Daniel Saul,
> Spitalfields weaver and that's all.

Strype was six years old when Charles I was beheaded. From St. Paul's School he went to Cambridge, and would be there, a youth of eighteen, when the Stuarts were restored. He must have heard a great deal about the Plague and the Fire of London, and have had interesting stories to tell about both these tragedies from personal experience.

He came to Theydon Bois in July 1669, and after a few months there moved on to his life's work at Leyton. At that time the Leyton living was worth less than twenty pounds a year; but later Strype received a sinecure living in Sussex and a lectureship at Hackney. He had been at Leyton five years before he was so much as licensed to preach. Strype saw the downfall of the Stuarts, the Revolution of 1688, the entry of William III into London. He lived through the reigns of Queen Anne, of George I, and ended his long life in the reign of George II. We cannot help regretting that this laborious old historian should have been so much the antiquarian that he took, apparently, no interest in all this clash and tumult, living a secluded, studious life in his vicarage, occupying himself with matters which he may have thought others were inclined to neglect.

Strype found the Leyton vicarage 'very ruinous and being at its best state but mean and unfit to receive a Minister and his Family.' He had to pay the greater part of the cost of rebuilding it, £140 10s., in fact, out of his own pocket. In spite of his preoccupation with the Reformation, Strype did interest himself in his parish, and he left us a description of the Leyton of his day: 'North from Stratford Langton,' he says, 'about a mile and a half, lyeth the Parish of Low Leighton, or Leyton. The Manour or Lordship whereof formerly belonged to the Abbot of the said Stratford: as another great Messuage in the Parish, now called the Forest House, once pertained to another great Abbot on the other Side, namely the Abbot of Waltham. This parish is washed along the West side of it by the sweet River of Lee or Ley (falling into the Thames) which giveth the Village its Name.

It lyes all upon a gentle Rising, ascending for two Miles or better, from the said River Eastward to the pleasant Forest of Waltham. On which side lyeth one Ward of the Parish, called Leyton Stone, pleasantly and healthfully situated. Low Leyton is planted on the Side of the Hill, as it is lower, so it standeth more warm, and is guarded from the North by the Hills of its Neighbour Town of Walthamstow. Both Parts of this Parish are furnished with divers fine and, some of them, magnificent Houses.'

We hope that Defoe in his *Tour of the Eastern Counties*, which we shall deal with presently, called upon Strype when he visited Leyton. It may have been from him that Defoe obtained such information as he provides of the district. Strype was well acquainted with Ruckholt Manor, which, as we have seen, was visited by Pepys and Charles II. It was from the second Sir William Hickes of Ruckholt that he gained access to, and even possession of, papers originally belonging to Lord Burghley, to whom Sir Michael Hickes, Sir William's grandfather, had been private secretary.

Strype also made use of material supplied to him by a descendant of John Foxe. Even his ninety-four years did not give him time enough to use all the material he collected so assiduously. Dr. Samuel Knight, visiting him in 1733, wrote to a friend: 'I made a visit to old Father Strype (at Hackney) when in town last; he is turned ninety years yet very brisk, and with only a decay of sight and memory. He would fain have induced me to undertake Archbishop Bancroft's life, but I have no stomach for it, having no great opinion of him on more accounts than one. He had a greater inveteracy against the Puritans than any of his predecessors. Mr. Strype told me he had great materials towards the life of the old Lord Burghley, and Mr. Foxe, the Martyrologist, which he wished he could have finished, but most of his papers are in character, and his grandson is learning to decipher them.'

Writing of himself to a friend at Cambridge, Strype says: 'I am much decayed by reason of my great age, and the distemper of the Strangury chiefly, and therefore am forced to keep at home and to be free from study (which hath been my delight) and all other business as I can, though I do often divert myself in looking over my vast collections. But I have done writing books, and I pray God what I have done may be of use to the Church and True Religion.'

His most valuable work was his contribution to Stow's *Survey of London,* from which the description of Leyton just quoted is taken, rather than his works for the use of 'the Church and True Religion.' But all these years he was also a faithful parish priest. In 1717 we find him writing: 'This I write on the eve of my birthday, being seventy-four years complete to-morrow, and in good health, I thank God, a kind of miracle of God's goodness to me, who in my younger days was very weak and sickly.' And over a year later: 'This last Christmas was the fiftieth I have been at Leyton, and preached and administered the Holy Sacrament each Christmas Day without any omission.'

His published works fill thirteen great folios, or twenty-seven volumes in the Clarendon Press edition, a monument to patient, honest, and erudite industry. He died at his daughter's house at Hackney in December 1737. An old portrait of him hangs in the vicar's vestry at Leyton parish church, for which he did so much.

In the eighteenth century the Church ceased to attract men like Fuller, Donne, Herbert, and Hall. Wrangles over outward forms had brought it into disrepute with men of liberal and enlightened minds. During the eighteenth century the parson was often little more than a superior kind of domestic. Mr. Collins, in Jane Austen, is probably quite a fair representative of one type of parson of his day. In writers like Fielding we meet another type, the sporting, drinking parson, who was the squire's boon companion. If Strype lacked the brilliance of the clerical men of letters we have already met in the Forest, we cannot honour him too much for his selfless service in days when such service offered few rewards. With a living so poor that nobody wanted it, or cared whether the parson was inducted or not, a vicarage ready to tumble in ruins, a church badly in need of repair, great houses round it, but occupied for the most part by men of a new and godless generation, Strype found little to encourage him. He was twenty-six when he settled at Leyton, a dull dog in the pulpit, a poor leader. There was plenty of money in the parish; but if anything needed doing he had to dip into his own pocket for the funds, with some assistance from the Hickes family. Few knew how industrious their parson was during the twenty-four years between his taking over the vicarage and the appearance of his first work. When he did go into print, volume followed volume in quick succession. Without a spark of inspiration to cheer his course he laboured on till at last, at that great age, his eyes grew dim, his hand unsteady, and his pen had to be laid aside.

CHAPTER XVIII

Daniel Defoe—The merry grant to Randolph Peperking—*Journal of the Plague Year*

WHILE Strype, with so much opportunity, left few eye-witness reports of the great events of his lifetime, Defoe left accounts so vivid of things he did not witness, that his deception is often more convincing than Strype's honesty. Defoe's account of Londoners coming out into the Forest to escape from the Plague is so realistic that it is difficult to believe he was only a child in 1665, and can have known little about the Plague until he was older. However, something very like what he describes must have happened.

Defoe was descended from an old Essex family named Foe, settled at Chadwell, near Tilbury, since the fifteenth century. In 1694 Daniel himself set up a pantile works there. He had a fine house near the Thames, and on it a pleasure boat. But he was not the man for such middling prosperity. When *The Shortest Way with Dissenters* appeared, he soon found himself lodged in Newgate, and the pantile business was ruined. Defoe was no sentimentalist. He scorned antiquities and the tumbledown picturesque. He liked a trim, cultivated countryside with corn and cattle, and with good clean modern houses for the people to live in, so he is not quite in the spirit of the Forest tradition. He was a Philistine, interested in trade and agriculture and practical affairs generally. But he was also an artist, and had a keen eye and ready pen. He had most of the virtues—and more than a few of the vices—that old Strype lacked, with a bigger harvest in his brain and less time to reap it. Strype had much honesty and little imagination; Defoe had much imagination and little honesty, and in literature imagination is more marketable than honesty. The paradox is that Defoe's fancies are often so much nearer the truth than Strype's facts. If he was guilty of filling in more than merely a detail here and there from his own imagination, the resulting picture was often a true one in the way that fiction can be truer to the essential nature of a situation than ascertainable fact.

His tour of the eastern counties began in April 1722. Leaving London by way of Bow Bridge, he noticed that all the villages through which he passed had greatly increased in size during the last twenty or thirty years. Stratford, he thought, must have doubled its population in that time. Every space had been built up with new houses, and two new hamlets had sprung up, one facing the road to Woodford and Epping, the other facing the road to Ilford.

The same growth was to be found at Leyton, Leytonstone, Walthamstow, Woodford, Wanstead, and West Ham. He noticed the increase in large and handsome houses, worth from twenty pounds a year to sixty. Indeed he found few houses worth less than twenty pounds a year. Most of these new houses were occupied either by wealthy London citizens who could afford two houses, one in the city and one in the Forest, or by retired merchants. 'The truth of this may at least appear,' says Defoe, and this is the Defoe method of convincing, 'in that they tell me there are no less than two hundred coaches kept by the inhabitants within the circumference of these few villages named above, besides such as are kept by accidental lodgers.'

He continues: 'This increase of the inhabitants, and the cause of it, I shall inlarge upon when I come to speak of the like in the counties of Middlesex, Surrey, &c., where it is the same, only in a much greater degree: but this I must take notice of here, that this increase causes these villages to be much pleasanter and more sociable than formerly, for now people go to them, not for retirement into the country, but for good company; of which, that I may speak to the ladies as well as other authors do, there are in these villages, nay, in all, three or four excepted, excellent conversation, and a great deal of it, and that without the mixture of assemblees, gaming houses, and publick foundations of vice and debauchery; and particularly I find none of those incentives kept up on this side of the country.'

A great change had come over the Forest. Kings and their courts had gone, leaving their parks and pleasances to bankers and merchants. Defoe was witnessing the beginnings of the Forest familiar to our grandparents and parents, the Forest that belonged not to the court but to the city. It did not differ much from the new suburbs being built in Middlesex and Surrey,

*E

except, Defoe noted, that it was a little more respectable, a
characteristic that remained throughout the next century, under
the strong influence of the great Quaker families who settled in
it.   This respectability only affected the villages close to London;
the deeper Forest became the haunt of gipsies, vagabonds, and
highwaymen.

Defoe continues his account with a reference to the remains of
the great stone causeway, the old highway from London into
Essex, then recently discovered in Hackney Marsh, and to the
Roman coins found at the same time, which had been lodged
with old Strype at Leyton.

'From hence the great road passed up to Layton Stone, a place
by some known, now as much by the sign of the Green Man,
formerly a lodge upon the edge of the Forest; and crossing by
Wanstead House, formerly the dwelling of Sir Josiah Child, now
of his son, the Lord Castlemain (of which, hereafter), went over
the same river which we now pass at Ilford; and passing that part
of the great forest which we now call Henault Forest, came into
that which is now the great road, a little on this side the Whalebone, a place on the road so-called because a rib-bone of a great
whale, which was taken in the River of Thames the same year that
Oliver Cromwell died, 1658, was fixed there for a monument of
that monstrous creature.'

Of the Forest he says: 'The Forest of Epping and Henault
spreads over a great part of this country still: I shall speak again
of the former in my return from this circuit.   Formerly ('tis
thought) these two forests took up all the west and south part of
the county; but particularly we are assured that it reached to the
River Chelmer, and into Dengy Hundred; and from thence again
West to Epping and Waltham, where it continues to be a forest
still.

'Probably this forest of Epping has been a wild or forest ever
since this island was inhabited, and may shew us, in some parts
of it, where enclosures and tillage have not broken in upon it,
what the face of this island was before the Romans' time; that is
to say, before their landing in Britain.

'The Constitution of this forest is best seen, I mean, as to the
antiquity of it, by the merry grant of it from Edward the Confessor, before the Norman Conquest to Randolph Peperking, one
of his favourites, who was afterwards called Peverell, and whose
name remains still in several villages in this county; as particu-

larly that of Hatfield Peverell, in the road from Chelmsford to
Witham. . . .

> 'Ich, Edward Koning, [King]
> Have yeven of my forest the keping
> Of the Hundred of Chelmer and Dancing
> To Randolph Peperking and his kindling, [heirs]
> Wyth heorte and hynde, doe and bocke,
> Hare and foxe, Catte and brocke,
> Wylde fowel with his flocke,
> Partrich, fesant hen, and fesant cocke,
> With green and wylde stob and stocke,
> To kepen and to yeinen-by al her might,
> Both by day and eke by night.
> And hounds for to hold,
> Good and swift and bold:
> Four greyhounds and six raches
> For hare and foxe and wilde cattes,
> And therefore Iche maac him my booke;
> Witness the Bishop Wolston,
> And book ylrede many on,
> And Swein of Essex, our Brother
> And teken him many other;
> And our steward Howelin,
> That by-sought me for him.'

There is a copy of this rhymed charter in the British Museum.
The Essex historian, Morant, believed it to be a forgery because
the language is that of the fourteenth century, but it is not at all
unlikely that it was a free translation of a genuine Saxon grant.

In west Essex Defoe found roads that were scarcely passable
by horse or man in winter, and towns, Chipping Ongar, Hatfield
Broad Oak, Epping, and others, famed for husbandry and good
malt, but of no other note.   To the south he found Waltham and
Wanstead both worthy of description, the one for its abbey, the
other for its great house.

Defoe's report of the unhealthiness of the Essex marshes has
frequently been quoted, and is too often accepted as fact.   The
region was bad enough before it was drained, but it was never
as bad as Defoe would have us believe.   He says 'that all along
this country it was very frequent to meet with men that had had
from five or six to fourteen or fifteen wives; nay, and some more.
And I was informed that in the marshes on the other side of the
river, over against Candy Island, there was a farmer who was
then living with the five-and-twentieth wife, and that his son,
who was but about thirty-five years old, had already had about
fourteen.'   His explanation was that while the men were bred in
the marshes and seasoned to life there, they took their wives from

the hilly country inland, and these unhappy girls rarely lived for more than a year in the damp atmosphere of the marshes. Later he confessed that one of his informers had 'fibbed a little.'

But his most interesting tale of the Forest is in the *Journal of the Plague Year*. We know that the merchants of London, many of whom lived in the Forest, transacted their business during the Plague in the parlour of 'The Spotted Dog' at Upton, an old hostelry that must have been well known to Dick Turpin. From Defoe we learn how poor people from the stricken city found shelter in the open forest. As we read his account we are reminded of that later and larger evacuation, when thousands flocked out into the same countryside during the air raids of the Second Great War. The characters in Defoe's *Journal* assuredly had their counterparts in fact.

He gives us a vivid and circumstantial account of the scene. More than five thousand persons were said to have died in five London parishes during the first three weeks in August. Rumours were about that poor people, distressed and starved, were up in arms and about to plunder the surrounding country. Constables were everywhere on guard. Defoe's first three characters pretended to be countrymen, so that the villagers would not be alarmed and turn them back. They carried with them enough food for two or three months, hoping that by the end of that time the cold weather would have checked the infection. But before long they joined a larger party less well provisioned.

Their first real difficulties came when they reached Walthamstow. There the constable refused to admit them. John, the leader, a resourceful ex-soldier, deceived the people of the village into believing that his friends were fully armed and ready to attack if permission to pass was refused. The people of Walthamstow complied, and John and his followers made their way into the Forest.

By this time all the neighbouring villages were alarmed by rumours of armed bands of robbers who had broken out of London, and had the plague upon them. John prudently decided that his company must split up into small parties to allay suspicion. He and his original two companions, taking the horse with them, went towards Waltham; the others, in two parties, towards Epping. Having thus gained access to the denser part of the Forest, the three parties reassembled near Epping. They pitched their camp under a cluster of pollard trees on the north side of the highway. The next day, or the day after that, was market day at Epping, and provisions were bought—bread, mutton, and beef. In the bustling market they were less likely to be recognized as strangers.

When the people of Epping did get news of them, it looked as though the Walthamstow experience might be repeated. John wisely decided to try other tactics this time. He met the angry people of Epping with friendly and persuasive arguments, and before long succeeded in winning their goodwill. The minister of a neighbouring parish sent two bushels of wheat and half a bushel of white peas. A gentleman who lived near sent them a cart-load of straw, with which to thatch their huts, hastily constructed of logs and branches. Others brought stools, old chairs, and household utensils, so that at the beginning of September they were as well supplied as an average gipsy encampment, and only concerned about the prospect of winter.

Then rumours came to them that the plague was already at Waltham Abbey on one side, and at Romford on the other. Before long it was at Epping also, at Woodford, and at most of the villages of the Forest. About a hundred and twenty persons were said to have died of the distemper in the villages near them. Now that the small towns and villages were full of fever, poor people were following their example and taking to the Forest. Many of these were already sick, and before long the plague was not only in the villages, but also in the tents and huts near them in the Forest. John became very worried about this, and paid a visit to the charitable gentleman who had been their principal benefactor. After discussing the danger of infection with him, John decided that his party must leave the place where they had been so well received and find other quarters.

They then moved to the marshes near Waltham Abbey, where they found a man who kept a weir on the river. This man so terrified them with his stories of the plague in Waltham, Enfield, Ware, and all the towns near the river, that they were afraid to go forward. Again they crossed the Forest, this time towards Romford and Brentwood. In this direction they found large numbers of Londoners taking refuge in Hainault Forest. These people were in a desperate plight. They had no Captain John to organize them and plead their cause with the villagers. Instead they lived by thieving and poaching, and even went so far as to kill cattle, so that the whole countryside went in fear of them. Others lived in hovels they had constructed by the road-side, where they waylaid travellers and supported themselves by begging.

John saw no prospect for his own well-conducted company on this side of the Forest, so he led them back to his old friend and benefactor near Epping, who found an uninhabited house for them, capable of sheltering them from the bad weather. Here they settled, resolved never to remove again. But they were still Londoners, and when the hard weather came they caught colds and longed for the city. About December they returned to London.

That is a brief outline of a story told with great skill. Lamb said of Defoe's fictitious narratives: 'In the appearance of truth, in all the incidents and conversations that occur in them, they exceed any works of fiction I am acquainted with. It is perfect illusion.' Defoe's degree of realism is still rare. Probably the secret of it was that he had studied effects on people by direct speech. His style is a direct, spoken style. Over and over again he had been obliged to use his command of language to get himself out of awkward corners. Twice he was sentenced to Newgate prison, and three times to the pillory, yet he was so popular that on one occasion the pillory was decked with garlands and the people drank his health in the streets. It is diverting to reflect that this prince of liars is buried in the same graveyard as honest John Bunyan. Near them lies Isaac Watts. Strange bedfellows!

CHAPTER XIX

THE eighteenth century brought exciting days to the Forest.
Towards the end of Strype's long life an Act of Parliament was
passed with the object of ridding the tract of gangs of ruffians
called Waltham Blacks. Its roads had long been infested by
them, though cavalry patrolled every night between Hackney
and Waltham. The fame of these Essex ruffians spread far.
Even John Byrom, the Lancashire poet best known as the author
of *Christians, awake*, wrote a ballad on an Epping Forest hold-up.

Most of these outlaws were ex-soldiers who had fought during
the Civil War, and had turned deer-stealers and highwaymen for
lack of regular employment afterwards. Their numbers steadily
increased during the first half of the eighteenth century, until
they became an organized menace. The most famous gang, the
Waltham Blacks, appeared about 1690. They were a murderous
horde of desperadoes, who once nearly captured William III
himself on his way through the Forest to Newmarket. This
particular gang camped in the Wake Valley, between Waltham
and Epping, in huts built of turf, covered with fern and brambles.
A few of them remained until late in the eighteenth century, when
Mr. Conyers of Copt Hall did something towards civilizing his
outlaw neighbours by building them small cottages.

Many stories were current in the neighbourhood about the
Waltham Blacks. Some were even romantic, like the story of
the Lady Millicent, who ran away from the nunnery at Cheshunt
to join her lover in the Wake Valley:

> Deep in the Forest's dreary tracks,
> Where rang'd at large fierce Waltham Blacks,
> There passengers with wild affright
> Shrunk from the horrors of the night;
> Where o'er the marsh false meteors beam,
> And glow-worms in the bushes gleam:
> There through the woods, o'er meadows dank,
> Where merry devils frisk and prank,
> Behold a maid still fearless rove,
> Fair Millisent, the child of love;
> From Cheshunt's dome she wanders darkling,
> Array'd in white, her eye-beams sparkling,

Astound, the curate, and mine host,
Exclaim, that 'they have seen a ghost!'
Yet Munchinsey does soon discover,
She 's a mortal to her favour'd lover.[1]

A certain Mr. Woods, writing to a friend in 1729, described how
his horse became lame while he was riding through the Forest,
so that he was compelled to take shelter for the night at a small
ale-house. The innkeeper received him civilly, but when Mr.
Woods asked if he might stay the night, both the innkeeper and
his wife appeared nervous. At first they said they had no room,
but when Mr. Woods promised to pay them well they became more
accommodating. His suspicions were thus aroused, and during
the night they were confirmed when the highwaymen arrived,
disguised so effectively that Mr. Woods confessed that he would
be unable to identify any one of them. They went through a
ridiculous kind of ceremony before their leader, who called himself 'King Orronoko, the King of the Blacks.'

At this time most of the cottages in lonely parts of the Forest
were occupied by deer-stealers. Honest men were not welcome.
These cottages had pits in the floor, near the hearth, into which
the deer was dropped. When the chance came it was taken out
and carried to one of the inns, where stolen venison was bought as
'black sausage.' Even in Charles II's reign keepers were not
allowed 'to keep victualling houses whereby idle people may be
encouraged to kill the deer.'

In spite of the death penalty the Blacks contrived to evade
capture. Some of them, like Dick Turpin's gang, were not deer-
stealers regularly, but fell back on the less risky adventure if no
wealthy traveller happened to come their way. Other gangs of
thieves worked in London itself, and came out into the Forest
for hiding. Some may have worked the other way round. We
find that one gang 'robbed Captain Cockburn, a Commissioner
and Comptroller of the Navy, near his own house at Woodriding,
in the Forest, and half an hour later, on their way to London,
robbed Mr. Clay of Goldings Hill as he was riding up Buckhurst Hill.'

One famous highwayman of the day was Jack Rann, 'Sixteen
String Jack,' so called because he appeared in the dock at the
Old Bailey with sixteen coloured ribbons 'streaming from the
knees of his breeches.' Rann is a name still common in the

[1] A better version of this story is found in *The Merry Devil of Edmonton*.

Forest. But the most famous highwayman of the Forest was
Dick Turpin himself. He was born at 'The Bell,' later called
'The Crown,' Hempstead, in 1704. His name still lives in the
district in such landmarks as Turpin's Ring, Turpin's Corner,
Turpin's Meadow, and Turpin's Oak. But he belongs to the
Forest. The stable is still standing at Buckhurst Hill where
Dick is said to have tricked his pursuers. This stable was
formerly behind Luctons, a large house where Dick had two
stables, the one remaining and another on the first floor of the
house. The second stable was a windowless closet opening from
one of the bedrooms. Dick would lead his sweating horse upstairs after a mad chase, and hide it in the closet, bringing another
horse down into the stable outside, so that when the king's men
arrived they would find an unridden horse, and Dick lounging
sulkily about the yard. A similar story was associated with an
old house at Ilford, named after Lord Salisbury, which, from
being a monastery first, became the Green Man Inn in the
eighteenth century, and a private residence later. Mrs. Wallis
of Shaftesbury, Dorset, who lived in this house as a child, was
told by her parents that when they first went to live there they
found rings in the wall of an upstairs room, where horses had been
stabled. Dick Turpin was believed to have used this indoor
stable exactly as he used the one at Buckhurst Hill. The stables
outside were haunted. A horse would be heard galloping up to
the gates, but when they were opened, nothing was there.

As a youth, Dick was apprenticed to a butcher in Whitechapel.
A song about him was sung in the Forest, one verse going:

> In London a long time ago,
> Dick Turpin he lived you must know;
> He was a non-sucher, and lived as a butcher,
> In that famous place, Whitechapel Row.

When the butcher discharged him 'for the brutality of his
manners' he became servant-man to a farmer who lived in
Richmond Street, Plaistow. While there he married Hester
Palmer of East Ham, and soon afterwards came to be suspected
of stealing cattle and cutting them up for sale. He was again
discharged. This time he revenged himself by stealing from his
last employer two fat oxen, which he drove to his own house at
East Ham and stripped off their hides. The hides were offered
for sale at Waltham Abbey market. There he was recognized.
A warrant for his arrest was issued, but when the constables

arrived at his house he slipped away through a back window, making his way down to the river, where he joined a gang of smugglers. Smuggling was rife at that time, and Dick's gang worked between Plaistow and Southend. Cargoes of tobacco and spirits were brought in by fishing smacks, landed in the marshes, and carried away at a convenient hour in carts fitted with false bottoms. The next day these carts were loaded with hay or straw, and driven to receiving agents.

For some reason, perhaps only a desire for change, or perhaps the promise of greater profits, Dick gave up this trade and joined as highwayman a man named King, whom he later shot on Plaistow Marsh. Their field of action was Epping Forest. Here they did so well that the Government issued a proclamation offering a reward of two hundred pounds for Turpin's arrest. The trade of highwayman was combined with that of deer-stealer; but this second pursuit had ceased to yield the profits Dick coveted. The number of keepers had been increased; the number of deer reduced. Common housebreaking offered better rewards. Dick and his associate, King, hit on a simple plan that served them well. They would knock at the door of a lonely farmhouse, and when it was opened rush in and grab whatever was within reach. If the farmer's wife happened to be alone, one of them would hold her while the other found more valuable property to carry off. At the house formerly called Trap's Hill Farm, Loughton, they held a blindfolded and terrified old lady over the kitchen fire until she told them where the money was hidden. They are said to have got four hundred pounds from her. Another time, inspired no doubt by motives of revenge, they broke into the house of a forest-keeper named Mason, beat him to death, wrecked his household possessions, and carried off one hundred and thirty guineas. One night Turpin and his gang robbed both Chingford and Barking churches, but failed to find the church plate, which had been carried home for greater safety by the church-wardens.

At the beginning of his career in the Forest, Dick lived for six months with his wife in a cottage at Sewardstone. At the end of this time he was recognized and took to a cave at High Beach, hidden by fern and brambles, from which he would sneak down to get food from his wife, who remained in the cottage. The cave was so artfully concealed that Turpin and King could see any one approaching along the road, while remaining hidden themselves.

This excavation, or what is claimed to be the one, is still pointed
out at the small ale-house called 'Turpin's Cave.' The cave
itself is twelve feet long, seven feet high. In Turpin's day it
was probably larger. Inside the inn are an old cutlass, with
rusty iron scabbard, the head of an old pickaxe, old horse-shoes
and horse-bits, two large padlocks, a pair of rusty handcuffs,
a flintlock pistol, and similar objects, which the visitor is assured
were discovered in the cave. On the walls of the little bar-
parlour hang several old prints with Turpin as subject. In one
he is shown shooting a game-cock with a pistol.

In 1737, after two of his gang had been hanged, Turpin, with
King, his chief confederate, decided to move back into the East
End. The cave was deserted. To-day Dick Turpin is a legendary figure, remembered chiefly from the exciting pages of
Harrison Ainsworth's *Rookwood*. On a moonlight night we may
fancy we see him sliding off the smoking flanks of Black Bess,
and hastily concealing himself behind the Forest brambles. We
recognize him by his short face, his broad cheekbones, dark scowl,
and pock-marked skin. He stands five feet nine inches tall.
Dick—Gentleman Dick, if you please!

If the glories of the Royal Forest had proved an insub-
stantial pageant, a reckless splendour had succeeded them.
There were highwaymen, young gallants riding to Newmarket
races, coaches, and flourishing—though notorious — wayside
inns. We can imagine the riders with their heavy coats
and spurred boots, their three-cornered hats upon their
powdered wigs.

Of the old Forest inns, none had a more romantic history than
the old 'Green Man' at Leytonstone, a favourite meeting place
in the eighteenth century. The innkeeper was in the confidence
of the highwaymen and gave them cover. One bedroom of this
famous old house held an enormous chest in which three or four
men could conceal themselves. Underneath the chest was a
trap-door, through which the fugitives escaped to a room below.
In the floor of the lower room there was another trap-door,
opening into a cave, with a passage leading to freedom in the
dense undergrowth of the Forest. Old pistols and other weapons
were found from time to time in or about the old inn.

The Forest was now the terror of all honest citizens. The
villages and great houses remained, but their character was
changing. Not far from the Wake Valley of the Blacks, Copt

Hall still stood on its hill. At the end of the previous century it
had been occupied by a character as wild and legendary as Dick
Turpin himself, though in a different way. He, too, must have
called at 'The Green Man' on his way out from London to Copt
Hall. Let us imagine three roistering fellows drinking in a
corner of the inn parlour. They are flushed with anticipation of
lusty pleasures awaiting them at the great house in the Forest.
There is pride in their dress and in the carriage of their
heads. One, a poet, jewels his conversation with learned
quotations; another mocks his bookishness. The third,
Charles Sackville, Earl of Dorset, the owner of Copt Hall,
laughs loudly at both, knowing well their hatred of each other
and their dependence upon himself. His speech is coarse but
good-natured. He shouts with gusto to the landlord, who runs
to his table.

There is a stir in the room as a traveller comes in with a tale
of being robbed on the road by a highwayman. Sackville silences
his companions and listens. The landlord has a knowing look
in his eye. Before long this highwayman will slip in through the
back door, and some of the traveller's money will be transferred
to his own greasy pocket.

An hour later our three gallants are riding through the Forest
towards Epping, with the image of Copt Hall in their minds.
One thinks how he will be able to pace the great avenues or
nearby glades, intoning his stanzas. The second thinks how
merry it will be to drink ale with the stolid farmers at Epping.
Sackville thinks of Nell Gwynn, who has gone on in the earl's
carriage. Nell Gwynn was the mistress of Charles Sackville
before she was passed on to the king, and always spoke of Sackville as her Charles I.

This Charles Sackville of Copt Hall was the Earl of Dorset who
vrote the song:

> To all you ladies now at land
>   We men at sea indite;
> But first would have you understand
>   How hard it is to write. . . .

He was a volunteer attending the Duke of York in the Dutch
War of 1665. He was in the battle on 3rd June, when eighteen
great Dutch ships were taken, fourteen others destroyed, and the
admiral blown up with all his crew. His famous song, which was
written to the ladies at Whitehall, was said to have been dashed

off the day before the battle, but the story is not true. The song
was written six months earlier, and Sackville took more than
one day over it.

The earl and his friends were the wildest set in England. On
one occasion Sackville, Sedley, and Sir Thomas Ogle got drunk
at the Cock Tavern in Bow Street. All three went out on to a
balcony, where Sedley stripped himself of all his clothes, and
harangued the crowd in the street below. The escapade cost
him five hundred pounds.

Dr. Johnson says that Sackville was 'eager of the riotous and
licentious pleasures which young men of high rank, who aspired
to be thought wits, at that time imagined themselves entitled to
indulge.' Pepys had an eye on him, but not everything he recorded about Sackville and Sedley appears in the popular editions
of the *Diary*.

While staying at Copt Hall on one occasion, Sackville and his
friends rode out in pursuit of thieves, and killed an innocent
tanner somewhere near Waltham Cross. They took away the
tanner's money, believing it to be stolen, and were apprehended
for robbery and murder. The grand jury, however, found a bill
for manslaughter only.

Copt Hall, as we saw in the chapter on Fuller, had come to
the Sackvilles by marriage with a Cranfield. It remained in
their possession until 1701, when the estate was sold for approximately twenty thousand pounds. The finest furniture, pictures,
and tapestries were removed to Knole, and may be seen there
to-day, including pictures of this mad, bad, but benevolent
Restoration earl, with the coarse and florid features, the heavy
jowl, and the merry eyes. England never had another patron of
letters like him. Pope, Dryden, Prior, Killigrew, Shadwell, and a
host of others, scholarly or licentious, jovial or satirical, had reason
to bless his name. Nothing that had merit came amiss to him.

Many stories of Sackville have come down to us. In one we
see him entering the Rhenish Tavern in Covent Garden, his eye
falling on the small pot-boy sitting in a corner with a book.
The earl asks what the boy is reading, and receives the surprising
answer: 'Horace.' He demands a translation, and is so surprised
that he immediately takes the boy under his patronage, sending
him back to Westminster School, which he had been obliged to
leave on his father's death, and later to Cambridge. The boy
is Matt Prior.

Though Sackville squandered his fortune upon poets and
mistresses, he regretted nothing:

> May knaves and fools grow rich and great,
>   And the world think them wise,
> While I lie dying at her feet
>   And all the world despise.

At Copt Hall he entertained most of the wits of his day.   One
of these reckless young men was disappointed because he was not
able to visit this famous rendezvous in the Forest.   Sir George
Etherege, like his companion, flouted the conventions and even
the decencies of civilized life, fleeing from the country after an
exceptionally disgraceful brawl.   He wrote to Sackville:

'I have lost for want of exercise the use of fancy and imagination, and am grown so very stupid that when I read a new poem
methinks the author should be invited to one of those reverend
cells the hermit Lee has quitted [a cell in Bethlehem Hospital,
where Nathaniel Lee, the dramatist, was twice confined for
insanity].   Lovers have been metamorphosed by the ancient
poets, though churches have not yet; you and I were ne'er so
bold to turn the fair Castle when she fled us into a tree, not dream-
ing she would grow as big as one of Evelyn's oaks, nor ourselves
into bulls when we carried the two draggle-tailed nymphs one
bitter, frosty night over the Thames to Lambeth. . . . I would
gladly be witness of the content you enjoy at Copt Hall now, and I
hope to surprise you there one day.'

Whatever Sackville's faults, he had the virtue of generosity,
though this attracted to him parasites who flattered him for gain,
and ranked him as a poet above his merits.   His verse was
described by Johnson as 'the effusions of a man of wit,' which is a
description that would do equally well for most of the poetry of
his day.   He wrote nothing else so good as his famous song, and
the extravagant praise he received as a poet was due to the
desirability of keeping in his good books.   Most of his admirers
were in debt to him.

For all his folly and vice, this notorious libertine retained the
genuine affection and admiration of all kinds of people.   His
brilliant conversation and engaging manners secured to him the
admiration of society.   The poor blessed him for his liberality,
and were always ready to take his part against the city watch.
It is said that not a day ever passed without some poor family
being better off for his interest in them.   He had reckless courage,

and not a trace of malice did he ever show towards anybody. Sackville was, in fact, the most popular man in the England of his day.

He also had the honour of bringing another princess into our Forest story. In 1688 the life of the Princess Anne, afterwards queen, was believed to be in danger, and Sackville was called upon to arrange her escape. Dr. Johnson tells us that he conducted her to Nottingham under guard. Macaulay's account of the escape is the most romantic. 'That evening,' he says, 'Anne retired to her chamber as usual. At dead of night she rose, and, accompanied by her friend Sarah [Churchill] and two other female attendants, stole down the back stairs in a dressing gown and slippers. The fugitives gained the open street unchallenged. A hackney coach was in waiting for them there. Two men guarded the humble vehicle. One of them was Compton, Bishop of London, the princess's old tutor; the other was the magnificent and accomplished Dorset, whom the extremity of the public danger had roused from his luxurious repose. The coach drove instantly to Aldersgate Street . . . there the princess passed the night. On the following morning she set out for Epping Forest. In that wild tract Dorset possessed a venerable mansion [Copt Hall], the favourite resort, during many years, of wits and poets.'

Of this incident the earl's grandson relates that 'one of her Royal Highness's shoes sticking fast in the mud, the accident threatened to impede her escape; but Lord Dorset, immediately drawing off his white glove, put it on the Princess's foot and placed her safely in the carriage.'

Morant, Wright, and other historians of the Forest who have copied them, tell us that the Princess Anne retired to Loughton Hall. As they do not also mention this escape to Copt Hall, and do not give any supporting evidence for the Loughton Hall story, it appears reasonable to conclude that the two halls have been confused, and that it was to Copt Hall, not Loughton Hall, that she escaped.

Among the poets entertained at Copt Hall was Shadwell, who wrote there his best comedy, *The Squire of Alsatia*, which caught the taste of the town and enjoyed popularity for many years. Shadwell brings the subject of satire into the Forest again by being the unfortunate victim of Dryden, his mortal enemy, in *Mac Flecknoe*, from which Pope derived the idea for his *Dunciad*. Shadwell had superseded Dryden as laureate, on Sackville's recommendation, when Dryden's religious views were no longer acceptable.

As Sackville was always an easy dupe, it is not surprising that his life ended in squalor with a common woman at Bath. His family, already estranged from him, were anxious to prove him insane, and sent Prior to report on his condition. Prior found him much the worse for wear, but still better in mind than most men, and told the family not to call him into court to give evidence against his old friend.. Congreve, after visiting Sackville on his deathbed, declared: 'Faith, he slabbers more wit dying than other people do in their best health.' And so we leave him, the personification of Restoration England.

Charles II was entertained at Copt Hall, and it is sometimes claimed that the loin of beef was 'knighted' there; another story places the ceremony at Pimp Hall, Chingford. The old ballad has it:

> The Second Charles of England
> Rode forth one Christmastide
> To hunt a gallant stag of ten,
> Of Chingford woods the pride.

The hunt was interrupted by a snowstorm, which drove the party to Pimp Hall for shelter. Inside all was hearty; blazing logs on the hearth; a loin of beef on the table:

> Quoth Charles: Odds fish! a noble dish,
> And noble made by me,
> By kingly rite, I dub thee knight—
> Sir Loin henceforward be.

The loin of beef had already been 'knighted' by James I at Hoghton Towers in Lancashire, and also, according to similar stories, by Henry VIII.

Charles I went through Epping in 1634. In John Baker's Trust Account we read of a payment: 'For taking upp the stulpes and settinge upp the same upon the highway leading througe Wintrie Wood, for his Maᵗⁱᵉˢ travelinge that way.' We read also that 'The Protector lay last night at Epping.' Charles II dined at Copt Hall in June 1660, and William III, on his way to Newmarket, dined and stayed the night there on 4th April 1698. With Henry VIII, Mary, Elizabeth, Charles II, Anne, William III, and perhaps others, the first two Copt Halls had an impressive list of royal visitors.

CHAPTER XX

Prior at Down Hall—Dr. Thomas Newton—Locke at High Laver

THE friend of Sackville who comes most prominently into the Forest story is Prior, who lived at Down Hall, between Hatfield Broad Oak and Harlow, when it was a house of more modest proportions. An engraving showing Down Hall as it was more than fifty years after Prior's day is reproduced in Sir Gurney Benham's pamphlet, *The Story of Harlow*.

Prior was imprisoned for two years on a charge of high treason. He was discharged without trial, and also, alas, without means. But he was not without friends. These persuaded him to publish his poems in a magnificent folio edition for wealthy subscribers, which produced four thousand guineas. To this Lord Harley, son of the first Earl of Oxford, added an equal sum for the purchase of the Down Hall estate as a residence for the poet, with the stipulation that it should revert to himself at Prior's death. The story of the poet's first visit to his new home is told in a lively ballad. Prior travelled with Lord Harley's land-jobbing agent, John Morley of Halstead, himself a picturesque old Essex character:

> I sing not old Jason, who travell'd through Greece,
> To kiss the fair maids, and possess the rich Fleece;
> Nor sing I Aeneas, who, led by his mother,
> Got rid of one wife, and went far for another.
> Derry down, down, hey derry down. . . .

> But I sing of exploits that have lately been done
> By two British heroes, called Matthew and John:
> And how they rid friendly from fine London town,
> Fair Essex to see, and a place they call Down.

where:

> There are gardens so stately, and arbours so thick,
> A portal of stone, and a fabric of brick.

The two set out for Harlow, and in an old engraving that went with the earlier editions of the poem, we see Morley and Prior lumbering along in an elaborately carved chariot, with Prior's Swedish servant mounted on his master's horse at the side.

They did not come through the Forest, but went round by Hoddesdon, and called at 'The Bull,'

> Near a nymph with an urn, that divides the highway,
> And into a puddle throws mother of tea. . . .

137

> So to Harlow they came; and hey! where are you all?
> Show us into the parlour, and mind when I call;
> Why, your maids have no motion, your men have no life;
> Well, master, I hear you have buried your wife.

After some merry talk in Harlow they set out again; but though they travelled a dozen miles round failed to find Down Hall. At last Morley saw it in the distance, and pointed it out to Prior, who looked, but could only see a windmill, until:

> 'O, now a low, ruin'd white shed I discern,
> Until'd and unglaz'd; I believe 'tis a barn.'
> 'A barn! why you rave: 'tis a house for a Squire,
> A Justice of Peace, or a Knight of our shire.'

In spite of the objections, Prior bought Down Hall with Harley's money, or—to be more correct—Harley bought it and gave Prior the use of it for life. Soon after acquiring the property, the poet sent a present of eight pigeons, with instructions to roast them 'properly incrusted with sweet breads and "sparagrass,"' to Lady Harley and her daughter, the poet's 'noble, lovely little Peggy.' Prior lived off and on at Down Hall, built one or two summer-houses, cut walks in the wood, and made a fishpond to hold ten carp. In James Gibbs's *Book of Architecture* there is a draught made by Prior: 'to have been built at Down Hall in Essex.' This project was never carried out. Of Prior at Down Hall, Dr. Johnson says: 'Prior had now what wits and philosophers have often wished for, the power of passing the day in contemplation and tranquillity.'

Prior never forgot Sackville's kindness to him as a boy. He dedicated his poems to his old patron's son, several of them addressed to members of the Copt Hall family. It is always disconcerting to political theorists to find poets rising from humble origins to high places in the State under the system of patronage more easily than under democracy. Apparently a high degree of economic security has to be reached before men can be persuaded to give the honour that is their due to these finer minds. Prior, from being a pot-boy when the gay earl found him, rose to be both a courtier and a diplomat. At the French court he was regarded as a man of great distinction. He played a notable part at Utrecht, and when misunderstanding arose by some mistake in the queen's orders, Bolingbroke wrote to him: 'Dear Mat, hide the nakedness of thy country, and give the best turn thy fertile brain will furnish thee with to the blunders of thy countrymen, who are not much better politicians than the French are poets.' He was the grandson of a peasant and the son of a carpenter; but whether as diplomat, courtier, or member of Parliament, he always conducted himself with sanity, dignity, and geniality.

Of all Prior's poems, the autobiographical *Ballad of Down Hall* reveals most clearly his characteristic traits, and shows what a gift for comedy he would have had if only he had been given the leisure to cultivate it. For all his humour he was more seriously minded than most of the wits of his age. He was haunted by a profound sense of man's lowliness before the infinite and the unknowable. Perhaps it is this shadow that makes his light verse less superficial than that of most of his contemporaries. 'The pleasures of life do not compensate for the miseries,' he wrote in the preface to *Solomon*. The humorous interest in chances and accidents of the road shown in *The Ballad of Down Hall* was a compensation for these darker broodings. From the same source springs the note of tenderness found in his poems on children.

At Wimborne, where Prior was born, a place still famous for its chained library, visitors used to be shown a chained copy of Raleigh's *History of the World* of 1614, with a hole in the pages. This was said to have been burned by young Matt Prior when dozing over the book with a taper in his hand. It is a pleasant story; but there is reason to believe that the book was not in the library when Prior was there as a boy. After the poet's death, Down Hall was altered extensively by Lord Harley, an indolent, good-natured man and a great connoisseur. It was he who completed the famous Harleian collection of manuscripts, begun by his father, which was acquired by Parliament and is now in the British Museum. In 1724 Lord Harley succeeded his father and became the second Earl of Oxford. He lived at Down Hall for the last fifteen years of his life, dying in 1741 of intemperance, aggravated by financial embarrassment. In forming his remarkable collection of manuscripts and pictures, Harley is said to have spent £400,000 of his wife's fortune. It could not have been spent to better purpose. The Harleian collection of manuscripts was sold by his widow for £10,000.

Prior was not the only writer of the age to gain here 'the power of passing the day in contemplation and tranquillity.' John Locke, our greatest English philosopher, lived for fourteen years with the Masham family at High Laver. And a few years later Shelley, between Moreton and Ongar, was the quiet retreat of another eminent scholar, Dr. Thomas Newton, who published, in 1749, an edition of Milton's *Paradise Lost*, with critical notes and a life of the poet, and wrote many learned dissertations on the Bible. Dr. Newton was Dean of St. Paul's from 1768 to 1782.

Oates, at High Laver, the house where Locke lived, has gone, though the site can still be identified. A ruined outhouse remains, a pond, and part of the philosopher's garden. Oates was a square, Tudor manor house with a turret above the entrance hall. Locke's study was over the parlour, and his bedroom adjoined his study—always a convenient arrangement. It seems most fitting to think of the philosopher in the seclusion of High Laver, though he, too, comes into the index of 'The Green Man' at Leytonstone. In August 1695 we find him writing to Edward Clarke from Oates that 'There were several people robed [robbed] in Eping Forest the same morning we passed it. We heard of it at The Green Man and our Ladys hearts went pitapat.' Even the tranquillity of High Laver was not entirely undisturbed by echoes from the great Forest to which it had once belonged.

Inside High Laver Church we read the epitaph which the philosopher composed for himself. In translation it reads: 'Stay, traveller. Near this place lies John Locke. If you ask what kind of man he was, he replies that he lived content with his own modest fortune. Bred a scholar, he devoted his learning only to the service of truth. This you will learn from his writings, which will bear more faithful evidence to his character than the dubious praises of an epitaph. His virtues, if he had any, were too humble to afford grounds of praise to himself, or a pattern for you. Let his faults be buried with him. If you seek an example in good living you have it in the Gospel. May you never seek an example of evil. Of mortality, examples are here and everywhere. May you profit by them.'

Locke had known Lady Masham as the daughter of his friend, the philosopher Ralph Cudworth, something of whose intellectual character she had inherited, so that Locke could say of her: 'You will not find many men to whom she is not superior in wealth of knowledge and ability to profit by it.' Sir Francis Masham, her husband, was a genial country gentleman who, though not a scholar himself, enjoyed the society of the men of learning invited by his wife to Oates. When Locke was induced to come out and try the air of Essex he found both the county and the Masham family completely to his taste. Besides being a scholar, Lady Masham had a sunny, equable nature, so that when she and Sir Francis pressed Locke to make his home with them he readily consented, with the one condition that he must be allowed to share the household expenses. It was agreed that he should pay twenty shillings a week and board himself and his servant, to whom he paid twenty shillings a quarter. This settled, the philosopher made High Laver his home and entered the happiest period of his life.

Locke required of his friends that they should think meanly neither of themselves nor of others. Virtue he set above wisdom and learning. In the Mashams he found all three, and in the right order. Plain living and high thinking were the established custom of the household. With Sir Francis he would ride on horseback through the lanes and villages of the Roothings; with Lady Masham and her friends he would enjoy cultivated society in the evenings.

Sir Isaac Newton was one of his visitors at Oates. We know that he was there in the January of 1691, and again in 1702, discussing theology, always an interesting subject at Oates, and a serious matter with Newton, who wrote books on the interpretation of prophecy and biblical criticism. Rarely can these subjects have been discussed with less tendency to dogmatize than at Oates. Locke was a delightful talker, humorous and easy. He enjoyed nothing more than a good story, for, like Fuller, his geniality equalled his learning. Writing to an Irish friend in 1698, while confined to the house with asthma, he says: 'I wish, nevertheless, that you were here with me to see how well I am; for you would find that, sitting by the fireside, I could bear my part in discoursing, laughing, and being merry with you, as well as ever I could in my life.'

Locke regularly attended the services at the village church. The rector, Samuel Lowe, was his very good friend. Together they would discuss, amongst other things, the writings of Samuel Hoard, who had been rector of the neighbouring parish of Moreton. Hoard, like Harsnett, had protested against the doctrine of predestination, publishing in 1635 a work presenting evidence of 'God's love to mankind . . . by disproving his absolute decree for their damnation.' Hoard's work was considered to be one of the best on the subject. A reprint in 1673 is sufficient testimony to its quality.

At the end of his life Locke said that he died in perfect charity

with all men, and in communion with the Church of Christ, by
whatever name it was called. He spoke the truth, for he was
himself an example of the tolerant understanding he preached.
Though frequently the object of attack for his views, he never lost
his mildness and urbanity in the heat of controversy.

Locke was born in Somerset. In 1670 he conceived the ideas
expressed in his most famous philosophical work, the *Essay on
Human Understanding*, but the book, which shows his gift for
patient, detailed inquiry, took nineteen years to complete. Of
its origin we are told that Locke was present at a dispute, which
appeared to him to have arisen purely out of verbal misunderstanding. How many disputes, he reflected, arise in this way.
So he set about studying the origin of ideas. He dismissed the
Cartesian doctrine that knowledge is innate. Knowledge is,
he believed, mostly derived from experience. He believed that
our natural faculties are capable of forming every notion that we
possess. They form them partly by direct sensation and partly
by reflection, or, in other words, partly by experience of the outer
world, and partly by personal, mental operations. Understanding comes with consciousness. Men of large understanding are
men of extended consciousness. We know right from wrong,
truth from falsehood, when we have so extended our personal
consciousness as to have a true awareness of the reality of things,
and are simply reasonable enough to conform with the reality of
which we have become aware. His point of view was thoroughly
English. The formation of abstract theories was of no use;
theories must conform with experience.

He wrote two treatises on government, in which, as we should
expect, he strongly opposed the idea of the divine right of kings
and the passive obedience of subjects, upholding what are still
held to be the principles at the root of constitutional government
in this country. If Sir Thomas Smith was ahead of his time in
visualizing England as a democracy, Locke was equally advanced
in declaring that political power exists and should be exercised
only for the public good. Those who hold power, he insisted,
must recognize that they hold it on trust, and only by the consent
of the governed. He wrote extensively on the reasonableness
of Christianity, and three fine *Letters on Toleration*. Locke had
all the sturdy honesty, independence, and tolerance of the
Englishman at his best, with a firm grasp of the vital necessity
of political and spiritual freedom for all men.

He suffered persecution for his principles, and had to live in Holland for a time, in concealment from his enemies. When he was able to emerge, he formed a literary society in Amsterdam, and occupied himself with liberal studies until he was able to return to England with William and Mary,

Locke did not cut himself off from the world at High Laver. He continued to write, and he had become so well known that he wielded great influence. His opinion was sought on every political and philosophical question that presented itself.

In the last winter of his life Lady Masham saw that the end was approaching. Her devoted attention delayed it until the following autumn. In the April of his last year he made his will, in which all his friends were remembered. He bequeathed twenty shillings to every servant in the household at Oates, a hundred pounds to the poor of High Laver, and a hundred pounds to the poor of Peblow and Pensford. In the early autumn he was able to bear a visit from his cousin, Peter King, and his bride. Peter King began his career in a grocer's shop in Exeter, and rose to be Lord Chancellor of England. On 28th October 1704 John Locke died. We have a moving picture of his last moments. The aged philosopher lay restfully in his room at Oates while his dear friend, Lady Masham, read to him from the Psalms. He listened to her quietly for some time, then interrupted the reading to say he felt tired and would sleep. She tells us that he smiled at her in his gentle way as she closed the book. It was a fitting end.

After reading Locke's epitaph in High Laver Church we may turn to the south wall of the chancel, and find there a memorial to the minister whose friendship the philosopher enjoyed so long, Samuel Lowe. He was, we read, minister of the parish for forty-seven years. There was only a year between the two in age.

CHAPTER XXI

Watts and Wesley—Aaron Hill's crazy schemes—John Adkins—Elizabeth Tollet—George Edwards—Edmund Burke at Plaistow—Sheridan at Waltham Abbey

IN the Forest, as elsewhere, minor poets abounded during the eighteenth century. Gone were the ribald days of the Restoration as well as the merry days of the Tudors. The Forest now had no poets to rank with the great ones we have already met, riding across its heaths, reflecting upon the comedy or the tragedy of life as the muse dictated. During the eighteenth century poem after poem was attributed first to this author and then to that, evidence of a sterile uniformity of style and subject.

In the eighteenth century the level of craftsmanship was high, but inspiration was at a low ebb. When it did overtake a writer it came as such a shock to the frigid sanity of the age that it was almost certain to throw the poet into a madhouse. The licentiousness of the Restoration writers produced a fruitful harvest for a few years, but it soon ran to seed, until grossness and vulgarity were met by frigidity and over-precision. The literary gardens of one age had too much manure, the gardens of the next too little, and slender stems had to be supported by prosodic canes and tied with Latin tags. Verse became too correct. Madness was one refuge; religion another, so we find some of our greatest hymns written at this time. Watts and Wesley both came into the Forest, and the volatile Philip Doddridge was related by marriage to the first minister of the Independent Chapel at Epping, John Nettleton, who afterwards moved to Ongar.

Isaac Watts was at Walthamstow frequently, and lived at Cheshunt for twenty-five years. John Wesley visited Plaistow in 1739, writing in his diary: 'I accepted a pressing invitation to go to Plaistow. At five in the evening I expounded there, and at eight again. But most of the hearers were very quiet and unconcerned. In the morning, therefore, I spoke stronger words. But it is only the voice of the Son of God which is able to wake the dead.' As we claim associations with both Watts and Wesley, it is interesting to recall that the first verse of Watts's most famous hymn, *O God, our help in ages past*, was partly

Wesley's work. Watts had written a verse beginning: 'Our God, our help in ages past,' which was published in 1719. In 1737 Wesley altered it. In Charlotte Brontë's *Shirley*, published in 1849, Mrs. Pryor still sings the verse as Watts wrote it:

> Our God, our help in ages past—.
> Our hope for years to come;
> Our shelter from the stormy blast;
> Our refuge, haven, home!

Apart from the fine hymns of these men of religious genius, and from the writings of men of disordered minds—and literature can stand a good deal of madness—we have in the eighteenth century a vast amount of innocuous vicarage verse and of 'the mild effusions of the female mind.' In Aaron Hill, John Adkins, and Elizabeth Tollet, the Forest had a representative group of minor poets. Aaron Hill, known to his friends as 'Hilarius,' is the most interesting. He demonstrates, at all events, that madness is not the only thing needful to produce a good poet. Perhaps the only prudent thing he ever did was to marry a lady of fortune, the daughter of Edward Morris of Stratford.

Aaron Hill's bonnet was a veritable hive of buzzing bees. No sooner had one impossible scheme ended in disaster than he thought of another equally impossible and equally disastrous. At one time he was full of proposals for improving the wool trade, at another for starting a company to extract oil from beechmast, of which there had once been a plentiful supply in the Forest. He formed a company with a capital of twenty-five thousand pounds, on which he promised to pay forty-five per cent after two years, besides making the entire nation happy with oil as sweet as olives. At Plaistow, to which he retired in 1738, he planted a hundred thousand French vines. Some of his vintage he sent to his friend Richardson, the novelist, politely hoping it would contribute to his health and happiness. Another of his schemes was for the manufacture of potash; another for raising plantations in Georgia; and another for making a new fuel, compacted of coal-dust and Thames mud. The highlands of Scotland he proposed to clear of timber for the use of the Navy. Not one of his practical ventures succeeded, though some of the ideas he voiced in his paper, *The Plain Dealer*, are still before us. He advocated the abolition of capital punishment, the advantages of inoculation, and the claims of women. In No. 69, 'Patty Amble' is made to ask: 'How are we represented, when none of our sex are

F

permitted to sit and vote for us? . . . Either let us as a distinct body have a right to govern ourselves; or admit an equal number of us to sit where laws are made for us.'

Pope likened Hill to the flying fishes, 'who now and then rise upon their fins, and fly out of the profound; but their wings are soon dry, and they drop down to the bottom.' Hill rejoined with an epigram, which stung Pope into giving him a place in *The Dunciad*. For this affront Hill so frightened Pope that for a time he always carried loaded pistols, and rarely went out without his great dog Bounce. Later the quarrel was patched up, and in 1731 we actually find Hill thanking Pope for his 'compassion.' Hill had just lost his wife.

Aaron Hill corresponded frequently with Richardson, who also corresponded with Hill's daughters, Astraea and Minerva—a third daughter was called Urania; and a son, Julius Caesar! Richardson once asked these girls what they thought of Fielding's *Tom Jones*, hoping, it is to be feared, that they would feed his vanity by telling him how much inferior to his own work they thought it. But the girls knew a good book when they read one, and praised the merits of *Tom Jones*. Richardson replied with asperity, drawing tears to the eyes of the girls, for they could not bear, they said, that Mr. Richardson should think them capable of approving 'of anything, in any work, that had an evil tendency.' They still had enough courage to suggest to the offended novelist that he should read the book for himself, promising that if he did so he would find a 'thread of moral meaning' running through it.

When Mrs. Hill died she was buried in the Great Cloister at Westminster Abbey, where Hill was buried later. The poet's excitable imagination turned to the question of a memorial. 'There is,' he said, 'a low and unmeaning lumpishness in the vulgar style of monuments which disgusts me.' He set about designing one more inspiring. It should rise from a pediment of white marble, standing on a black marble 'mountain.' In the side of this representation of a mountain there should be a craggy path, with the figure of Time in white marble, in the attitude of one climbing. His progress should be obstructed by little cupids, some rolling rocks into his path from above, others throwing nets round his feet, others again shooting arrows at him. Death should appear in a cleft of the mountain, indicating that it might not be necessary for the traveller to toil to the summit. A quicker way might be found.

It is interesting to find Hill being read by a later poet of the Forest. In Clare's journal for 1824 we find this note: 'I have been much struck with some passages in the Poems of Aaron Hill. He seems to struggle to free his ideas from the turnpike hackneyisms of sounding rhymes and tinkling periods then in fashion, for most of the rhymers of that day seem to catch their little inspiration from Pope.' One of Aaron Hill's epigrams hints that he may not have been as foolish as he appears:

> Tender-handed stroke a nettle,
> And it stings you for your pains;
> Grasp it like a man of metal,
> And it soft as silk remains.
>
> 'Tis the same with common natures,
> Use them kindly, they rebel;
> But be rough as nutmeg-graters
> And the rogues obey you well.

Hill's house at Plaistow was large and old, with a shady and well-cultivated garden. The climate, however, did not suit him, and it appears to have been one of the few things he did not believe himself capable of improving, though he did devise a scheme for repairing the Thames embankment at Dagenham Breach. Plaistow, he said, had 'a moist, malignant air.' Richardson described it as a 'terrible marsh-pit.'

John Adkins, the author of *A Voyage to Guinea, Brazil and the West Indies*, came to live at Plaistow while Hill was there, and Elizabeth Tollet still has her memorial on the floor of the chancel in the parish church: 'Elizabeth Tollet, daughter of George Tollet, Esqr. Commissioner of the navy in the reign of Queen Anne, died 1754, aged 60. Religion, justice and benevolence appeared in all her actions, and her poems in various languages are adorned with extensive learning applied to the best purposes.' Her talents were matched by her modesty. No collection of her poems was published during her life, but they enjoyed a fair degree of popularity later.

Plaistow was then a small, highly respectable village. Only one coach a day travelled into London, and those who wished to use it were required to book their seats a day in advance. The fare for the return journey was three shillings. A royal duke, it may be remembered, the Duke of Cumberland, had a house and racing stables at Plaistow—Cumberland House at the end of Balaam Street. As late as 1801 Barking and Ilford together had a population of only 4,000, Leyton of 2,500, East Ham of 1,000, and West Ham of only 6,500.

West Ham is proud of having been the birthplace of George Edwards, one of our most distinguished Essex naturalists. He was born in 1693, and after attending a clergyman's school at Leytonstone was apprenticed to a merchant in Fenchurch Street. His interest in natural history, however, soon led him away from commerce. He became librarian to the Royal College of Physicians. *The History of Birds*, four quarto volumes which occupied all his leisure for twenty-one years, was his greatest work. His coloured drawings of animals and birds commanded high prices, and in the course of his life he produced hundreds of these remarkable studies. The *History* was followed by three additional volumes entitled *Gleanings in Natural History*. At the age of seventy-one he retired and settled at Plaistow with his two sisters, enjoying the society of a large circle of friends until he died of cancer in 1773 at the age of eighty-one. The cancer affected one eye, which must have been particularly hard for an artist to bear. He was buried in West Ham churchyard, but the stone over his grave has disappeared.

The Forest just missed a better poet than those already mentioned in this chapter. The father of Thomas Gray, author of the *Elegy in a Country Churchyard*, spent the last few months of his life, and squandered the greater part of his fortune, in building a country house at Wanstead. The poet and his mother appear to have known nothing about this enterprise until after Mr. Gray's death, when they found themselves in reduced circumstances.

In the political world we find a distinguished association at this time. Edmund Burke lived at Brunstock Cottage, Balaam Street, Plaistow, for two years from 1759 to 1761, that is to say, from his thirty-first to his thirty-third year. When he left, an old portrait was found in the house, later believed to be a likeness of Pepys. In 1756 Burke had published his treatise on *The Sublime and the Beautiful*, which his father acknowledged with a bank bill for one hundred pounds. In the same year he wrote *A Vindication of Natural Society or A View of the Miseries and Evils arising to Mankind from Every Species of Civil Society*, containing views which he explained in later life were not intended to be taken seriously.

Burke was already a figure in London society when he came to live at Plaistow. The previous Christmas he had had the temerity to contradict Dr. Johnson himself, who was twenty years his senior, to the amazement of their fellow guests at David Garrick's table. The doctor was not offended, and was, in fact, very fond of his young Irish friend.

In the second of Burke's two years at Plaistow he came under the eye of Horace Walpole, who wrote: 'I dined at Hamilton's yesterday; there were Garrick and young Mr. Burke, who wrote a book in the style of Lord Bolingbroke, that was much admired. He is a sensible man, but has not worn off his authorism yet, and thinks there is nothing so charming as writers, and to be one. He will know better one of these days.' It was this friendship with Hamilton—known as 'Single Speech Hamilton'—that took Burke away from Plaistow. The two first met some time in 1759, and their acquaintance so ripened during the following two years that when Hamilton became Chief Secretary in Ireland he persuaded Burke to go with him as his own secretary. Hamilton found Burke's brains extremely helpful, and wished to purchase them for his own exclusive use. This he tried to do out of public money by obtaining for Burke a pension of three hundred pounds a year. The pension was acceptable enough; but when Burke realized what Hamilton's designs were he became furious.

It was from this point that Burke went forward to his great career. No man in the history of our politics, with the single exception of the present member for Epping, Mr. Winston Churchill, who will be remembered with pride in future histories of the Forest, has brought to the conduct of national affairs a mind so splendidly endowed with vision and purpose, and a tongue of such impassioned eloquence. The love of liberty has burned like a beacon for both.

The events which brought another Irishman, Richard Brinsley Sheridan, to Waltham Abbey, form a romantic story. At nineteen Sheridan fell in love with a beautiful singer named Miss Linley, at that time a girl of little more than sixteen, but already the cause of much rivalry among the young men of Bath, where both she and Sheridan were living. She had even been on the point of marrying a Mr. Long, an elderly gentleman of considerable fortune who lived in Wiltshire. Fortunately, she recognized the unsuitability of the match in time, and the gentleman demonstrated the unselfishness of his affection by breaking the engagement, and settling on her the sum of three thousand pounds. To this disinterested action Sheridan owed not only his bride, but also the means of supporting her during the early years of their life together.

Sheridan and Miss Linley made a runaway marriage. When they left home, Miss Linley intended to enter a nunnery in France, and Sheridan was pretending to help her to escape from her parents. As soon as they were safely out of the country he disclosed his real purpose and persuaded her to marry him. Mr. Linley, however, was quickly in pursuit. The lovers were overtaken and induced to return to England, though not before they had been married at a village near Calais. On their return, Sheridan became involved in a quarrel with another jealous admirer of his bride, a married man named Captain Mathews. These two fought a duel, which ended, according to Sheridan, in Mathews pleading for his life. Mathews gave a different account. It is probable that neither told the truth, but however that might be the parents were so incensed by the scandal that the two lovers were parted, and Sheridan decided that further residence in Bath was impossible. It was under these circumstances that he came, in August or September 1772, to pass several months at Waltham Abbey, where he lived with his friends, Mr. and Mrs. Parker, at Farm Hill, on the Forest side of the abbey.

At Waltham, Sheridan occupied himself with study, nearly filling a quarto volume of more than a hundred pages, closely written, with a history of England. There is also evidence that while living here he studied the works of Sir William Temple, paying special attention to Temple's use of idiomatic expressions, studies which helped him to form his own dramatic style. So his period in the Forest, as with so many others we have mentioned, was turned to good account. It is certain that at no other time did he give himself so passionately to the studies necessary for the development of his great gifts. Anxiety and adventure had combined to raise his mind to a pitch of excitement that made some sort of activity essential. Barred from physical exertion as a result of the duel, and frustrated in his love, he found compensation in the ardours of study. He had gained the hand and heart of the lady he loved; but for the time being saw no promise of normal life with her. His enemies were constantly misrepresenting him. The whole world appeared to be against him, yet within his spirit burned the proud consciousness of genius. In all his letters written from Waltham Abbey there is a strain of despondency and almost of despair, alternating with vigorous outbursts of power and ambition. A remarkable feature is that in none of these letters does he mention the fact of his marriage with Miss Linley. He even appears to have been induced by his father to promise that he never would marry her. His mad jealousy took the course of warning all his acquaintances against her irresistible charms. He was frantically determined that if he might not possess her himself, neither should any one else if he could prevent it. All this time his wife was being guarded by her family from any communication with him.

The following Lent Miss Linley appeared in the oratorios at Covent Garden, and Sheridan, in his own phrase, 'trod upon the heels of perilous probabilities,' by frequently seeing her in public, though not in private. Amongst other stratagems which he contrived for a closer view of her, he more than once disguised himself as a hackney-coachman and drove her home from the theatre.

A famous beauty could not avoid the attentions of admirers, and it came to be rumoured that Miss Linley was about to be married to a titled gentleman. Sheridan was thrown again into the desperation of violent jealousy. Renewed attempts at reconciliation were made. This time Mr. Linley, seeing the impossibility of keeping the two apart much longer, consented to their 'marriage,' and on 13th April 1773, the *Gentleman's Magazine* announced the marriage of 'Mr. Sheridan of the Temple to the celebrated Miss Linley of Bath.'

CHAPTER XXII

Elizabeth Fry of Plashet—Lord Lister—John Fothergill—Luke Howard
—Famous Quaker families—Mary Wollstonecraft—William Sotheby

BURKE defended the rights of the people he called 'constitutional dissenters.' His defence must have been remembered in the Forest, where so many distinguished Quaker families made their homes. The Gurneys, the Frys, the Buxtons, the Howards, came in order to be near London, where they were establishing their businesses and prospering in the approved Quaker fashion. They built their great houses on the edge of the Forest, thee'd and thou'd each other with serene Quaker decorum, married their cousins, and raised large families to the glory of God and the credit of each other's finances. Thrift was next to godliness, and godliness was a mighty good aid to thrift. The Lord prospered the righteous. As Tyndale's translation has it: 'The Lorde was with Joseph, and he was a luckie felowe.'

The nonconformity of the Puritans had produced rebellion; the Quakers diverted their zeal into mysticism. Rebellions disturbed credit.

Elizabeth Fry was one of the Gurneys of Earlham. She was born at a time when every one kept a diary and wrote long letters, which were tied together carefully with tape or ribbon and put away in a drawer. Families held together. The whole world held together. Life at last appeared to have become secure, and to none was it more secure than to the Quaker bankers. Their sons entered the family banks, and their daughters married the sons of other bankers.

The Gurneys were not of the stricter sort of Quakers; they permitted music and dancing in their home. Elizabeth was brought up to a life of freedom and gaiety. In her youth she was to be seen riding along the lanes about Norwich in her scarlet riding-habit. She was once so bold as to attend meeting in a pair of purple boots laced with scarlet. Later in life she became a 'plain Quaker,' with the more serious interests that led to her great work of prison reform. In 1811 she became one of the ministers of the Society of Friends, preaching as well as giving practical help, charming every one with her smile, her generous sympathy, and her simple-hearted goodness.

152

She made a good match with the son of the wealthy William Storrs Fry of Plashet, East Ham, whose estate was described as sumptuous. 'I accepted my Joseph more from duty than anything else,' she confessed, 'and how much I now love him.' Samuel Gurney married Elizabeth Sheppard of Ham House, not far from Plashet. Fowell Buxton married Hannah Gurney— vowing when he was sixteen that she should be his wife. Later, the Buxtons were to live at Warlies, Upshire, where Samuel Foxe had lived. Most of them, Buxtons, Frys, Gurneys, and also Listers, lived about Upton.

Lord Lister, the greatest healer of his day, was born at West Ham, facing Upton Park. The house is now marked by a tablet. Henley's lines in his honour deserve to be quoted:

> His brow spreads large and placid, and his eye
> Is deep and bright, with steady looks that still.
> Soft lines of tranquil thought his face fulfil—
> His face at once benign and proud and shy.
> If envy scout, if ignorance deny,
> His faultless patience, his unyielding will,
> Beautiful gentleness, and splendid skill,
> Innumerable gratitudes reply.
> His wise, rare smile is sweet with certainties,
> And seems in all his patients to compel
> Such love and faith as failure cannot quell. . . .

According to an old story, Lister narrowly missed being killed as a young boy, when shot splintered the window of the room in which he was standing. The shot is said to have been fired by one of the Buxtons, who was shooting rabbits in the park.

Another famous doctor, John Fothergill, the Quaker from Wensleydale who founded Ackworth School, lived at Ham House. What is now West Ham Park was formerly his garden. Here he had no fewer than three thousand four hunded different species of plants and trees. After Kew, these gardens were the finest in Europe from the horticulturist's point of view. Dr. Fothergill was one of the great characters of his time, abounding in good works that added as much to his fame as did his distinction either as naturalist or as physician. The people of West Ham doffed their hats when his famous green coach went by, driven by a portly coachman who invariably wore a white wig.

The security that the good Quakers thought had been achieved was soon shattered by Napoleon. The day came when he had an army encamped at Boulogne, and a flotilla of flat-bottomed boats ready for the invasion of England. Joseph Fry saw

*F

preparations being made for flooding the Essex marshes. Families were preparing to evacuate. The beacons which had flared through the night when England was threatened by the Spanish Armada were again ready. Farmers were warned not to burn rubbish in their fields lest these smouldering fires should be mistaken for beacons. But Napoleon was overcome and the country settled down. It is interesting to note that the *Téméraire*, the second ship in Nelson's line, was commanded by Captain Harvey (Sir Eliab), of Rolls Park, Chigwell.

But of all these famous people, the one best remembered is Elizabeth Fry. She loved the Forest, especially during spring, when she could take her children out to pick wild flowers and laugh at the odd ways of the squirrels. Her daughter gave us a happy picture of Mrs. Fry and her family going into the Forest with baskets and trowels to dig from the sunny banks primroses, later to be planted at Plashet. Elizabeth Fry was a mother before everything else. She was a mother to her family, a mother to the wretched women for whom she did so much. She was no theorist. Her work was not the result of any convictions about economics, but of warm-hearted sympathy and practical common sense. When she stepped alone into Newgate prison, and the gate clanged behind her, it was her mother instinct that saved her from the violence of those clamorous women. She picked up a child:

'Friends, many of you are mothers. I too am a mother.' She was one of them. That was the secret of her success. Her attitude was not that she who was good had come to help those who were sinful, but, 'All we like sheep have gone astray; we have turned every one to his own way; and the Lord hath laid on him the iniquity of us all.'

'What struck me as most remarkable in her speaking,' reported a clergyman who watched her at work, 'and no doubt that which won its way so powerfully to the hearts of those abandoned women, was that she always seemed to class herself with them; she never said "You," but "Us."'

By a strange irony the Upton Lane house where Elizabeth Fry lived became the headquarters of the 3rd Volunteer Battalion of the Essex Regiment. The husky voices of sergeants sounded through the rooms once full of Quaker tenderness. In this house Mrs. Fry was visited by the King of Prussia in 1842. 'I walked with him into the drawing-room,' she records in her journal, 'where all was in beautiful order—neat and adorned with flowers. I presented to the king our eight daughters and daughters-in-law . . . and afterwards presented twenty-five of our grand-children. We had a solemn silence before our meal, which was handsome and fit for a king, yet not extravagant—everything most complete and nice. I sat by the king, who appeared to enjoy his dinner, perfectly at his ease, and very happy with us. He partook twice of oyster soup, a dish he had never heard of before, and which he highly commended.'

Elizabeth Fry's descendants still live in the Forest, along with the descendants of the Buxtons, the Howards, the Gurneys, and the rest of them. No names are more honoured.

Another great Englishwoman, one whose outlook was very different from Mrs. Fry's, Mary Wollstonecraft, was born either at Hoxton or in Epping Forest—there is some doubt which. Her earliest recollections were of the Forest, where she lived in an old house near the whalebone at Chadwell Heath, mentioned by Defoe. This may have been Whalebone House itself, which was bombed and demolished during the Second Great War. After the publication of her *Rights of Women*, Horace Walpole gallantly described her as a 'hyena in petticoats,' and a 'philosophizing serpent.' She had committed the unpardonable indelicacy of expressing her thoughts at a time when women were not expected to have any.

Mary Wollstonecraft was born into an unhappy household. According to her own account, which is perhaps not entirely to be trusted, her father was a drunken tyrant. Allowing for some exaggeration, we may at least conclude that whereas Elizabeth Fry had to learn that not all families were happy, Mary Wollstonecraft had to learn that not all were miserable.

To Mary's independent heart and oversharpened brain, marriage appeared to be an evil institution. But she was beautiful as well as clever, so in spite of her theories she found herself involved in relationships with members of the despised, tyrannical sex. Nature, she discovered, is as strong as reason, and the two do not always agree. She formed alliances with more than one lover, but marriage was still unthinkable. These emotional entanglements produced extreme misery, if also brief, unrestrained happiness. Twice she attempted suicide. After the second attempt failed, she settled down to make the best of life, even marrying when she found that for the second time she was about to become a mother.   This marriage of Mary Wollstonecraft with William Godwin gave the world Mary Godwin, destined to become the wife of Shelley.

Though Mrs. Godwin died at thirty-eight, she had already won fame as a pioneer in proclaiming the rights of women.   To-day, few but feminist fanatics can read her turgid, opinionated writings. If she had lived a little longer, Godwin, who was at least a man of taste, might have helped her to free herself from such militant feminism as hers, operating so disastrously on the king's English. Her foolish and incoherent rhetoric must have been a sore trial to him.

Returning to the Quakers, we have Luke Howard, the manufacturing chemist of Plaistow who founded the firm now so long established at Ilford.   Luke Howard was born in 1772, and lived to the great age of ninety-two.   In 1806 he began to keep a register of meteorology, which led him to conclusions first published in 1818–20 in *The Climate of London*.   It was Luke Howard who, in defining the principal modifications of the clouds, gave them the names by which they are still known—cirrus, cumulus, nimbus, stratus, and so on.

Goethe, in whom literary and scientific interests were so nobly balanced, became interested in cloud formations in later life, and took daily observations at Jena for several months in 1820. When Howard's classification became known to him it was adopted with enthusiasm.   Goethe addressed Howard as 'Our Master,' and composed in his honour a poem entitled *Howards Ehrengedächtnis*.   He also dedicated to him a shorter poem entitled *The Atmosphere*:

> The earth and her great dome of sky
> Spreading so far, so broad and high,
> Beautiful, solemn visions brought,
> But how to make them food for thought?
>
> Truth in the infinite to find,
> Distinguish first, then group in mind;
> So my winged song commends to fame
> The man who gave each cloud a name.

At the end of the Napoleonic wars a large sum of money was collected for relief work by a committee of London citizens, many of whom were Quakers.   Luke Howard was entrusted with the task of distributing these funds.   In recognition of his good offices he received diamond rings from the King of Prussia and another

German prince, and a present of fine porcelain, specially made for the purpose, from the representatives of the kingdom of Saxony.

At Goethe's request, Howard wrote a long, autobiographical essay, which was forwarded to the poet by John Christian Huttner, a clerk at the London Foreign Office. In acknowledging the manuscript Goethe wrote: 'Nothing has for a long while given me so much pleasure as the receipt of the biography of Mr. Howard, which I read yesterday evening and have been thinking of ever since.

'If you have any opportunity of thanking this excellent man for it, I beg that you will not neglect to do so. Here, too, experience has afresh shown, that delicate minds, those of finer mould, are the most susceptible of the pleasures arising from the observation of natural phenomena.'

This association of Luke Howard with Goethe reminds us of that of William Sotheby, poet, and friend of Sir Walter Scott, Byron, and Wordsworth, with Wieland. Members of the Sotheby family were lords of the manor of Sewardstone for two hundred years, living at the manor house at High Beach. The poet himself lived at Fairmead Lodge, which stood close to the Fairmead Oak. The beginning of the drive to this house is still discernible, and there are still fruit trees in Fairmead Bottom which were formerly in Sotheby's garden. The house itself has gone, and the grounds are restored to the Forest.

William Sotheby published a volume of *Poems* in 1790, and a number of historical tragedies. He translated both the Iliad and the Odyssey, but his translation of Wieland's *Oberon* was his most successful work. Wieland himself possessed an intimate knowledge of the English language. He had translated Shakespeare into a German version that was later used extensively by Schlegel, who sometimes transposed large passages literally.

Oberon, clearly, was inspired by *A Midsummer Night's Dream*. The plot is fantastic, with a complete indifference to probability. Wieland took a malicious delight in the failings of his characters, turning the most tragic situations into occasions for jesting. Sotheby cannot have found translation an easy task. Perhaps it was the Forest that put him in the mood for it. The opening line is: 'There rode into the old romantic land,' which evokes an atmosphere in harmony with the romantic wilderness about Fairmead. The story belongs to a time when the word romantic applied particularly to subjects derived from medieval sources.

That the Forest is naturally kindly to such moods was to be shown later in William Morris's work.

When Wieland received Sotheby's translation he was most agreeably surprised, and praised it as a masterpiece, possessing all the grace, ease, and elegance he had aimed at in the original, and at the same time being a model of fidelity in translation. 'England,' he said, 'had hitherto wanted such intelligent friends of German literature.'

In Sotheby's *Oberon* the elves of *A Midsummer Night's Dream* sport under the beeches on Fairmead side. They vanish, and another poet glances at us shyly from behind a hawthorn bush. His name is John Clare.

CHAPTER XXIII

John Clare with Dr. Allen at High Beach

ALMOST any day between 1837 and 1841 a small, sensitive man, with keen eyes, high forehead, and fine features, might be seen wandering about Fairmead. He was John Clare, the peasant poet, who spent four years in Dr. Allen's private asylum there.

The sad story of this poet son of a Northamptonshire farm labourer has often been told. The strange boy who sat in the candlelight of his cottage home, copying out the verses he had composed while digging in his master's fields, is now a familiar figure. There is so much in both his story and his character to appeal to the sentimental side of popular taste. But there is a sharper side to the story. Clare was first the sport of nature, and afterwards the sport of fame. It is the custom of society to be ever on the look-out for fresh means of diversion, and, other means failing, a performing peasant may become an acceptable adornment of a fashionable drawing-room. Poor Clare became the victim of blue-stocking society. He did not know that the restless desire for novelty which brought him into fashion would as quickly bear him out again. For a short time he experienced the intoxication of fame. London was all agog about him. But the interest did not last, and when it vanished the memory of it made the delving and ditching harder than ever. By this time Clare had to provide for a family of seven children. It is hardly surprising that his brain gave way.

By the timely intervention of his publisher, John Taylor, he was brought to High Beach and given into the care of Dr. Allen, a man of humane and enlightened views. Dr Allen, by his natural courtesy, had the gift of being able to win the confidence and affection of his patients. He was also a man of culture, and therefore well equipped both by nature and knowledge to be a healing companion to the poet.

Dr. Allen selected High Beach as the ideal place for his purpose as a pioneer in modern methods of healing, and opened his asylum there in 1825. Here, he wrote, 'together with domestic comfort, diversity of occupations and amusements suited to their various states, the retirement, pure air and sweet scenery around, afford ample scope for walks without annoyance, and apparently

without restraint, which, with judicious moral and medical
management combine many acknowledged requisites to assist
the disturbed and diseased mind to regain its tranquillity.'
Of the three houses the doctor used, one, Fairmead House, was
demolished more than eighty years ago. The other two, Lip-
pitt's Hill Lodge and Springfield House, remain. One of the three
houses was reserved for women, who were under Mrs. Allen's
care, another for men, and the third for those needing the doctor's
constant attention.

The three houses were altered structurally to meet the special
needs of the patients. The back part was divided into cubicles
for those who had to be isolated. Along the front of these cubicles
ran galleries, from which the patients might look into the front
part of the house, which was designed to be as much like a normal
dwelling as possible. Here the patients who were sufficiently
recovered lived a family life with the doctor and his assistants.
To see the privileges enjoyed by those who had regained a measure
of mental and moral control gave the backward patients an
incentive towards recovery. The life at the front of the house
was happy and enlightened. Social visits were arranged between the three houses; games were played; the patients even
edited a newspaper. Many of these patients went in and out at
will, owning their own door-keys, and Dr. Allen tells us that few
took unfair advantage of the privileges he allowed them.

Allen deplored the lack of mental occupation in the public
asylums of his day. The judicious exercise of mind and body,
he argued, was essential in any treatment. Clare could not have
fallen into better hands. He was encouraged to take walks in
the Forest and write poems. Even more important, he was
relieved of the pressing necessity of earning money for the support
of his family. Writing in 1840 of the poet's improved condition
after rather more than two years at High Beach, Allen says that
when he came he was 'exceedingly miserable, every instant bemoaning his poverty, and his mind did not appear so much lost
and deranged as suspended in its movements by the oppressive
and permanent state of anxiety, and fear, and vexation, produced
by the excitement of excessive flattery at one time, and neglect
at another, his extreme poverty and over exertion of body and
mind, and no wonder that his feeble bodily frame, with his
wonderful native powers of mind, was overcome.

'I had then not the slightest hesitation in saying that if a small pension could be obtained for him, he would have recovered instantly and most probably remained well for life.'

Clare was soon able to forget his troubles in his enjoyment of the great Forest at his door. He wrote to his wife: 'The place here is beautiful . . . the country is the finest I have ever seen.' There are few traces of mental disturbance in the poems he wrote:

> I love the Forest and its airy bounds,
> Where friendly Campbell takes his daily rounds:
> I love the breakneck hills, that headlong go,
> And leave me high, and half the world below;
> I love to see the Beech Hill mounting high,
> The brook without a bridge and nearly dry,
> There's Bucket's Hill, a place of furze and clouds,
> Which evening in a golden blaze enshrouds. . . .

The 'Campbell' referred to was the only son of the poet Thomas Campbell; Bucket's Hill was the local name for Buckhurst Hill, and the brook without a bridge still runs across Fairmead. In the distance he could see London:

> While giant London, known to all the world,
> Was nothing but a guess among the trees,
> Though only half a day from where we stood.

One of his favourite haunts was 'Fern Hill at the back of the chapel, a beautiful retreat from a madhouse.' Fern Hill is quite unchanged, but the chapel was dismantled when the present church at High Beach was built in 1872. The old church, a small brick building erected in 1836, dedicated to St. Paul, stood on ground which has now been restored to the Forest. The site was on the Forest side of the road, between High Beach vicarage and 'The Suntrap,' which occupies the site of Fairmead House. The Rev. William Watson, who was curate in charge while Clare was with Dr. Allen, lived in Loughton from 1839 till his death in 1869, acting during the greater part of this time as assistant curate without stipend at the parish church.

In a small pocket-book used by Clare at High Beach we have glimpses of his life in the Forest:

'Easter Sunday, 1841. Went in the morning to Buckhurst Hill Church and stood in the Churchyard, when a very interesting boy came out while the organ was playing, dressed in a slop frock like a plough boy and seemingly about nine years of age. He was just like my son Bill when he was about the same age and as stout made. He had a serious, interesting face and looked as weary with the working days as a hard-working man. I was sorry I did not give him the last half-penny I had and ask him a few questions as to his age and name and parents, but perhaps I may see him again.' Clare had probably gone up to see his old friend Mr. Watson, who was curate in charge of St. John's, Buckhurst Hill, for about a year from a date in 1841, the date when he left High Beach, after five years' ministry there. The following day Clare wrote:

'Easter Monday. At the Easter Hunt I saw a stout, tall, young woman, dressed in a darkish fox-red, cotton gown as a milkmaid or farm-servant. I stood agen her for some minutes near a small clump of furze. I did not speak to her, but I now wish I had and cannot forget her.'

The diffidence shown in these two entries was characteristic of his malady. Clare was inclined to be distrustful both of himself and of others, and for this weakness Allen was an excellent doctor. It was an essential part of his method that the complete confidence of the patients should be won. Truth must never be violated in dealing with them. Dr. Allen would not allow his nurses to resort to deception even in bringing patients from their own homes. There must be no deception anywhere. Where force was necessary, it must always be pointed out that they were all working together towards the end where moral restraint, and the self-restraint born of goodwill and mutual responsibility, should take the place of the physical restraint necessary for the moment. Under Dr. Allen's care the poet became stout and sunburnt, full of high spirits and fun. A smile continually played about his lips.

There remained the difficulty that the doctor saw must be overcome before full recovery would be possible: Mrs. Clare and the seven children. If Clare became strong enough to return to them the old grind would begin again, with the old despondency following. Allen was fully conscious of this. To one who asked for something in the poet's handwriting he wrote:

'MY DEAR SIR,

'I enclose at your request some of Clare's writing. Why show respect to the mere handwriting, and no humanity to the man nor his family?

'I pledge myself, that if a small annuity could be secured for him, he will very soon recover and remain so—and yet people desire the autograph of a man who but for me would have been

a hopeless case permanently confined and lost in the mass of
paupers in some public Establishment or perhaps what is worse
exposed to the idle gaze of fools.'

An appeal for five hundred pounds was made.   In response, the
queen dowager sent twenty guineas, Lord FitzWilliam 'a handsome subscription,' and the Marquess of Northampton promised
five pounds a year.   But the total amount fell short of the modest
sum required, and the hope of finding an easy life outside the
asylum disappeared.   With prospects so gloomy, it is not surprising that the poet gave way to despair whenever he reflected
on his condition:

> My mind is dark and fathomless, and wears
>   The hues of hopeless agony and hell;
> No plummet ever sounds the soul's affairs,
>   There, death eternal never sounds the knell,
> There, Love, imprisoned, sighs the long farewell.

His mind could only find refuge in evasion and the sheer animal
satisfaction of living for the moment only:

> Thus all are blessed indeed—
> The weak, the strong, the timid and the bold.
> Thus will the hare feel safe in its retreat
> Where lay the murdering fox an hour before;
> And upon boughs warm with the falcon's feet
> The wren will perch and dream of harm no more.
> Kind Providence amid contending strife
> Bids weakness feel the liberty of life.

He found refuge also in the compensations of fancy.   The figure
most constantly in his mind was that of Mary Joyce, his first love.
It might be said that the real contest for Clare's mind was between the kindly doctor and the lost sweetheart, who was, in fact,
dead.   Everywhere he saw her image:

> How beautiful this hill of fern swells on,
>   So beautiful the Chapel peeps between
> The hornbeams, with its simple bell; alone
>   I wander here, hid in a palace green.
>   Mary is absent, but the Forest Queen,
> Nature is with me; morning, noon and gloaming,
>   I write my poems in these paths unseen.

Forest scenes must have remained with Clare to the end of his
life, and must often have cheered him in the public asylum where
he was condemned to spend the last twenty-two years of his life.
   In 1841 his longing for home became more than he could bear.

On 18th July he wrote in his note-book: 'Sunday. Felt very melancholy; went a walk in the forest in the afternoon; fell in with some gipsies, one of whom offered to assist in my escape from the madhouse by hiding me in his camp; to which I almost agreed, but told him I had no money to start with, but if he would do so I would promise him fifty pound; and he agreed to do so before Saturday. On Friday I went again, but he did not seem so willing, so I said little about it. On Sunday I went and they were all gone. I found an old wide-awake hat, and an old straw bonnet of the plum-pudding sort was left behind. I put the hat in my pocket, thinking it might be useful for another opportunity, and, as good luck would have it, it turned out to be so.'

Clare was longing for freedom. Three days earlier, a thunderstorm had broken over the Forest, and Clare had written:

> My soul is apathy, a ruin vast,
>   Time cannot clear the ruined mass away;
> My life is hell, the hopeless die is cast,
>   And manhood's prime is premature decay.
>
> Roll on, ye wrath of thunders, peal on peal,
>   Till worlds are ruins, and myself alone;
> Melt heart and soul, cased in obdurate steel,
>   Till I can feel that nature is my throne.
>
> I live in love, sun of undying light,
>   And fathom my own heart for ways of good;
> In its pure atmosphere, day without night
>   Smiles on the plains, the forest, and the flood.
>
> Smile on, ye elements of earth and sky,
>   Or frown in thunders as ye frown on me;
> Bid earth and its delusions pass away,
>   But leave the mind, as its creator, free.

Clare was in defiant mood. On 20th July he left Dr. Allen's roof for the last time. His account of the next three days is a remarkable document. In those three days he tramped the eighty miles between High Beach and Northborough in Northamptonshire, his old home. What he must have suffered on this journey can hardly be imagined. He had only the few particulars about the road picked up from the gipsy, and he set out without a penny in his pocket.

The first day he reached Stevenage, a distance of more than twenty miles, without once tasting food. On 24th July he wrote: 'Returned home out of Essex, and found no Mary. She and her family are nothing to me now, though she herself was once the dearest of all; and how can I forget?' After this entry begins what is headed 'Journal.' The entry for 18th July has been given. The account continues:

'19th July, Monday.—Did nothing.

'20th July, Tuesday.—Reconnoitred the road the Gipsy pointed out and found it a legible one to make a movement, and having only honest courage and myself in my army, I led the way and my troops soon followed. But being careless in mapping down the route as the Gipsy told me, I missed the lane to Enfield Town, and was going down Enfield Highway, till I passed the Labour in Vain public-house where a person I knew, coming out of the door, told me the way. I walked down the lane gently and was soon in Enfield Town, and by and by on the Great York Road, where it was all plain sailing.'

That night he slept in a shed near Stevenage, lying down with his head towards the north so that he would know his direction in the morning. Early the following day a man rode by on horseback and threw him a penny, which bought half a pint of beer. On the third day he had to appease his hunger by eating grass from the roadside. By the time he reached Stilton he was 'completely foot-foundered and broken down.' Still he pressed on, and before he reached Peterborough a man and woman pulled up beside him in a cart. They proved to be old neighbours of his. After hearing his story they gave him fivepence and passed on. At the next inn he bought two half-pints of beer and two pennyworth of bread and cheese.

At Werrington, the journal tells us, 'a cart met me with a man and a woman and a boy in it. When nearing me, the woman jumped out and caught fast hold of my hands and wished me to get into the cart; but I refused and thought her either drunk or mad. But when I was told it was my second wife Patty, I got in and was soon at Northborough. But Mary was not there, neither could I get any information about her further than the old story of her being dead six years ago. . . . But I took no notice of the blarney, having seen her myself about a twelvemonth ago, alive and well and as young as ever. So here I am, homeless at home.'

The following December he was placed in Northamptonshire County Asylum on the ground of having spent 'years addicted to poetical prosings.' Nearly twenty years later he wrote to a Mr. Hopkins:

'DEAR SIR, I am in a madhouse. I quite forget your name or who you are. You must excuse, for I have nothing to communicate or tell of, and why I am shut up I don't know. I have nothing to say, so I remain, Yours faithfully, JOHN CLARE.'

In spite of his complaints, Clare's years in Epping Forest were probably as happy as any he had ever known. They were certainly happier than the twenty-two that followed. Dr. Allen had done his best for him. At the end of August 1841, after having been at home a month, Clare wrote a letter to Allen, pouring out his troubles. Allen replied with friendly advice, adding:

'Whenever you like a little change you are welcome to come here and get Bed and Board for nothing, and be at liberty to go and come as you choose, provided you do nothing to make you unpleasant as a Visitor. You might lead the life of a Hermit as much as you choose, and I would contrive to get you some place for the purpose.' (Clare had expressed a wish to live as a hermit.)

Allen, the kindly and genial, was soon to be broken himself. A rash business enterprise ruined him, and brought him to an untimely death. We shall find him under these altered circumstances when we look in upon Tennyson at Beech Hill House. After Allen's death the asylum was continued by his widow, who lived at Fairmead House with the women patients. At Springfield House a Dr. Forest had charge of the worst patients. Seventy acres of ground were cultivated by the patients under the charge of Mrs. Allen and Dr. Forest.

CHAPTER XXIV

CLARE mentioned the famous Easter Hunt, which is commonly believed to have originated with the Forest Charter of Henry III, 1226, but there is some doubt about this. Whatever its origin, the Easter Hunt was an important event in the Forest calendar. If we do not know when it started, we do know when it ended. It was formally abolished in 1858, but the old custom died hard and continued for twenty-four years after that date, degenerating into a scene of rowdy merrymaking, until it was finally suppressed in 1882.

The head of the stag hunted in 1858, at the last official hunt, was presented to the City of London Corporation by Colonel George Palmer in 1875, and is probably still to be seen in the Guildhall, with the inscription:

'Head of the stag hunted in Epping Forest on Easter Monday, 1858, on which occasion the Right Honourable Lord Brougham was present with some of the Aldermen of the City of London.'

In its heyday the Epping Hunt was an important civic occasion. The Lord Mayor of London and his party came out to Fairmead Glade, and about midday a fine buck, its great antlers decked with ribbons, was released from a cart, The poor creature must have been half dead with fright before the hunt began. In its last days the Easter Hunt was an event which only the pen of Charles Dickens could have described adequately.

Many reports of days with the hunt may be found. Perhaps the best is in Hone's *Every-day Book*:

'. . . The huntsmen of the east were all abroad by nine o'clock, trotting, fair and softly, down the road, on great nine-hand sky scrapers, nimble daisy-cutting nags, flowing-tailed chargers . . . some in job-coaches at two guineas a-day; some in three-bodied nondescripts, some in gigs, some in cabs, some in drags . . . while some on no stages at all, footed the road, smothered by dust. . . .

'At that far-famed spot, the brow above Fairmead Bottom, by 12 o'clock, there were not less than 3,000 merry lieges then

167

and there assembled. The greensward was covered with ever moving crowds on foot, and the pollard oaks, which skirt the meadow on either side, were filled with men and boys.

'But where the deuce is the stag all this while? One o'clock and no stag Two o'clock and no stag. . . . Precisely at half past two o'clock the stag-cart was seen coming over the hill by the Baldfaced Stag. Hundreds of horsemen and gig-men rushed gallantly forward to meet and escort it to the top of Fairmead Bottom, amid such whooping and hallooing as made all the forest echo again.

'For a moment, all was deep, silent, breathless anxiety; and the doors of the cart were thrown open, and out popped a strapping four-year-old red buck, fat as a porker, with a chaplet of flowers round his neck, a girth of divers coloured ribbons, and a long blue and pink streamer depending from the summit of his branching horns.

'He was received, on his alighting, with a shout that seemed to shake heaven's concave, . . . Presently, he caught a glimpse of the hounds and the huntsmen, waiting for him at the bottom, and in an instant off he bounded sideways through the rank, knocking down and trampling all who crowded the path he chose to take, and dashing at once into the cover, he was out of sight before a man could say " Jack Robinson."

'Then might be seen gentlemen running about without their horses, and horses galloping about without their gentlemen; and hats out of number brushed off their owner's heads by the rude branches of the trees; and everybody asking which way the stag was gone, and nobody knowing anything about him . . . yet nothing at all to be seen, though more than enough to be heard; for every man, and every woman too, made as loud a noise as possible.

'Meanwhile the stag, followed by the keepers and about six couple of hounds, took away through the covers towards Wood-ford . . . he there turned back, sweeping down the bottom for a mile or two, and away up the enclosures towards Chingford, where he was caught, nobody knows how, for everybody returned to town, except those who stopped to regale afresh, and recount the glorious perils of the day. Thus ended the Easter Hunt of 1826.'

To-day the hunt is remembered chiefly through Hood's comic ballad and Tom D'Urfey's *Pills to Purge Melancholy*, of 1719, which is frequently quoted in popular accounts of the event:

Next once a year into Essex a hunting they go;
To see 'em pass along, O! 'tis a pretty show,
Through Cheapside and Fenchurch Street, and so to Aldgate Pump,
Each man with 's spurs in 's horse's sides, and his back-sword 'cross his
·rump.
My Lord Mayor takes a staff in hand to beat the bushes o'er,
I must confess it was hard work he ne'er had done before,
A creature bounceth from the bush, which made them all to laugh,
My lord he cried, 'A hare! a hare!' but it proved an Essex calf.

Hood's ballad is too long to quote. It was written while the poet was living at Winchmore Hill, and published in a small pamphlet in 1829, with six illustrations by George Cruikshank.

Hood came to live in the Forest at Lake House, Wanstead, in 1832, but did not remain there many years. Financial difficulties made it expedient for him to retire to the Continent in March 1835, and he did not take up residence in England again until 1840. Wanstead was probably in his mind when he wrote *Our Village*, an interesting example of the skilful use of rhyming prose in humorous writing. Everything in *Our Village*, of course, must not be taken as literally applicable to Wanstead, but there, with numerous other inns, was 'The Green Man,' reckoned the best because it boasted a postilion, 'two deplorable lame white horses, and a ramshackled "neat postchaise."'

Hood's description could not be called enticing. You might go and whistle for hollyhocks at cottage doors, for honeysuckle, or jasmine. All that could be found in the way of flora were dandelions and thistles interspersed with cabbages. The fruit trees that did bear fruit were regularly stripped by thieves. There was a small day school, kept by a respectable Mrs. Gaby, and a select establishment for those who could afford it. But we cannot give an adequate summary of Hood's village simply by extracting a few features. The reader must turn to the poet himself.

While at Lake House, Hood wrote a novel entitled *Tylney Hall*, in which he does better justice to his surroundings. Lake House had been a summer-house, or banqueting hall, for the great Wanstead House, built by the first Earl Tylney in 1715. The trees in the long avenues radiating from Wanstead House had been planted by the earl's father, Sir Josiah Child, under the direction of John Evelyn, the diarist and author of *Sylva*. Visiting the earlier Wanstead House in 1683, Evelyn wrote:

'I went to see Sir Josiah Child's prodigious cost in planting walnut trees about his seat, and making fish ponds, many miles in circuit, in Epping Forest, in a barren spot, as oftentimes these suddenly monied men for the most part seat themselves.'

Among other famous visitors to Wanstead House was Horace Walpole, who visited the earl's palatial mansion in 1755, and wrote to Richard Bentley: 'I dined yesterday at Wanstead: many years have passed since I saw it. The disposition of the house and prospect are better than I expected, and very fine. The garden, which, they tell you, cost as much as the house, that is £100,000, is wretched; the furniture fine but without taste.'

The last Earl Tylney died in 1784, and Wanstead House passed to the Tylney Longs, whose heiress married the Hon. Wellesley Pole, a nephew of the Duke of Wellington. Such was the reckless extravagance of this gentleman that within ten years of acquiring prodigious wealth he was obliged to flee from his creditors. The great house was pulled down, and after being closed for many years the ornamental gardens were acquired by the Corporation of London.

If we want to know what Wanstead House represented to society at the height of its fame, we must look at Hogarth's 'The Wanstead Assembly,' which appeared in 1728, and was the artist's first challenge to the art world of his day. His style was not yet fully developed, but the little groups playing ombre, or drinking tea, depict with satire and humour the social life of the period.

Lake House, where Hood lived, had only one good room, the old banqueting hall itself, which had a Grinling Gibbons fireplace, carved in fruit and flowers, and also a beautifully painted ceiling. The seasons were represented in the style of Watteau round the panelled walls. But even this sumptuous room was in a bad state of repair.

From his window Hood looked across part of the old gardens towards a small lake, from which the house took its name. One day boys were caught robbing this garden, and Hood had them brought into the house. There the poet's father-in-law, an imposing old gentleman, was called upon to act as magistrate, and a mock-trial was staged. The boys were sentenced to immediate execution, the old gentleman ordering them to be hanged from the cherry-tree. At this point the poet's son entered the room to plead for mercy. The boys promised never to steal again and were duly pardoned.

In this absurd scene we may imagine Hood, a small man of clerical appearance, dressed sombrely in black. He had delicate, regular features which bore evidence of his continual ill health. The melancholy of his expression gave no indication of his wit. Lamb, his great friend, who lived for some time at Enfield, and died at Edmonton, was of different aspect. Lamb was a sturdy man of middle height, with a brown and rather ruddy complexion in spite of his long years of office confinement. When the Lambs moved to Enfield, Charles wrote to Hood:

'I fear to invite Mrs. Hood to our new mansion, lest she envy it, and hate us. But when we are fairly in, I hope she will come and try it.'

Lamb was near the end of his life when Hood moved to Wanstead; but he lived to read *Tylney Hall* and to be 'infinitely amused' by it. His letter acknowledging the book was one of the last he wrote.

Hood found a great deal to amuse him at Wanstead, as everywhere. He describes in one place a literary society, that 'waited on ladies and gentlemen at their own houses.'

'Our Minerva, allegorically speaking, was a motley personage, in blue stockings, a flounced gown, Quaker cap, and kerchief, French flowers, and a man's hat. She held a fan in one hand and a blow-pipe in the other. Her votaries were of both sexes, old and young, married and single, assenters, dissenters, High Church, Low Church, No Church; Doctors in Physics, and Apothecaries in Metaphysics; dabblers in Logic, Chemistry, Casuistry, Sophistry . . . Conchology, Demonology; in short, all kinds of Colledgy-Knowledgy-Ology, including "Cakeology," and tea and coffee.

'Like other Societies, we had our President—a sort of Speaker who never spoke; at least within my experience he never unbosomed himself of anything but a portentous shirt frill. According to the usual order of entertainment, there was—first, tea and small talk; secondly, an original essay, which should have been followed, thirdly, by a discussion, or great talk; but nine cases in ten, it chanced, or rather mumchanced, that, between those who did not know what to think, and others, who did not know how to deliver what they thought, there ensued a dead silence. . . . To make this awkward pause more awkward, some misgiving voice, between a whisper and a croak, would stammer out some allusion to a Quakers' Meeting, answered from right to left by a running titter, the speaker having innocently, or perhaps wilfully forgotten, that one or two friends in drab coats, and as many in slate-coloured gowns, were sitting, thumb-twiddling in the circle.'

We read little of Lamb on the Forest side of the Lea, but his love for Izaak Walton must have led to many pleasant reflections on the banks of the angler's favourite stream. Perhaps his delight in Fuller brought him into Waltham for long soliloquies in the abbey church. We do not know. But we read in his letters of a tramp to Waltham Abbey, and of a journey across the Forest from Epping to Enfield, on which he amused himself composing verses for a friend.

The letter in which Lamb informs us that he had crossed the Forest is dated 2nd April 1830, and it was in this same month that the famous roadmaker, McAdam, was appointed surveyor to the Epping and Ongar Highway Trust. McAdam took up his new duties in June, and sixteen days later produced a plan for a new road through the Forest from Wake Arms to Woodford. This new method of road making put an end to the old abuse of gravel stealing. Gravel- and sand-pits were to be found in every part of the Forest. To-day they form ponds, that add a new beauty to the woodland scene.

A greater poet than Hood, John Keats, comes into our Forest record as a visitor to Walthamstow. While still children, the Keats family were left in the care of their grandmother, Mrs. Jennings, and at her death were placed in the guardianship of a wholesale tea merchant, named Richard Abbey, who lived in Marsh Street, Walthamstow. Mr. Abbey took Fanny, the poet's sister, into his own home when she was a girl of fourteen, and sent her to a school in Marsh Street kept by a Miss Càley, who had a good reputation as a teacher.

The Keats children had little affection for the Abbeys. Fanny was unhappy with them, and John regarded them as little better than ogres. John was living at Edmonton at this time, not a long distance away from his sister, but his visits to Walthamstow were not encouraged. He was delicate, too, and in one of his letters to Fanny he said the walk frightened him. One morning, however, Fanny received the joyful news that he was coming to see her. He had written: 'This morning I scarcely know what I am doing. I am going to Walthamstow.' On arrival he found his sister looking better than she had looked for some time. We do not know what he thought of Walthamstow itself.

On the other side of the Forest we find James Smith, of the *Rejected Addresses*, who had been at Chigwell School as a boy, revisiting the Forest. He walked up Vicarage Lane, Chigwell, crossed to Chigwell Row, and went down Gravel Lane to Abridge, returning to Chigwell along the main road, rhyming as he walked:

> I pass the vicar's white abode,
> And pondering take the upward road,
> 'By busy thoughts o'erladen,
> To where the pride of Chigwell Row
> Still lives—a handsome widow now,
> As erst a lovely maiden.
>
> Here hills and dales and distant Thames,
> And forest glens, green proof proclaims,
> Of Nature's lavish bounty,
> And dub thee, lofty region still,
> Surrey's tall foe, the Richmond Hill
> Of this our Eastern County.
>
> Diverging from the road, the sod
> I tread which once, a boy, I trod,
> With pace not quite so nimble.
> But where's the Maypole next the lane,
> Who dared to banish from the plain
> That wreath-encircled symbol?
>
> Abridge, her tank and waterfall,
> The path beneath Sir Eliab's wall
> I once again am stepping,
> Beyond that round we rarely stirred;
> Loughton we saw—but only heard
> Of Ongar and of Epping.

CHAPTER XXV

Tennyson at High Beach—Matthew Arnold at Woodford—Sarah and Eliza Flower—*Nearer, my God, to Thee*—Coventry Patmore and his domestic angels

To High Beach in 1837 came Alfred Tennyson, a young man of twenty-eight with deep, emotional brown eyes under brooding eyebrows, a powerful head, a sulky mouth. The blood of yeomen ancestors invigorated his frame, but with it mingled a strain of melancholy and rebellion. 'We Tennysons,' he growled, 'are a black-blooded race.' The strong and the sensitive had combined in him to produce an artistic temperament of abnormal complexity.

When Tennyson was a young man English poetry had lost its vitality. Shelley, Keats, Byron, Coleridge, Scott were dead—all the great ones except Wordsworth, who published *Yarrow Revisited* in 1835. And Wordsworth had long ago wasted his substance, not in riotous but in righteous living. His best work had been completed thirty years earlier. In 1834 *Fraser's Magazine* complained that we had 'no sun, no moon, no stars in the poetic heavens—nothing but a miserable sprinkling of wretched glow-worms.' Public taste was as low as it could be, so low that well over one hundred thousand copies of Tupper's *Proverbial Philosophy*, published in 1838, were sold, bringing the author £20,000 reward, while the five hundred copies of an edition of Wordsworth lasted years.

Tennyson had all the emotional flux of a great lyric poet, reserves of passion, and personal magnetism. But he allowed himself to become muffled in the thick homespun of Victorian moralism, which hampered the free movement of his genius. He wished to be read, and his contemporaries required to be edified as well as entertained. They wanted books like Tupper's. They wanted to be reassured about the divine purpose of life, and Tennyson allowed himself to gratify them.

Tennyson's poems appear conventional enough now. In time the great poet creates the taste by which he is appreciated. Talent can usually be recognized at once, genius rarely. Tennyson had both talent and genius, and while critics of his early work recognized his talent, they did not recognize his genius. Even Coleridge said: 'The misfortune is that Mr. Tennyson has begun to write verses without very well understanding what metre is,' and complained that he could 'scarcely scan his verses.' The wounds from such criticism as this healed slowly, so we have what is called 'the silent and morose decade,' from 1832 to 1842, in which the High Beach period falls. The other cause of this temporary clouding of his powers was the death in 1833 of Arthur Hallam in Vienna, at the age of twenty-two.

Hallam's death, following the ridicule of critics, produced an acutely neurotic condition. *In Memoriam* brought some relief. It was begun at this time, though not completed till seventeen years later. Curiously, the first stanzas to be composed are not the most agonizing. For a record of the emotion felt when the blow fell we have to read *Break, break, break*, and *The Two Voices*. And so Tennyson,

> Vex'd with a morbid devil in his blood
> That veil'd the world with jaundice, hid his face
> From all men, and communing with himself,
> He lost the sense that handles daily life.

We hear of him in the Lake District in 1835, being 'very gruff and unmanageable,' refusing to go over to Rydal Mount to see Wordsworth.

In 1836 the cloud lifted for a short time when he met Emily Sellwood. Charles, his brother, was being married to Emily's elder sister, and Alfred conducted Emily as bridesmaid to the church:

> And all at once a pleasant truth I learn'd,
> For while the tender service made thee weep,
> I lov'd thee for the tear thou could'st not hide,
> And prest thy hand, and knew the press return'd,
> And thought, 'My life is sick of single sleep:
> O happy bridesmaid, make a happy bride!'

In 1837 they became engaged; but the wedding did not follow until thirteen years later.

It is against this background that we must think of Tennyson at High Beach. How he felt about the wrench from the open marshes and grey wolds of his native Lincolnshire we read in sections 100 to 103 of *In Memoriam*. Beech Hill House, High Beach, was chosen because it was in rural surroundings and yet near London. The house was enlarged and altered so much in 1850, when its name was changed to Beech Hill Park, that if the poet could return he would have difficulty in recognizing his old home. He had a study over the dining-room, 'with a bay' window, red curtains and a Clytie on a pedestal in the corner.' In winter he might be seen in his long blue cloak, skating on a pond in the park:

> At Francis Allen's on the Christmas-eve,—
> The game of forfeits done—the girls all kiss'd
> Beneath the sacred bush and past away—
> The parson Holmes, the poet Everard Hall,
> The host, and I sat round the wassail-bowl,
> Then half-way ebb'd: ánd there we held a talk,
> How all the old honour had from Christmas gone,
> Or gone, or dwindled down to some odd games
> In some odd nooks like this; till I, tired out
> With cutting eights that day upon the pond,
> Where, three times slipping from the outer edge,
> I bump'd the ice into three several stars,
> Fell in a doze:

Most of the time he was restless and unhappy. Writing to Emily Sellwood in 1839 he laments:

'I have been at this place in Epping Forest all the year, with nothing but that muddy pond in prospect, and those two little sharp-barking dogs.

'Perhaps I am coming to the Lincolnshire coast, but I scarcely know. The journey is so expensive, and I am so poor. . . . The far future has been my world always.'

Poor Miss Sellwood must have sighed over this letter. Clearly if he could not afford the price of a journey to Lincolnshire, he could not afford to marry. And what comfort could there be in the assurance that the far future was his world always?

The Forest pleased the mother no better than the son. To the end of his life Tennyson remembered her distress during a thunderstorm. Again to Emily Sellwood he wrote:

'What a thunderstorm we had the other night! I wonder whether it was so bad at H——. It lasted the whole night, and part of the previous afternoon. Lewis Fytche, who was with us then, was looking out of my window at half-past 11 o'clock, and saw a large fire-ball come up the valley from Waltham, till it seemed to come quite over our pond; it then according to his account grew on a sudden amazingly large. "How large?" I asked him. He said: "Like a great balloon, and burst with an explosion like fifty batteries of cannon." I am so sorry not to have seen it, for it was a thing to remember; but I was just gone to my mother's room; she was grovelling on the floor in an extremity of fear when the clap came, upon which she cried out,

"Oh, I will leave this house; the storms are very bad here."
Such a scene, almost ludicrous in its extreme.'

We wonder how the highly strung Tennysons would have
endured the heavy raids on London of just a hundred years later,
when Lewis Fytche's balloon would have been a land mine, and
his fifty batteries of cannon no mere figure of speech.

Mrs. Tennyson was a timid, gentle woman, given to shedding
tears. Once when the poet found her crying, he exclaimed:
'Oh, dam your eyes, mother! dam your eyes.'

Tennyson complained about the absence of birds at High
Beach, which he cannot have looked for, and, with more reason,
about the absence of men. Soon after he arrived he wrote to
Mrs. Rawnsley:

'You hope our change is for the better. The only advantage
in it is that one gets up to London oftener. The people are
sufficiently hospitable, but it is not in a good old-fashioned way,
so as to do one's feelings any good. Large set dinners with stores
of venison and champagne are very good things of their kind, but
one wants something more; and Mrs. Arabin seems to me the only
person about who speaks and acts as an honest and true nature
dictates; all else is artificial, frozen, cold, and lifeless.'

This description of his new neighbours may not be as prejudiced
as it sounds. The history of the Forest is sufficient to account
for a tradition of suspicion and closeness.

Tennyson must have met Clare in the Forest, for we read in
one of James Spedding's letters: 'Alfred Tennyson has reappeared.
. . . He has been on a visit to a madhouse for the last fortnight
(not as a patient), and has been delighted with the mad people,
whom he reports the most agreeable and the most reasonable
persons he has met with. The keeper is Dr. Allen, with whom
he has been greatly taken.' This association with Dr. Allen
was calamitous for both. Soon after Clare left High Beach,
Allen became enthusiastic about a scheme for wood-carving
by machinery. The Patent Decorative Carving and Sculpture
Company was formed, and Tennyson was persuaded to invest in
it all the family money he could lay his hands on. At the start
he was as keen about the scheme as Dr. Allen. When the company failed and Allen became a bankrupt, Tennyson forgot his
own enthusiasm and blamed the doctor for his loss. It is fortunate that we are not dependent on Tennyson's accounts for our
knowledge of Dr. Allen. They are bitter in the extreme. It has

G

been said truly that Dr. Allen nearly cured one poet and nearly drove another insane. The complete story is much less to Tennyson's credit than to Allen's. In any case, we should have thought better of the poet if he had spent the money on making a home for Emily Sellwood. When the business failed, Tennyson's lamentations found their way into verse. Of Dr. Allen he snarled:

> He is fled—I wish him dead—
> He that wrought my ruin—
> O the flattery and the craft
> Which were my undoing.

Again, the unfortunate doctor is described as 'the scoundrel of the supple-sliding knee.'

Misfortune and calumny hastened Allen's end. When he died in 1845 it was found that his life had been insured for part of the debt, so the poet's loss was less than expected.

One other Forest resident appears in Tennyson's pages. He is Sir Thomas White, who founded and endowed St. John's College, Oxford, and who lived at Salisbury Hall, Walthamstow, granted to him by Queen Mary in 1560. In Tennyson's play, *Queen Mary*, Sir Thomas says:

> I am Thomas White.
> Few things have fail'd to which I set my will.
> I do my most and best.

There are few direct references to High Beach in Tennyson's poems. Perhaps there may be one in the following lines:

> A mound of even-sloping side,
> Whereon a hundred stately beeches grew,
> And here and there great hollies under them;
> But for a mile around was open space
> And fern and heath.

Lying in the Forest in the drowsy heat of a summer afternoon, watching the dragonflies darting backwards and forwards in front of us, we may be reminded of those two lines:

> He dried his wings, like gauze they grew—
> A living flash of light he flew,

and forget the melancholy of the man who composed them.

Returning home from London late one night, and looking back from the crown of the hill, he remarked upon the lights of London, 'flaring like a dreary dawn,' another description that was all too apt a hundred years later.

The importance of this period in Tennyson's life is not to be looked for in his experience of the Forest. His interests were in London. He loved solitude, but one half of his complex nature found relaxation in growling and smoking with kindred spirits at the Cock Tavern. *Will Waterproof's Monologue* was written to the head waiter there. At the Sterling Club, founded as the Anonymous Club in 1838, he would meet Carlyle, Rogers, Thackeray, and Dickens, and it is Carlyle who gives us the best portrait of him at this time:

'Some weeks ago, one night, the poet Tennyson and Matthew Allen were discovered here sitting smoking in the garden. Tennyson had been here before, but was still new to Jane—who was alone for the first hour or two of it. A fine, large-featured, dim-eyed, bronze-coloured, shaggy-headed man is Alfred: dusty, smoky, free and easy; who swims, outwardly and inwardly, with great composure in an articulate element as of tranquil chaos and tobacco smoke; great now and then when he does emerge; a most restful, brotherly, solid-hearted man.'

'The silent decade' is a relative term, referring to publication rather than writing. In his first year at High Beach he contributed *St. Agnes* to *The Keepsake*, and *Oh! that 'twere possible*, one of his best lyrics, to Lord Northampton's volume, *The Tribute*. Part of *In Memoriam* was written at High Beach, including the stanzas inspired by the bells of Waltham Abbey—'Ring out, wild bells.' *The Talking Oak* and *Locksley Hall* were both written in the Forest, and during the three years spent there his mind was being prepared for some of his most popular work, part of which must have been written at Beech Hill House—parts of *Maud*, for instance. He must have begun if not completed in the Forest many of the poems that appeared in the 1842 volume. He was standing on the threshold of his great career. Throughout the forties his reputation steadily increased, until in 1850 he reached a peak of honour such as few poets have known, married Emily Sellwood at long last, and became Poet Laureate.

In Memoriam is one of the two great commemorative poems written by Victorians. The other is Matthew Arnold's *Thyrsis*, and it is interesting to find, that though the background of that poem is the countryside about Oxford, which Arnold wished to be associated with Clough's memory, some of the best stanzas were inspired in the Forest. Arnold was at Woodford in

1864, and there he heard 'the cuckoo I have brought in in *Thyrsis.*'

> So, some tempestuous morn in early June,
>> When the year's primal burst of bloom is o'er,
>> Before the roses and the longest day—
> When garden-walks, and all the grassy floor,
>> With blossoms, red and white, of fallen May
>> And chestnut-flowers are strewn—
> So have I heard the cuckoo's parting cry,
>> From the wet field, through the vext garden-trees,
>> Come with the volleying rain and tossing breeze:
>> *The bloom is gone, and with the bloom go I!*
>
> Too quick despairer, wherefore wilt thou go?
>> Soon will the high Midsummer pomps come on,
>> Soon will the musk carnations break and swell,
> Soon shall we have gold-dusted snapdragon,
>> Sweet-William with its homely cottage-smell,
>> And stocks in fragrant blow;
> Roses that down the alleys shine afar,
>> And open jasmine-muffled lattices,
>> And groups under the dreaming garden-trees,
> And the full moon, and the white evening-star.
>
> He hearkens not! light comer, he is flown!
>> What matters it? next year he will return,
>> And we shall have him in the sweet spring-days,
> With whitening hedges, and uncrumpling fern,
>> And blue-bells trembling by the forest-ways,
>> And scent of hay new-mown.

Robert Browning we can claim only through his friendship with the two gifted sisters, Sarah and Eliza Flower. These two ladies were the daughters of Benjamin Flower, a staunch nonconformist who edited the Cambridge *Intelligencer*. Browning had the greatest admiration for Eliza's musical talent, and for Sarah so strong an affection that it has been the subject of romantic speculation, though she was seven years his senior. It was by Sarah Flower's influence that Browning's first poems were accepted for publication. She was born at Harlow on 22nd February 1805, and grew up to be a tall and extremely attractive girl. Her humour and vivacity made her a delightful companion. After marrying William Brydges Adams, she became an actress, and attracted the attention of Macready, who had a high opinion of her gifts. She left the stage after a breakdown in health, and turned to literature. For some time she lived at Woodbury Hill, Loughton, in a house that stood where Sunnybank was built later. There she wrote the hymn, *Nearer, my God, to Thee,* which finds a place in nearly every Christian hymnal throughout the world. The tune was composed by her sister Eliza. It will be a long time before Englishmen forget how this great hymn was sung on board while the *Titanic* sank down into the deep waters of the Atlantic.

Another eminent Victorian, Coventry Patmore, was born at Woodford. He spent much time as a boy, along with his younger brothers, at the country house in Epping Forest of his uncle, Robert Stevens. The house he was born in has not been identified.

Patmore's most famous work was *The Angel in the House*, in which poetry was purposely subordinated to conjugal philosophy of a moralizing, Victorian character. His great-grandson explains that Patmore regarded marriage as the earthly symbol of the union between God and the soul. Patmore was a genuine poet when his tendency to moralize was overcome, but normally he got his values sadly confused. Of his beautiful Amelia he wrote:

> To look on her moved less the mind
> To say 'How beauteous!' than 'How good and kind,'

which is not the way of poetic love, however well calculated to produce domestic happiness.

The poet's household was a virtuous and impressive establishment. The children rose to their feet when the great man entered the room for breakfast, and dutifully played whist with him in the warmly curtained Victorian evenings.

The lady honoured as 'The Angel in the House' was Emily Augusta Andrews. When she died, her poet was fortunate enough to find a second inspiration, apparently no less angelic, of whom he wrote that he 'had never beheld so beautiful a personality.' This beauty, mercifully, was not in a form to disturb her lover's philosophy. It was, we learn, 'the pure effluence of Catholic sanctity.'

Fifteen years later a third 'angel' had the joy of becoming the object of this devout poet's matrimonial adoration. 'Lovers,' the poet continued to maintain, 'are nothing else than Priest and Priestess to each other of the Divine Manhood and the Divine Womanhood which are God.' So far as we are able to learn, all three marriages were serenely happy.

In spite of his smugness, Patmore remained a poet. Besides the happiness bestowed upon him at the hearth, he caught a glimpse of 'The Unknown Eros,' and the windows of his soul were found to be open whenever the heavy Victorian curtains could be drawn back.

At Woodford, too, was born Sydney Smith, but his birthplace cannot be discovered. Of both Patmore and Sydney Smith we know little more about their connection with the Forest than that they were born in one of its villages.

CHAPTER XXVI

The Taylors of Ongar—David Livingstone

ONGAR and Stanford Rivers are still quiet enough, astonishingly quiet and sequestered when we remember that they are only twenty miles away from the heart of London, and only half that distance from the teeming boroughs of Greater London. Yet to the Taylors life appeared to be losing its orderly and tranquil ways even in Ongar.

The Taylors were a wonderful family: they had two supreme joys, one was to acquire knowledge, the other to impart it, and they learned both from the head of the household. When Isaac Taylor senior—who was the son of an Essex mother—married, he was sure of only half a guinea a week. This he received as wages for three days' work done for his brother Charles, a publisher and engraver. During the remaining three days he worked hard at whatever presented itself as a means of supplementing the half-guinea. Regularity and industry were ingrained in him. He rose early, so that he would be able to spend the hour from six to seven in private devotions, which included praying aloud and singing one hymn, a practice continued throughout his life. Josiah Gilbert remembered 'when the voice was cracked with age, hearing the cheerful though quaking notes — cheerful, whether heard through the open window of the study in summertime, or in the darkness and chill of winter mornings.' Articulate prayer, Mr. Taylor maintained, prevented 'vagrancy of thought.'

Mrs. Taylor was as remarkable in her way as her husband. In early married life they were poor, and children came quickly. Mrs. Taylor was in danger of losing her intellectual interests through pressure of domestic duties. The danger was brought home to her when an acquaintance warned her that 'the affections of a man of taste cannot fix permanently on a mere plod.' What could she do about it? They could not afford servants, and even intellectuals must be fed. The danger, however, was real. Already her husband, withdrawn from her most of the time, was reading at meals. She found a solution. She would read to him herself at breakfast and tea, thus improving her own mind, her children's minds, and attracting her husband's attention to herself. So after toiling in the kitchen to prepare the meal, she sacrificed more time to feed their minds as well, maintaining the custom for forty years.

The whole family was taught that every waking moment must be usefully employed. When he entered the breakfast-room, 'my father,' we read, 'brought under his arm a drawing case, which he lodged on a side-table. The moment that he had finished his own breakfast, and while my mother continued her reading aloud, he commenced drawing—probably a flower from nature, just brought in from the garden.' These drawings were afterwards copied by the children. It was the same in church when Mr. Taylor became a minister. Every text he used in the pulpit was carefully construed by the listening children.

The Rev. Isaac Taylor, as Mr. Taylor had become some years previously, received his call to Ongar in July 1811, and ministered to the little congregation at the Independent chapel for the remaining eighteen years of his life. His flock were 'friendly and pious, though plain, people'; notwithstanding 'some dashing silk pelisses and feathers on a fine afternoon.'

Fortunately, this industrious and serious-minded family had a strong sense of humour, and took a lively interest in the oddities of local characters at Ongar and elsewhere. There was old Orford, who had not sat in a pew for half a century. He was very deaf, and sat high up on the pulpit steps with his ear-trumpet. Nor was old Orford the only one on the pulpit steps. Another old man claimed the top step as his right, and leaned against the pulpit door. 'His venerable and rheumy countenance, his drab knee breeches gaping above his corded grey stockings,' were remembered by the family to the end of their lives. They remembered especially a famous occasion 'when his huge tin snuff-box slipped from his pottering fingers and rolled bump, bump, down the uncarpeted stairs with portentous noise.' While the snuff-box was being recovered the parson pursued his learned way through the sermon undistracted.

At Ongar, Jane and Ann, the Reverend Isaac's accomplished daughters, reached marriageable age, and an 'intellectual and cultivated gentleman,' the Rev. Joseph Gilbert, a childless widower, presented himself to solicit the heart and hand of Miss Ann. They were married in 1813. But the unity of the family must be preserved, so the Taylors in conference agreed that on the night of every full moon, at nine o'clock, they would each stand alone and look into the face of the moon, meeting in thought.

At the first full moon after Ann left home she sat quietly waiting for the finger of the clock to reach nine. At the precise moment she rose sedately and retired behind the curtain to gaze through the window at the moon. Alas! it was invisible.

Mr. Taylor, with characteristic thoroughness, provided Ann with a list of full-moon nights when she left Ongar, and with the list an ode in thirty-two stanzas, addressed to the moon herself, consecrating the chosen hour. Apparently the pagan moon did not wish to encourage his clerical advances.

The Taylors lived at the Castle House for their first three years in Ongar, and loved it. In 1814 they moved to Peaked Farm, where their astonishing industry was continued. Even Mrs. Taylor had surprised them all by taking to authorship. She had produced a tale in three weeks of mental fever, completing it just as her husband received seventy pounds for a book of his own. Jane, in the quiet of her room, solicited her own muse for favours. Isaac, her brother, was busy with his miniatures and illustrations. Once when Ann expressed surprise at the amount of work Isaac the younger could get through, he replied: 'There is no real mystery in getting through with a good deal in the year; or if there be, one Taylor need not explain it to another. Only observe the simple rule of staying at home, and sitting so many hours every day to the business in hand, and the thing is done. If free from care and well in health, I should not scruple to undertake getting out two bouncing octavos per annum, and all original.'

Bouncing octavos! With how much gusto Isaac must have written those words. It was Isaac Taylor the younger who complained about the penny post because it had ended 'the dispensation of letters, bringing in the dispensation of scores of notes, each as brief as Saxon can make it. The locust swarms of scraps in an envelope has eaten up almost every green thing in the fields and gardens of soul-land. This is what we have come to under Whig administration!'

The most famous volume produced by Jane and Ann, *Original Poems for Infant Minds*, was translated into German, Dutch, and Russian. As writers of verse for children, the Taylors were practically the first in the field. When Jane sat down to write one of her rhymes she would shut her eyes and imagine a child standing in front of her. She attributed her success to this little imaginary being, and when she had failed she believed it was

* G

because she had said: 'Now you may go, my dear, I shall finish the hymn myself.'

Authorship was inevitable with the Taylors, though, strangely enough, both parents were against their children taking up writing as a profession. Of the two sisters, Ann, who found other creative work to do when she married, and so put her pen away, was the more dramatic. She wrote about people, while Jane wrote chiefly about nature. Ann was sociable and practical, Jane shy, sensitive, and mercurial. It was Ann who wrote:

> Dance, little baby, dance up high,
> Never mind, baby, mother is by;
> Crow and caper, caper and crow.
> There, little baby, there you go;
>
> Up to the ceiling, down to the ground,
> Backwards and forwards, round and round;
> Then dance, little baby, and mother shall sing,
> While the gay merry coral goes ding-a-ding, ding.

Jane's best known poem is *The Star*, of which every one knows the first verse:

> Twinkle, twinkle, little star,
> How I wonder what you are!
> Up above the world so high,
> Like a diamond in the sky.

The two sisters were separated by Ann's marriage, but she could still write to Jane:

> The seasons vary, but we stand,
> Dear girl, as ever, hand in hand.

Towards the end of their lives, Ann noticed that the public seemed inclined to forget that there were two sisters. She wrote: 'We were, perhaps, rather sought after as "clever girls," and of the two, Jane always conceding a large share of birthright to me, I seemed to be generally accepted as the cleverest. The mistake has been rectified by the public since, and indeed, so as to swing a little beyond the mark, attributing to her many productions that were really mine. Publishers have frequently given a convenient wink and announced "By Jane Taylor" when "Ann Taylor" was the guilty person.

'Dear Jane never needed to steal, while I could not afford to lose. But what signifies it?'

Describing a scene in the Roding Valley, Jane wrote:

'Twilight already stealing over the landscape shades yonder

sleeping cornfield, whence the merry reapers have this day borne away the last sheaf. A party of gleaners have since gathered up the precious fragments. Now all are gone: the harvest moon is up. A low mist rising from the river floats in the valley. There is a gentle stirring amongst the leaves of the tall elm that shades our roof. All besides is still.'

The Rev. Isaac Taylor, his wife, and Jane lie buried at Ongar. The old chapel has been enlarged, and their graves are now inside the building, near the vestry door. Their stones may be seen by lifting the floor boards. Isaac the younger lies with his wife at Stanford Rivers, while Ann is buried with her husband at Nottingham, far from the secluded valley of the Roding and the peace of Ongar.

Ongar is outside the Forest itself; but signposts bearing the name are seen as we wander about its lanes. Jane Taylor always remembered reading one on a picnic in the Forest in 1810, little knowing that it was to be her home, and that her name was to be so intimately linked with it. Every member of the family loved the old town. Nothing would have pleased them better than to know that they would be remembered as The Taylors of Ongar. When Mr. Taylor visited the place before taking up the appointment, he leaned over a gate, looked across the modest cluster of houses, and murmured to himself: 'I could be content to live and die in that spot.'

Isaac the younger lived for forty years with his wife and family at Stanford Rivers, in retirement most of the time, but visited by many thoughtful men his work attracted. Sometimes he had to leave his cherished seclusion to conduct experiments in the application of some of his ideas to practical affairs. One such experiment took him to the cotton mills of Lancashire, where he spent his time, as he said, 'in the rumbling intestines of this world of machinery.' His work there was in connection with the engraving of calico patterns and the process of calico printing. He was a man of profound intellect, possessing at the same time all the family aptitude for cultivating the arts and graces of life.

The Taylors were a remarkable example of heredity. To be a Taylor was to be born with personal gifts and delight in exercising them given to few. Like the Brontës they lived in a remote part of the country, and loved its solitude. They had none of the turbulent passions of the Brontës, and were entirely different in temperament and outlook. Perhaps we might say that the difference betwen them was the difference between genius and talent. Or was it only the difference between the bleak moors of Yorkshire and the sunny Essex meadows? Whatever it was, the Taylors' was the happier lot.

Ongar is proud of another association. David Livingstone studied there with the Rev. Richard Cecil, who trained men for work in the mission field. In addition to their theological studies, Mr. Cecil required his students to share the housework, chop firewood, assist in the garden, and grind corn. This, he argued, was a necessary part of training for men who would have to do so much for themselves when they were cut off from civilization. It must have been as useful to Mr. Cecil himself as to his students.

Livingstone, a great walker, explored all the countryside about Ongar. His connection with Essex is best remembered from one incident. One Sunday he went out from Ongar to preach at the Independent chapel at Stanford Rivers. The service went well enough until the time came round for the sermon. The congregation settled down in their pews and looked eagerly towards the pulpit. The words of the text were read with great deliberation; but not a word of the sermon could the nervous young man utter. He had to confess to the astonished villagers that he had forgotten every word he intended to say.

CHAPTER XXVII

Writers for children—The Howitts at Theydon Bois—Dr. Southwood Smith—Caroline Smith—Octavia Hill—The Commons Preservation Society—The foundation of the National Trust—*Old Mother Hubbard* —Thomas Day—Daniel Day and Fairlop Fair—Borrow and the gipsies

THERE were other writers for children in the Forest besides the Taylors. William and Mary Howitt lived for a short time at Long Running, Theydon Bois. They were married in 1823, and in that year published together a book of poems entitled *The Forest Minstrel*. Like the Taylors, they were pioneers with books for children, William with *A Boy's Adventures in the Wilds of Australia*, Mary with her delightful verses. It was Mary Howitt, too, who introduced Hans Andersen to English children.

In his *Year Book of the Country*, William writes: 'We break the spell of town dreariness and are once more in the woods. We take our first flight into the near Forest of Epping. We walk for miles in green glades and beneath the close covert of the hornbeam trees.' The Howitts did not remain long in the Forest, or anywhere else for that matter. From Theydon they went to live in Staffordshire. Next we hear of them tramping through Scotland, and settling again for a short time at Nottingham, where we hope they talked about the Forest with Ann Taylor. From 1840 they lived for three years in Germany, where William made a collection of student songs. During their next period of residence in England, Mary, on 16th July 1844, visited John Clare at Northamptonshire County Asylum. He gave her a manuscript copy of his poem *The Sleep of Spring*. In the fifties William and his two sons were in Australia—Mary did not go with them—returning to England to live for eighteen years at Highgate. Still they were not settled. The Howitts' next home was in Italy, where William died in 1879.

William Howitt's most pleasing books are those in which English life and scenery are described, rather in the manner of Miss Mitford. Both he and Mary contributed regularly to the periodicals of the day. William had the true instinct of the countryman. 'But as for the village green,' he wrote, 'the common lying near a town, the forest, and the moorland that has a poetical charm about it, felt and acknowledged by the public—may the axe and

189

the spade that are lifted up against them be shivered to atoms, and a curse, worse than the curse of Kehama, chase all commissioners, land surveyors, petitioning lawyers, and every species of fencer and divider out of their boundaries for ever and ever!'

Of the old hunting lodge at Chingford he wrote: 'The hand of the past is impressed upon thee, and has given thee a character. It has invested thee with the poetry of nature.' In verse William was never as good as his wife. Such poems as those on the squirrel, and many other nature verses by Mary, are as fresh as when they were written. The simple lilt of her *Spring Song* cannot fail to captivate the unsophisticated reader:

> See the yellow catkins cover
> All the slender willows over;
> And on mossy banks so green
> Star-like primroses are seen;
> And their clustering leaves below,
> White and purple violets grow.
>
> Hark! the little lambs are bleating,
> And the cawing rooks are meeting
> In the elms—a noisy crowd;
> And all birds are singing loud,
> There, the first white butterfly
> In the sun goes flitting by.

Thomas Hood was an admirer of the Howitts. 'Whilst I am thus closeted in the confessional,' he wrote, 'it may be as well, as the pelican said, to make a clean breast of it, and at once plead guilty to all those counts—and some from long-standing have become very Old Bailey counts—that haunt my conscience.' Among his numerous 'crimes' are the inevitable unanswered letters and unacknowledged books. He singled out for special mention a book by William and Mary Howitt, and grieved that he never told them how much it pleased him.

At Highgate these gentle Quakers, the Howitts, lived close to their friends, Dr. Southwood Smith and his family, who had previously lived at Loughton, in the house where Sarah Flower Adams wrote *Nearer, my God, to Thee.* Dr. Southwood Smith laboured throughout a great part of his life with single-hearted devotion to improve the conditions of factory workers. He was particularly interested in the employment of children in mines. At the time he was living in Loughton he was attached to a London fever hospital. There he saw that the patients who came in such numbers during fever epidemics were the victims of insanitary conditions, especially bad in the congested East End. For years he fought against vested interests and apathy, until squalid housing conditions were recognized as a public responsibility when the first Public Health Act was passed.

Dr. Southwood Smith was a man of serene temper, who refused to be discouraged by the slow progress of his schemes for reform. His pioneering spirit was inherited by his daughter Caroline, whose articles on education attracted the attention of a banker named James Hill. Caroline Smith became governess to the Hill children, and later their stepmother. She had three daughters of her own, the youngest of whom became famous as Octavia Hill, bearing the doctor's proud standard into a third generation. Mr. Hill was not successful, and when his bank failed, Dr. Southwood Smith settled the family in a cottage at Epping.

The close friendship between the Howitts and the Hills developed out of a children's party at Highgate, to which the Howitts invited the Hill children. Mary Howitt had the greatest admiration for the way Mrs. Hill was bringing up her family. The play of fancy was encouraged in them, and what frolics they had! They went out looking for fairies together; they imagined goblins in the cellar, and performed nightly rites of propitiation.

If Mrs. Howitt admired Mrs. Hill, the Hill children loved Mrs. Howitt. Octavia wrote: 'I shall never forget the atmosphere of love . . . in the long winter evenings with her, I used to sit on a little stool at her feet, she used to take down my hair and I can feel her soft, gentle touch . . . can see the firelight flicker on her face as she worked and Mr. Howitt read.' In summer Mr. Howitt took the children for walks, explaining the life of the countryside to them. Sometimes they went bathing. 'It is so delicious bathing,' wrote Octavia, 'we stay in so long and try to float and splash and dash and prance and dance—I am so happy; you don't know how happy—they are all so sweet and kind to me, and it's so beautiful here.'

Octavia, like her mother and grandfather, had a vision of better social conditions. One aspect of her work interests us especially. William Howitt had taught her the value of life out of doors, and it may have been as a result of this that she became associated with the Commons and Footpaths Preservation Society. Sir Robert Hunter, the solicitor who did so much towards winning Epping Forest for the people, was her friend, and together they awakened the nation to the value of such open spaces as the Forest, laying the foundations of the National Trust, which was founded in 1895. The beauty of our own Forest was doubtless an inspiring memory to both the Howitts and the Hills, and must have influenced Octavia in her endeavour to do for the whole country what was done for London in Epping Forest.

The name Sarah Catherine Martin conveys nothing; but we all know *Old Mother Hubbard*. Sarah Martin was the author of this popular rhyme, and her grave is to be found in St. Nicholas's churchyard, Loughton. It is the second grave surrounded by iron railings to the right on entering the small gate nearest Chigwell. There she rests in the family vault with her parents. The grave is neglected, but the inscription can still be read: 'Sarah Catherine Martin, daughter of Sir Henry and Lady Martin, who departed this life on the 17th day of December, 1826.' She was born in January 1768, and was about thirty-seven when she wrote *Old Mother Hubbard*.

Little is known about the connection of the Martin family with Loughton. Only the entries of the family burials are to be found in the Loughton parish registers, but we know that the Martins were related to the Powell family, who owned estates in the Loughton and Theydon Bois districts, and lived in what is now called Newnham House, Loughton.

The Taylors, the Howitts, and the Hills all understood children. Their writings still delight young minds. We can hardly say the same of Thomas Day with his *Sandford and Merton*. Day was, of course, much earlier than the others. He might have understood children better if he had been born a hundred years later. No one ever had better intentions. He was really a good, kind, gentle soul, and anxious to do good in the world. But he was eccentric in the extreme. In his innocence he believed that if he could find a healthy, untutored girl, and train her mind himself, the result would be the ideal Mrs. Day. More and Milton suffered from the same delusion. Of the three, Day was the most sensible: first, because he saw that he must catch his victim young; secondly, because he trained two girls in case one should be a failure; thirdly, because he did not, in fact, marry either.

He took his first victim, a flaxen-haired girl of twelve, whom he named Sabrina, from an orphanage at Shrewsbury. The second he took from a foundling hospital in London and named Lucretia. Both were bitter disappointments. Lucretia was the more fortunate in that she was the first to be given up as a failure. She suffered from excessive interest in dress, and Day was glad to get her apprenticed to a milliner in Ludgate Hill, where feminine vanity would have more scope. When she married a prosperous draper a few years later, Mr. Day settled five hundred pounds on her.

Sabrina was reserved for further trial. She was not so vain as Lucretia, but proved lacking in endurance when her kind benefactor applied his prepared tests. She winced when melted sealing-wax was dropped on her arms; she screamed when pistols were fired at her garments. Clearly she would never be worthy of the honour of becoming Mrs. Day. The sensitive Sabrina was thereupon lodged in a boarding school for three years, with a personal allowance of fifty pounds a year. On leaving school she married a barrister and, like Lucretia, received five hundred pounds from her disappointed guardian.

His experiments in training a wife having failed, Day married a Miss Milnes of Wakefield, a lady who is said to have agreed with him in everything. They lived in Hampstead immediately after their marriage; but when Day had accustomed his bride to the extraordinary ideas which he considered essential to virtuous happiness, he proposed that they should move out into the country. He had long been considering a scheme for the amelioration of the conditions of agricultural labourers, and he wished to put it to the test. A house and small farm were acquired for the purpose at Stapleford Abbots, a remote and rural village on the Hainault side of the Forest. The house had only one good room; the land was heavy, water-logged clay in a stretch of undrained forest. Such trifles as these, however, were unworthy of the consideration of the redoubtable Mr. Day. He had a plan for rendering the soil fertile, as well as a plan for easing the lot of the labourer who cultivated it. When the house was found to be unfit for habitation, he was also obliged to conceive a plan for rebuilding that.

Numerous workpeople were engaged to execute his designs; but the plan failed to work. The most distressing part of the new tasks was that they interrupted his intellectual conversations with his wife, prevented their leisurely walks in the neighbouring Forest and their application to studious habits in the house. Day was deep in a treatise written by an enthusiastic agriculturist to prove that deep ploughing would make any land fertile. But he could not apply himself to the treatise thoroughly if he had to be constantly interrupted to answer frivolous questions about the position of the window in the new room on the first floor of the house, or if the carpenter continued that insufferable hammering.

His dear friend, Mr. Edgeworth, ever ready to assist in any noble project, came on a visit and desired to help. Together they applied themselves to this urgent question of the position of the window. In the middle of their deliberations, the mason entered the room to ask if the wall might not be started, and the position of the window decided later. This, at all events, would occupy the mason. Mr. Day and Mr. Edgeworth agreed that there was no reason why the wall should not be started, while they continued examining their plans for the proposed window. The mason set to work. The wall grew higher and higher, and still the position of the window had not been determined. It had been made clear to the workmen that the building would never be completed if the master was always being disturbed while making his designs. The mason, anxious to oblige, did not disturb him again, and the room was completed without any windows at all. Mrs. Day kept it as a dressing room for three years, using candles in broad daylight. It was then decided to turn it into a lumber room.

Essex labourers were found to be churlish; Essex land unresponsive to treatment. Finally, Mr. Day was obliged to admit defeat in his designs upon the Forest. He moved over into Surrey to continue his experiments there. In the end, his theories cost him his life. He was thrown by a young horse, which he refused to have trained in the usual way. The accident proved fatal. Mr. Day rebelled against any form of restraint; so, unfortunately, did the horse.

When Mr. Day published his *Sandford and Merton*, he stated in the preface that he had written it because he had observed a great lack of books for children's reading. 'The least exceptionable that I could find for this purpose,' he stated, 'were Plutarch's *Lives* and Xenophon's *History of the Institution of Cyrus*, in English translations.' No doubt the translation was allowed in order to inspire gratitude in the reader. He approved also 'some part of *Robinson Crusoe* and a few passages in the first volume of Mr. Brooke's *Fool of Quality* and *Mary and Florence, or Grave and Gay*, by Miss Fraser Tytler.'

Day's educational theories were shared by the virtuous Mr. Edgeworth, who came into Essex to discuss the position of the window with him. Mr. Edgeworth was an Irishman whom providence had blessed with ample opportunities for putting such theories to the test, without resort to unbroken horses or foundling infants. He had, in orderly succession, four wives, fifteen children, and always a large retinue of servants and dependants. According to himself, he ruled his household as a benevolent despot, admired, adored, and obeyed by all. 'I do not think,' he observed reflectively, 'that one tear per month is shed in this house, nor the voice of reproof heard, nor the hand of restraint felt.' To both Mr. Edgeworth and Mr. Day virtue and utility were the important principles; poetry and romance were to be guarded against.

While living on the edge of the Forest, Thomas Day was interested to hear of the adventures of his namesake, Daniel Day, the well-to-do Wapping block and pump maker, who was in the habit of visiting the great Fairlop Oak on the first Friday in every July, the day on which he came out into Essex to collect rents. Daniel Day used to bring out with him his friends from Wapping, and friends and tenants would join together under the giant oak for a feast of beans and bacon. The custom was begun about the year 1725. Before Daniel's death in 1767 the event had developed into an annual fair. Shipbuilders, block and pump makers, came out in two or three fully-rigged model ships mounted on carriage frames, each drawn by six horses, and attended by postilions and outriders. These model ships were used because, after a road accident, Daniel had an aversion to travel by carriage. He and his friends came down to Barking Creek by boat. From there the procession came by way of Stratford, Forest Gate, Manor Park, Ilford, Fulwell Hatch, and 'The Bald Hind,' to the oak. The postilions were dressed in blue and gold, and bands played on board the ships throughout the journey.

The seventeen branches of the great tree overspread an area three hundred feet in circumference. About three feet from the ground the trunk had a girth of thirty-six feet. When one of the branches was torn off in a gale, Daniel took the fall as an omen of his approaching death. He had a coffin made from the wood, and took the precaution of lying in it to make sure that his limbs would not be cramped when he set out on his last ceremonial procession.

Like the Epping Hunt, Fairlop Fair became a saturnalia, and had to be stopped. The pulpits of St. Pancras Church and Wanstead Church were made from the oak of this famous tree, which, in its day, had witnessed many spectacles not normally associated with the ministry of the church. An old song, once popular at Fairlop, goes:

> To Hainault Forest Queen Anne she did ride
> And beheld the beautiful Oak by her side;
> And after viewing it from bottom to top,
> She said to her Court, 'It is a Fair-lop!'

Fairlop Oak was set on fire in 1805 by gipsies. In February 1820 it was blown down in a gale. It was under the branches of Fairlop Oak that Borrow saw the beautiful young gipsy in the red cloak and large beaver, telling fortunes. When the Forest came under the control of the London County Council the gipsies had to break camp and find other shelter. Now they are no longer to be seen, sprawling on the grass, watching their ragged, dark-skinned children playing about amongst the gorse and fern. They may have been a nuisance to neighbouring farmers, but the Forest became poorer when the raven-haired gipsy women, with their gleaming teeth and massive ear-rings, their gaily coloured handkerchiefs and shawls, were compelled to leave.

There were famous gipsies in the Forest in the old days; there was Old Mike, an Irish gipsy who spent the summer on Wanstead Flats, where the family of Gipsy Smith, the world-famous evangelist, lived. Most of the gipsies cared little about religion, but they always had their babies christened, because it was good for business. The nearest clergyman was invited to the gipsy camp, and he usually brought with him some of the ladies of his congregation, who wished to witness the ceremony. These ladies brought presents for the gipsy mother and child. Most of the gipsies had scriptural names, which some authorities have thought were traditional, and evidence that the gipsies were one of the lost tribes. They were also sabbath observers. Sticks for the Sunday fires were always collected on the Saturday. There was no making of baskets, clothes-pegs, or tinware on Sunday. The Smiths were great fortune-tellers, and one might often be found entertaining the company at 'The King's Head,' Chigwell.

CHAPTER XXVIII

DISRAELI, writing to a Mr. Heath, said: 'I am not surprised that the ancients worshipped trees. Lakes and mountains, however glorious for a time, in time weary. Sylvan scenery never palls.'

The love of woodlands was born in the future Prime Minister when he was a boy attending Cogan's school at Walthamstow. His home was at Enfield. His father, who had made a fortune by the time he reached middle life, cultivated his Italian garden there, entertained his friends, played whist with Sir Horace Mann, ate macaroni dressed by the Venetian consul, and sang canzonettas. Mr. Disraeli senior was never forgiven by his wife for bearing a foreign name; his son was an enigma and a disappointment to him; but the old man enjoyed life and lived to be nearly ninety.

Benjamin Disraeli's family background was as flamboyant as his own character; but while his father was a romantic, Mr. Cogan, his headmaster, was a plain, hard-working man, an eminent nonconformist with a great reputation, especially among dissenters, as a Greek scholar. Dr. Blomfield, Bishop of London, considered Cogan the first Greek scholar in England. He was an untiring worker. The only recreation he allowed himself was an hour in the Forest on horseback after morning school.

Mr. Disraeli met Mr. Cogan in a bookseller's shop. On discovering that his new acquaintance was a schoolmaster, he resolved then and there to place Benjamin in his charge. At that time Walthamstow was a residential district for well-to-do city bankers and merchants. It had many highly respectable academies for the education of favoured youth, Mr. Cogan's school being different from the rest because it admitted nonconformists and Jews as well as sons of the Church of England.

Disraeli tells us that he was thirteen when he entered Cogan's school, which was then at Higham Hall, an old manor house two miles out of Walthamstow. 'Nothing was thought of there,' he tells us, 'but the two dead languages.' Cogan was acknowledged to be an admirable instructor, and his pupil says that after being with him four years he was fit for a university, adding, however, that he was no more advanced than other boys of his own age, and confessing that he never reached the first class.

The first class, we learn, dealt with Aeschylus, Aristophanes, Aristotle, Plato, and the Greek orators. 'I never could reach this stage,' confessed Disraeli, 'though I listened to many of the interpretations and expositions of the master with interest and admiration. Though a very reserved, shy, calm man, his whole being became animated when he was interpreting a great classic writer. However, though I never reached the first class, and was not eminent even in the second, I learnt, or rather read, a great deal in those years.'

One of his biographers says that 'if Waterloo was won on the playing fields of Eton, Disraeli reached Westminster and the Cabinet by way of Walthamstow.' Perhaps he also reached his fame as a novelist by the same route. In *Endymion* he describes a country mansion on the border of a forest, from which Bishopsgate Street may be reached in an hour. The name of the mansion is Hainault House.

While at Walthamstow, Disraeli spent much time reading old romances. His imagination was always active. He would invent stories and tell them to his school friends as they lay in bed at night. Shy and reserved, he would wander alone in the Forest, sometimes accompanied by Mr. Cogan's dog.

Disraeli was very fond of Mrs. Cogan, and used to visit her many years after he had left her husband's school. Once, as he rose to leave, he smiled and said: 'I am sorry I cannot stay any longer, Mrs. Cogan, but, you see, when I reach home there is the bore of a little dinner and dressing for the opera to be undergone.' Mrs. Cogan smiled back at him and replied: 'Don't talk nonsense, Disraeli; you know you would not like to live any other life.'

Walthamstow had many distinguished and cultivated residents at that time, amongst them the Forsters. Several members of this scholarly family have brief notices in the *Dictionary of National Biography*. More than one became a well-known naturalist, and Mr. Bosworth of Walthamstow has very properly taken care that they shall not be forgotten. But Walthamstow is proudest of having been the birthplace of William Morris. No name is more frequently recalled than his in notes on the Forest.

William Morris was born at Elm House, Clay Hill, on 24th March 1834. His parents were prosperous but undistinguished. Their home was a roomy, Victorian house, with a large lawn surrounded by shrubberies, and a kitchen garden that boasted a fine mulberry-tree. All this has now been swept away by the tide of modern building.

Describing the Essex scene in a restored and recivilized England, Morris gives us, in *News from Nowhere*, a glimpse of the countryside about Walthamstow as it was in his boyhood:

'Eastward and landward it is all flat pasture, once marsh, except for a few gardens, and there are very few permanent dwellings there, scarcely anything but a few sheds and cots for the men who come to look after the great herds of cattle. What with the beasts and the men, and the scattered red-tiled roofs and the big hay-ricks, it does not make a bad holiday to get a quiet pony and ride about there on a sunny afternoon of autumn, and look over the river and the craft passing up and down, and on to Shooter's Hill and the Kentish uplands, and then turn round to the wide green sea of the Essex marshland, with the great domed line of the sky, and the sun shining down in one flood of peaceful light over the long distance.'

No doubt, even in 1840, such a description would be considered poetic rather than accurate.

Morris was a delicate child who had to be kept alive with calves'-foot jelly and beef tea. As he was unable to romp with other children, he took to reading instead. When he was four, we are told, he was already deep in the Waverley novels. And so we imagine him as a boy, lying under the trees throughout the long days, peopling the Forest with all the characters of romance.

When he was six, the family moved to Woodford Hall, a spacious Georgian mansion, which stood in fifty acres of park along the London to Epping road. The estate included about a hundred acres of farmland between the hall and the river Roding; only a fence separated the park from the Forest. Woodford Church was alongside, the churchyard being reached from the hall grounds by a private doorway. The old village pound and stocks stood on the green opposite. 'When we lived at Woodford,' Morris wrote to his daughter, fifty years later, 'there were stocks there on a little bit of wayside green in the middle of the village: beside them stood the cage, a small shanty some twelve feet square, and as it was built of brown brick roofed with blue slate, I suppose it had been quite recently in use, since its style was not earlier than the days of fat George. I remember I used

to look at these two threats of law and order with considerable
terror, and decidedly preferred to walk on the other side of the
road; but I never heard of anybody being locked up in the cage
or laid by the heels in the stocks.'

J. W. Mackail, in his life of Morris, says: 'The park abounded
in wild birds and beasts from the neighbouring Forest.   It was an
ideal home for a boy with healthy outdoor tastes.   There Morris,
rambling with his brothers on foot or on Shetland ponies through
the Forest, formed his intense love of nature and his keen eye
for all sorts of woodland life.   He never ceased to love Epping
Forest, and to uphold the scenery of his native county as beautifully and characteristically English.   The dense hornbeam
thickets, which even in bright weather have something of solem-
nity and mystery in their deep shade, and which are hardly found
elsewhere in England, reappear again and again in his poetry
and his prose romances.   Fifty years later, when the treatment
of the Forest by the Conservators had been the subject of much
public criticism, he went over the familiar ground and reported
on the changes that had been made on it.   "I was born and bred
in its neighbourhood," he then wrote, "and when I was a boy
and young man I knew it yard by yard from Wanstead to the
Theydons and from Hale End to the Fairlop Oak.   In those
days it had no worse foes than the gravel stealer and the rolling-
fence maker, and was always interesting and often very beautiful.

'"The special character of it was derived from the fact that
by far the greater part was a wood of hornbeams, a tree not
common save in Essex and Herts.   It was certainly the biggest
hornbeam wood in these islands, and I suppose in the world.
The said hornbeams were all pollards, being shrouded every four
or six years, and were interspersed in many places with holly
thickets.   Nothing could be more interesting and romantic than
the effect of the long poles of the hornbeams rising from the trunks
and seen against the mass of the wood behind.   It has a peculiar
charm of its own not to be found in any other forest."'

Though healthy outdoor exercise strengthened the boy's constitution, he continued to be a great reader.   His sister remembered reading exciting romances with him in the rabbit
warren near their home at Woodford, and becoming so excited
that they were both afraid to cross the park on their way home.
Forest scenes still familiar to us imprinted themselves on his
young mind.   'Well I remember,' he writes, 'as a boy, my first

acquaintance with a room hung with faded greenery at Queen Elizabeth's Lodge by Chingford Hatch in Epping Forest . . . and the impression of romance it made upon me.'

At nine he was sent to a preparatory school in Walthamstow, kept by the Misses Arundale, and rode the two miles from his home to school on his pony. A year or two later the school was moved to George Lane, Woodford. Morris remained there until his father's death in 1847.

Mr. Morris's wealth had been increased towards the end of his life by a fortunate speculation. He had acquired shares in a copper mine near Tavistock, coming into possession of them, it is believed, as part payment of a debt. They were pound shares, and Mr. Morris held two hundred and seventy-two. Within a few months these shares were changing hands at eight hundred pounds each, and Mr. Morris's shares rose to be valued at over two hundred thousand pounds.

William Morris moved from one forest to another when he entered Marlborough in 1848. Savernake Forest was as great a joy to him as Epping had been. He never played either cricket or football, but spent all his holidays rambling across the downs or through the forest itself. The loose organization of Marlborough at this time enabled him to plan his own recreations in a way not possible at most schools.

When Mr. Morris died, the family returned to Walthamstow to live at Water House, a square, Georgian building of yellow brick, stolid, dignified, and spacious, within half a mile of the old house at Clay Hill. A broad staircase of Spanish chestnut leads from the hall to a gallery, where William would spend the greater part of the day when home on holiday, reading in one of the window seats. The house got its name from a moat, forty feet wide, surrounding an island planted with aspens. The Morris children spent a great deal of their time rowing round this island in a small boat they had. During the summer months they fished in the moat for perch and pike, and in winter they skated on it. The island, with its hollies, hawthorns, and chestnuts, was an island of romance. Island, house, and moat reappear time after time in his poems:

> Many scarlet bricks there were
>   In its walls, and old grey stone,
>   Over which red apples shone,
> At the right time of the year. . . .

Deep green water fill'd the moat . . .

and again:

White swans on the green moat,
Small feathers left afloat
By the blue-painted boat.

In an early story, contributed to a university magazine, Morris described the Lea valley: 'People called it an ugly country, I know, that spreading of the broad marsh lands round the river Lea; . . . but I was so weary with my hard work that it seemed very lovely to me then.'

Marlborough was not at its best when Morris was there. In 1851 he was taken away and prepared for matriculation by the Rev. F. B. Guy, afterwards a canon of St. Albans, who took a few private pupils at his home in Hoe Street, Walthamstow. Mr. Guy was then assistant master at the Forest School. Later he became headmaster. He was a man of splendid character, and profoundly influenced all who passed through his hands. Morris and he remained friends for life. Besides being a man of taste and wide sympathies, Mr. Guy had an extensive knowledge of painting and architecture. Few men can have influenced the poet more.

When Morris took up architecture with the intention of making it his career, he was articled to George Edmund Street, the designer of the Law Courts and author of books on architectural subjects, who was a native of Woodford. Thus Forest associations persisted. His next major influence was Dante Gabriel Rossetti, who was also a friend of the Howitts, using their garden studio at The Hermitage, Highgate. It was Rossetti who persuaded Morris that he would serve his generation better as a painter than as an architect.

Tennyson left the Forest in 1840; Clare a year later. As Morris was not born until 1834, he would not meet either of them there. At Oxford he found Tennyson's influence dominant, but adopted an attitude of 'defiant admiration' towards the older poet. Sir Galahad he thought 'rather a mild youth,' and of *Locksley Hall* he said, when he heard it read aloud: 'My dear fellow, if you are going to make that row, get out of the room, that's all.' Tennyson's technique he admired to the full. It was felt in Morris's time at Oxford that Tennyson had taken verse-craft to the utmost limit of perfection. No further development was thought possible.

During vacations, Morris went 'a-brassing' in village churches. After one such excursion he wrote to a friend: 'The Church that this last brass came from was I think one of the prettiest Churches (for a small village church) that I have ever seen; the consecration crosses (some of them) were visible, red in a red circle; and there was some very pretty colouring on a corbel, in very good preservation: the parson of the parish shewed us over this Church; he was very civil and very, very dirty and snuffy, inexpressibly so, I can't give you an idea of his dirt and snuffiness.' We wonder if he knew the Harsnett brass at Chigwell.

The atmosphere of old churches, and the priestly character, appealed to Morris strongly at this time. He had thoughts of devoting his entire fortune to founding a monastery, no doubt with the intention of making it a centre of religious art as well as of devotion. The brotherhood idea remained, as we know, when the monastic disappeared.

Morris was a man who tingled with vitality. Whatever he did was done with gusto and ease, even to writing epics. 'Well, if this is poetry,' he said, 'it is very easy to write.' Inevitably, he fell in love as easily as he did everything else. In youth, Morris and his friends desired to paint a certain young lady, at that time conspicuous in the streets of Oxford. She had all the romantic features that enthralled them—entrancing eyes, set wide apart, a full-lipped sensuous mouth, with a curve that caught the light in a fascinating and tantalizing way, and a neck that was irresistible. She consented to sit for Morris; but after looking at her for some time without making a stroke, he turned the canvas to her, and on it she read: 'I cannot paint you; but I love you.'

This is not the place to write of Morris's life after he left Essex. The story is well known. The grand, burly man, with the crop of dark, curly hair, and the generally unkempt appearance, is one of the figures of the age. His splendid courage, force, and vigour of mind left their impress on a generation, and started movements in thought and action that still continue. He was a man of imperious temper, with a passion to right wrong. The dreamer and the practical man of affairs joined forces in him, and with them went all the strange, conflicting characteristics of the unusual combination. On the one hand, he had sanity and stout common sense, on the other, a morbid and haunting fear of death and decay. His dreaminess alternated with fits of hot passion, so that with all his ideas about no man being good enough to be another man's master, he did not scruple to hurl a folio at the head of an offending workman.

To Morris, morals and social ethics were involved in everything. Art was an expression of faith. Another Walthamstow worthy, Roger Ascham, had scoffed at Malory's *Morte d'Arthur*. Morris admired it. The Round Table went straight into the idea of a working men's club. Malory and the working man were both part of a splendid dream. Morris might say: 'That talk of inspiration is sheer nonsense. I may tell you flat—there is no such thing; it is a mere matter of craftsmanship.' He might claim, and appear, to be simple and practical; but his conception of life was as complex as his personality, and sprang from its splendid diversity. 'He had,' we are told, 'the incessant recklessness of a wild creature.'

No man was more truly a son of the Forest. His strength was formed as he tramped through its hornbeam thickets, his imagination was fired by its moods and movements in sun and wind, and in his work our Forest scene is projected on to a plane where past and future blend. His genius was from the gods; but we may claim that its direction and character were largely influenced by his Forest boyhood.

Another poet, born in the same year as Morris, the Hon. Roden Noel, lived at Webster's Farm, Upshire, and wandered much about the nearby fields and woods, especially of Warlies, where his sister, Lady Victoria Buxton, lived. He wrote a great part of the volume entitled *Beatrice* while living in the Forest.

CHAPTER XXIX

THERE is no place in the Walthamstow of to-day where we can indulge the fancy of believing ourselves in a forest village; but Chigwell still retains its rural atmosphere where John Willet's 'Maypole Inn' and Samuel Harsnett's church and grammar school blink at each other on a summer afternoon. If we turn towards London, the village atmosphere is soon lost. We must go towards Abridge, climb through a hedge, and lie against a hay-cock, if we would win to the spirit of nineteenth-century Chigwell. Writing to John Forster, Dickens said: 'Chigwell, my dear fellow, is the greatest place in the world. Name your day for going. Such a delicious old inn opposite the churchyard—such a lovely ride—such beautiful forest scenery—such an out-of-the-way rural place—such a sexton! I say again, name your day.'

'His promise,' Forster assures us, 'was exceeded by our enjoyment; and his delight in the double recognition of himself and of Barnaby by the landlord of the nice old inn, far exceeded any pride he would have taken in what the world thinks the highest sort of honour.'

What, then, was Chigwell like in those days? It still retains enough of its former character to make Sir Walter Besant's description of it in *All in a Garden Fair* credible.

'The rurality of the place,' we read there, 'to one fresh from town, seems overdone, an affectation of rurality, a pedantry and pretence, somewhat overacted, of rusticity. Thus, nowhere are the roads more liberally edged with broad belts of grass, as if land was plentiful and cheap; nowhere will you find such broad, ugly, uncared-for ditches, with pollard willows and old oaks beside them, blackberry bushes and brambles scrambling over them, and tall weeds, reeds, and strange wild flowers growing in them; nowhere will you find the ducks waddling by the roadside with more perfect trustfulness, as if there were no tramps or gipsies in the world. . . .

'The roadside inns are picturesque and dirty; their signs— brave old signs, such as the "Good Intent" and the "Traveller's Rest"—hang creakily over the wooden trough full of water for

the horses.   There is generally a horse and cart waiting; the horse
drinks at the trough, the driver, leaning against a door-post of
the inn with a mug of beer in his hand, drinks and exchanges
opinions with the landlord; the people in the road roll as they
walk, with hands in pockets, lifting feet accustomed to a clay
soil, quite as if they were hundreds of miles from London.   Nowhere else so near to London can you hear such singing of birds;
nowhere else so near do you get the nightingale; nowhere else so near
does the dove coo.   You may hear the tinkle of a sheep-bell just as
if you were on Dartmoor.   You may see a hawk hovering in the
air as if you were on Malvern Hill.   You may hear the sharpening
of the scythe, the hammer of the blacksmith, and the *wo-wo-ing*
of the ploughboy.   On Sunday evening you may watch the
ploughboy making love.   And never an omnibus, or a tram, or
the whistle of a train.'

'Never an omnibus,' said Besant.   Yet strangely enough the
very word was coined by a Chigwell man, George Shillibeer, who
ran the first buses in London.   The tablet to his memory in
Chigwell Church was placed there by the London busmen.

On the road between Abridge and Theydon we may still find
the 'wild and ghostly' deserted churchyard, described by Besant.
But we are wandering too far from the heart of the village, The
King's Head, or 'The Maypole' of *Barnaby Rudge*.

The novel opens with a description of this famous house on the
border of Epping Forest, as the novelist imagines it to have been
in the year 1775:

'. . . an old building, with more gable ends than a lazy man
would care to count on a sunny day; huge zig-zag chimneys, out
of which it seemed as though even smoke could not choose but
come in more than naturally fantastic shapes, imparted to it in
its tortuous progress; and vast stables, gloomy, ruinous, and
empty.   The place was said to have been built in the days of
King Henry the Eighth; and there was a legend, not only that
Queen Elizabeth had slept there one night while upon a hunting
excursion, to wit, in a certain oak-panelled room with a deep
bay window, but that next morning, while standing on a mount-
ing-block before the door with one foot in the stirrup, the Virgin
Monarch had then and there boxed and cuffed an unlucky page
for some neglect of duty. . . .

'Whether these, and many other stories of the like nature, were
true or untrue, the Maypole was really an old house, a very old

house, perhaps as old as it claimed to be, and perhaps older, which will sometimes happen with houses of an uncertain, as with ladies of a certain, age. Its windows were old diamond-pane lattices, its floors were sunken and uneven, its ceilings blackened by the hand of time, and heavy with massive beams. Over the doorway was an ancient porch, quaintly and grotesquely carved; and here on summer evenings the more favoured customers smoked and drank—aye, and sang many a good song, too, sometimes—reposing on two grim-looking high-backed settles, which, like the twin dragons of some fairy tale, guarded the entrance to the mansion.

'In the chimneys of the disused rooms, swallows had built their nests for many a long year, and from earliest spring to latest autumn whole colonies of sparrows chirped and twittered in the eaves. There were more pigeons about the dreary stable yard and out-buildings than anybody but the landlord could reckon up. The wheeling and circling flights of runts, fantails, tumblers, and pouters, were perhaps not quite consistent with the grave and sober character of the building, but the monotonous cooing, which never ceased to be raised by some among them all day long, suited it exactly, and seemed to lull it to rest. With its over-hanging storeys, drowsy little panes of glass, and front bulging out and projecting over the pathway, the old house looked as if it were nodding in its sleep. . . . The bricks of which it was built had originally been a deep dark red, but had grown yellow and discoloured like an old man's skin; the sturdy timbers had decayed like teeth; and here and there the ivy, like a warm garment to comfort it in its age, wrapped its green leaves closely round the time-worn walls.

'It was a hale and hearty age though, still: and in the summer or autumn evenings, when the glow of the setting sun fell upon the oak and chestnut trees of the adjacent forest, the old house, partaking of its lustre, seemed their fit companion, and to have many good years of life in him yet.'

The story is introduced in the twilight of a March evening, the wind howling dismally through the bare branches, rumbling in the wide chimneys, and driving the rain against the windows of the old 'Maypole.' The landlord, John Willet, is drawn in the best traditional style: 'A burly, large-headed man with a fat face, which betokened profound obstinacy and slowness of apprehension, combined with very strong reliance upon his own merits.' Even better is the parish clerk, Solomon Daisy, with his little round black shiny eyes, his rusty black breeches and coat, his long flapped waistcoat with queer little buttons that twinkled and glistened like his eyes in the firelight.   A highwayman disturbs the serenity of the inn parlour and gives the right dash of romance to the scene, in the true character of the Forest.   Talk about the church and the great house, probably Loughton Hall, fills in the background, imagined through a mist of rain.   Solomon Daisy tells his story, a story that belongs to the house and that no other is allowed to tell.   He tells it to the accompaniment of the rattling latch and the creaking hinges, his strange figure dancing in the flickering firelight of the chimney corner, with the heavily timbered ceiling above and the panelled walls behind him.   The quiet world of Chigwell becomes the enchanted world of Dickens, with Solomon Daisy weaving the spell.

We are taken out into the cold churchyard, with its chill tombstones.   Solomon Daisy goes through with his lantern, on his way to toll the bell.   In one hand he carries the great iron key of the church.   He enters, sets down his lantern on the stone seat near the bell-rope, and falls into a reverie.

Returning to the old inn, we are led by John Willet up the wide staircase to the best apartment: 'It was spacious enough in all conscience, occupying the whole depth of the house, and having at either end a great bay window, as large as many modern rooms; in which some few panes of stained glass, emblazoned with fragments of armorial bearings, though cracked, and patched, and shattered, yet remained; attesting by their presence, that the former owner had made the very light subservient to his state.'

But it is in the kitchen that Dickens becomes lyrical: 'Within, what· carpet like its crunching sand, what music merry as its crackling logs, what perfume like its kitchen's dainty breath, what weather genial as its hearty warmth!   Blessings on the old house, how sturdily it stood!   How did the vexed wind chafe and roar about its stalwart roof; how did it pant and strive with its wide chimneys, which still poured forth from their hospitable throats, great clouds of smoke, and puffed defiance in its face; how, above all, did it drive and rattle at the casement, emulous to extinguish that cheerful glow, which would not be put down and seemed the brighter for the conflict!

'The profusion too, the rich and lavish bounty, of that goodly tavern!   It was not enough that one fire roared and sparkled on its spacious hearth; in the tiles which paved and compassed it, five hundred flickering fires burnt brightly also. It was not enough that one red curtain shut the wild night out, and shed its cheerful influence on the room. In every saucepan lid, and candlestick, and vessel of copper, brass, or tin that hung upon the walls, were countless ruddy hangings, flashing and gleaming with every motion of the blaze, and offering, let the eye wander where it might, interminable vistas of the same rich colour. The old oak wainscoting, the beams, the chairs, the seats, reflected it in a deep, dull glimmer. There were fires and red curtains in the very eyes of the drinkers, in their buttons, in their liquor, in the pipes they smoked.'

To the quiet village of Chigwell and its honest inn came, according to the story, though not in fact, all the rowdyism of the Gordon rioters. John Willet's cook and housemaid ran screaming upstairs, to lock themselves in one of the garrets. The rioters came up from London 'shouting and whooping like savages.' They raided the bar, which was 'changed all at once into a bear-garden, a madhouse, an infernal temple: men darting in and out, by door and window, smashing the glass, turning the taps, drinking liquor out of china punchbowls.' When tired of their orgy of destruction at the inn, they assembled outside.

'To the Warren!' shouted Dennis.

With a loud yell the others followed, and before long those who stood at the door of 'The Maypole' heard 'the loud and rapid tolling of an alarm-bell, and then a bright and vivid glare streamed up, which illumined not only the whole chamber, but all the country.

'It was not the sudden change from darkness to this dreadful light, it was not the sound of distant shrieks and shouts of triumph, it was not this dread invasion of the serenity and peace of night, that drove the man back as though a thunderbolt had struck him. It was the Bell. If the ghastliest shape the human mind has ever pictured in its wildest dreams had risen up before him, he could not have staggered backward from its touch, as he did from the first sound of that loud iron voice . . . still, still, the Bell tolled on and seemed to follow him—louder and louder, hotter and hotter yet. The glare grew brighter, the roar of voices deeper; the crash of heavy bodies falling, shook the air; bright streams of sparks rose up into the sky; but louder than them all—rising faster far, to Heaven—a million times more fierce and furious—pouring forth dreadful secrets after its long

H

silence — speaking the language of the dead — the Bell — the Bell!'

We recall these two features of the story, the inn and the tolling of the bell, because both had local foundations. But though they had local foundations, it is the novel that gives them their title to fame. The quotations from *Barnaby Rudge* may seem unduly long, but the real 'Maypole' is in its pages and can be found nowhere else. He would be a bold man who would take over, as it were, the licence of 'The Maypole' from Charles Dickens, and try to dispense its bounty on his own behalf.

We see Dickens at 'The King's Head' most realistically in a story told by Fred Roe in his fine book, *Essex Survivals*:

Next day the landlord, a fine old-fashioned specimen of his class, allowed me every facility to make a finished study of the elaborate carved fireplace in the 'Chester Room.' I well recall a narrative which he regaled me with, and will repeat it, as nearly as possible, in his own words.

'A good many years ago, before I became licensee, I was told by my predecessor that one day two gentlemen came in and ordered a meal. They had a table in this room, by the window, close to where you are sitting. At the finish they called the landlord up, and asked if he could let them have a bottle of good port to end up with. He said, "Yes, gentlemen, I can," and went down to the cellar and brought up a bottle of 18—. He served them with this and they tasted it. One of them said politely, "Will you take a glass of wine with us, landlord?"

'"Thank you, sir, I will. Here's my best respects."

'"They had a bit of a chat about the old house, and my predecessor could see that it was not the first time the gentleman had been here. Landlord drank his wine up, and was just going to leave the room when the gentleman who'd been talking to him said,

'"I suppose, landlord, you don't happen to know me?"

'"No, sir," he said, "I haven't that pleasure."

'"My name is Charles Dickens," says the gentleman.

'"And mine," says the other, rather pompously, "is John Forster."'

That Dickens had 'The King's Head' in mind when he wrote *Barnaby Rudge* is established beyond all doubt, even if the name did come from 'The Maypole' at Chigwell Row—that is to say, from the old inn of that name, not the present one. But what about the fire at the great house, and the tolling of the bell? *Barnaby Rudge* was published in 1841. In December 1836 a fire broke out at Loughton Hall, destroying fifty rooms. The butler was awakened by the library bell, which was set ringing by the fall of burning masonry. It is more than likely that Dickens heard about this fire and the eerie clamour of the bell on one of his visits to Chigwell. The story would be told frequently at 'The King's Head.' He may have heard it from the lips of a village character not unlike Solomon Daisy himself. Did he not say 'such a sexton!' in his invitation to John Forster, quoted earlier? The old parish clerk is so real that we take his human actuality for granted, and wonder what other stories he had to tell. How we should have liked to ask him about the old body-snatchers, for instance. We wonder what he thought of the spring invented by a Barking man for securing the bodies of the dead in their coffins. This body-snatching was a dangerous undertaking. To exhume the coffin entirely took time, so the body-snatchers dug a hole over the head, wrenched a portion of the lid off the coffin, and by means of ropes dragged the body through the broken lid. How we should have enjoyed discussing this topic with Solomon Daisy, while we sat with him on a tombstone one moonlight night.

Chigwell will change; its green pastures will be built over. Even the old inn will change. But Solomon Daisy and John Willet will never change. They and their little world, mysteriously called into being one day when Charles Dickens sat musing by a window at 'The King's Head,' looking across the road towards the churchyard, remain untouched and undying, a part of our Forest inheritance for ever.

CHAPTER XXX

Trollope at Waltham House—Trollope in the field—Henry Doubleday,
the Epping naturalist

AT Waltham House, Waltham Cross, lived another Victorian novelist, Anthony Trollope, from 1859 to 1871, thriving and abounding. The house, he tells us, 'was a rickety old place, requiring much repair and not as weathertight as it should be. But for strawberries, asparagus, green peas, out-of-door peaches, for roses and such everyday luxuries, no place was ever more excellent.' Trollope took the house on lease, but after spending a thousand pounds on improvements he bought it. He wanted, he confides, a house in which he could entertain his friends, grow cabbages and strawberries, make butter, and kill pigs. When he left Waltham after twelve happy years there, he sold the house at a loss of eight hundred pounds. 'As I continually hear,' he says, 'that other men make money by buying and selling houses, I presume I am not well adapted for transactions of that sort.'

At Waltham, Trollope glowed with good humour. He had wife and family about him in house and garden; he had hunters in the stable. In summer friends came to dinner, and afterwards sat out on the lawn with him, where wines and fruit were laid under the cedar-tree. At Christmas there were parties for the children, where games like those at Noningsby in *Orley Farm* were played. No one enjoyed these games more than Trollope.

Anthony Trollope at Waltham, broad, bushy, and boisterous, was much more popular during these years than Mr. Trollope, Surveyor-General to the Post Office. He was perfectly candid about it. His sworn enemy was Rowland Hill, the inventor of the penny post. 'With him,' confesses Trollope, 'I never had any sympathy, nor he with me. . . . It was a pleasure to me to differ from him on all occasions; and, looking back now, I think that in all differences I was right.' Trollope frankly admits that he was given to interfering in departments that were not his concern. 'I have no doubt,' he owns, 'that I often made myself very disagreeable. I know that I sometimes tried to do so.'

Edmund Yates, who published his recollections of the post office in 1884, was a fellow official who disliked Trollope heartily; but he left a good picture of Hill and Trollope in opposition:

'Sir Rowland Hill was far too cautious and reserved ever to put his likes and dislikes into print. But he hated Trollope very cordially, and could not avoid showing it when they were brought into contact. Trollope would bluster and rave and roar, blowing and spluttering like a grampus; while the pale old gentleman opposite him, sitting back in his arm chair and regarding his antagonist furtively under his spectacles, would remain perfectly quiet until he saw his chance, and then deliver himself of the most unpleasant speech he could frame in the hardest possible tone.'

Yates concludes his paragraph with a two-line anecdote:

'I differ from you entirely!' Trollope is alleged to have roared at the speaker who preceded him. 'What was it you said?'

Most of Trollope's best novels were written at Waltham, starting with *Framley Parsonage*, which was received with acclamation when it appeared as a serial in the *Cornhill*. When his *Autobiography* was published, and the sentimental Victorian public learned of the methodical way in which the novels were written, they were horrified. Here was a man who did his writing like any clerk at his desk, without any soliciting of the muse or fevers of inspiration. It was unthinkable that works of genius should be accomplished in such a way. Clearly the man was a humbug, masquerading as an artist.

Few men can ever have been busier than Trollope was at Waltham Cross. Besides his work at the post office and his novels, he wrote articles on politics, sport, and every phase of social life. He did the round of London society. He played whist at the Garrick. And he spent six weeks of every year abroad. How did he do it all? The answer is simply that he rose early and retired late: 'It was my practice to be at my table every morning at 5.30 a.m.; and it was also my practice to allow myself no mercy. An old groom, whose business it was to call me, and to whom I paid £5 a year extra for the duty, allowed himself no mercy. During all those years at Waltham Cross he was never once late with the coffee which it was his duty to bring me. I do not know that I ought not to feel that I owe more to him than to any one else for the success I have had. By beginning at that hour I could complete my literary work before I dressed for breakfast.

'All those I think who have lived as literary men—working daily as literary labourers—will agree with me that three hours a day will produce as much as a man ought to write. But then

he should so have trained himself that he shall be able to work
continuously during those three hours—so have tutored his mind
that it shall not be necessary for him to sit nibbling his pen, and
gazing at the wall before him, till he shall have found the words
with which he wants to express his ideas. It had at this time
become my custom—and it still is my custom, though of late
I have become a little lenient to myself—to write with my watch
before me, and to require from myself 250 words every quarter
of an hour. I have found that the 250 words have been forth-
coming as regularly as my watch went.'

At least twice every week Trollope hunted from the kennels at
Harlow. In *Can You Forgive Her?* he satirizes himself as Mr.
Pollock, 'the heavy-weight sporting literary gentleman' in
spectacles, who was declared to be 'as ignorant of hunting as
any tailor,' but who followed the chase undeterred and derived
a great deal of pleasure from it.

In Trollope's day, the master was the Rev. Joseph Arkwright
of Mark Hall, grandson of the inventor of the spinning frame.
In Trollope's *Autobiography* we read: 'Essex was the chief scene
of my sport, and gradually I became known there almost as
well as though I had been an Essex squire, to the manner born.
Few have investigated more closely than I have done the depth,
and breadth, and water-holding capacities of an Essex ditch.
It will, I think, be accorded to me by Essex men generally that
I have ridden hard. The cause of my delight in the amusement
I have never been able to analyse to my own satisfaction. In the
first place, even now, I know very little about hunting—though
I know very much of the accessories of the field. I am too blind
to see hounds turning, and cannot therefore tell whether the fox
has gone this way or that. Indeed, all the notice I take of hounds
is not to ride over them. My eyes are so constituted that I can
never see the nature of a fence. I either follow someone, or ride
at it with the full conviction that I may be going into a horse-
pond or a gravel-pit. I have jumped into both one and the other.
I am very heavy, and have never ridden expensive horses. I am
also now too old for such work, being so stiff that I cannot get
on to my horse without the aid of a block or a bank. But I ride
still after the same fashion, with a boy's energy, determined to
get ahead if it may possibly be done, hating the roads, despising
young men who ride them, and with a feeling that life cannot,
with all her riches, have given me anything better than when I

have gone through a long run to the finish, keeping a place, not of glory, but of credit, among my juniors.'

Trollope was as big a nuisance in the field as he was at the post office. He could not see the hounds himself, so he kept close behind someone he knew would be well forward in the hunt. At the end of a day's sport it was not unusual to hear a tired rider grumbling that his day had been spoilt because Trollope had ridden at his horse's tail the whole time.

The novelist's hunters were two heavy animals, Banker and Buff. They were more like coach horses than hunters; but Trollope required safe rather than showy mounts.

In 1864 Trollope did a series of hunting sketches. Field sports had always been to him an essential part of the English scene, their cultivation an essential part of the English character, and whenever they were attacked he was in hot pursuit of the attacker. Often when he met the man he had attacked furiously in print, he shook hands with him warmly. His emphatic, impulsive speech inflicted many wounds; but as many were healed by his underlying good humour and kindliness of heart. Life was too short for delving into mysteries. Trollope was satisfied to believe that things were what they appeared to be. He had unbounded zest for ordinary, everyday life, and this gave him his extraordinary power of making the commonplace dramatic and exciting. It was so to him, and it becomes so to his readers. As a man of the world, he had acquired a quick eye for summing up character. Trollope's characterization is uncommonly convincing. Because he relished life, he was able to transmit it. Essex was congenial to him—an honest, unpretentious county, with no aesthetic nonsense about it.

In 1867 Charles Buxton, described by Trollope as 'a man whom I greatly loved,' persuaded the novelist to offer himself to Essex electors as a candidate for Parliament at the next election. Disraeli's Government was expected to fall in the near future. But with the passing of the Reform Bill, Essex was divided into three instead of two divisions, and though Trollope was proposed by Charles Buxton as a candidate for one of the new divisions, he was persuaded to withdraw in favour of another candidate.

When Trollope rode through Epping on his way to Harlow, he would pass the grocer's shop of Henry Doubleday, who conducted his business in a large brick building, formerly the Black

Boy Inn, on the south side of the street. His father had kept
the business before him, and Henry was born in the same house
in 1808. But the Epping grocer had other interests besides
serving the people of the little market town with tea and sugar.
As a boy he had developed an interest in the insect life of
the surrounding Forest. In later life he became a well-known
authority and writer on entomology and ornithology. All his
knowledge was gained at first hand. Before opening his shop
in the morning, he would go out into the Forest and smear a kind
of treacle on the tree trunks. At night, after closing for the day,
he would go out again and collect the specimens his treacle had
trapped, going from tree to tree with his lantern and box on
dark evenings. Between the years 1846 and 1873 he was only
twice away from home at night. The old Forest provided all
the pleasure he desired.

Doubleday contributed many notes to Yarrell's *History of
British Birds*, which appeared in two volumes in 1843. His own
Synonymic List of the British Lepidoptera was issued between
1847 and 1850. The work was well done, and was used as a
reference book by later classifiers. He was also an excellent
taxidermist.

Doubleday is quoted several times by Darwin in the *Descent
of Man*. The two corresponded, and Darwin is said to have had
great respect for the Epping naturalist. In regard to the pro-
portion of sex among moths, for instance, Darwin believed that
no man spoke with greater authority. Some of Doubleday's
collections are preserved in the Bethnal Green branch of the
South Kensington Museum.

In 1848 Henry Doubleday was appointed treasurer to the
Epping Highway Trust, in succession to his father, who had held
the office since 1824. Like others of his family, he was a Quaker,
and attended the little meeting-house at Epping. He died
in 1875.

CHAPTER XXXI

The People's Forest—Enclosures—The Epping Forest Acts—Lopping
rights—Queen Victoria declares the Forest open

HENRY DOUBLEDAY would see half the Forest enclosed between
1851 and 1871, and must have been saddened to think that within
a few years it might be only a memory.   He did not live to see it
thrown open to the public in 1878, three years after his death,
when the old Royal Forest became the People's Forest; but he
did live to see the process of enclosure reversed, and must have
taken a keen interest in the events leading up to the decisive Act.
After all the anxiety, he was able to die happy in the faith that
his beloved Forest would at last be saved.

The history of the Forest enclosures bristles with conflicting
evidence.   The story of old Tom Willingale has now become a
legend, in which fact and fiction are as romantically mingled as
they were in the legends recalled in the first chapter of this book.
Grants to enclose land, Fisher informs us, had been made by
licence from early times.   These enclosures, like the one at
Wanstead, for instance, are shown on old maps; but before
1850 only about six hundred acres had been enclosed in more than
two hundred years.   When the right to enclose was granted, only
low fences were permitted, so that the deer should not be denied
pasture.   In the first year of the eighteenth century Sir Bernard
Whetstone, lord of the manor of Woodford, was sued for making
illegal fences, and in defending himself complained that the deer
did so much damage that the landowners were forced 'to give
over ploughing and sowing their arable land, of which the greater
part of the demense of his manor consisted.   He was still obliged
to pay compensation, in wheat and oats, for the King's household,
though not a foot of the demesne had been ploughed for the last
ten years, by reason of the number of deer, which would utterly
destroy the corn; and the cessation of ploughing caused the
increase of deer, by reason that the barren and dry fallows were
converted into sweet and fresh green pastures to layer and feed
the cattle.'

Between 1851 and 1871 large tracts were enclosed illegally;
but not without the knowledge of the Government.   The Forest
had long been a source of trouble.   It was difficult to supervise

properly, and as a result it provided cover for illegal practices. In a utilitarian age it was regarded as little less than sinful that all these thousands of acres should not be turned to some useful purpose. The enclosing of land, therefore, was not only connived at but encouraged. In 1848 a parliamentary committee recommended that Hainault Forest should be disafforested, and that the Crown should sell its forestal rights in Epping Forest to the lords of its nineteen manors.

Since enclosed land, and even towns and villages, had always been found in royal forests, it was held that the peculiarity of such a forest does not consist in the region being either woodland or open space, but in its being an area subject to the Forest Laws. At a perambulation made in the first session of the Long Parliament, the area of Waltham Forest was found to be sixty thousand acres, which would be ten times its present size. Four-fifths of this area was cultivated, but it was held by various landowners, subject to the sporting rights of the Crown. Very little of the actual land in the Forest had ever been held by the Crown. Most of it had belonged to the abbeys before the Dissolution, and afterwards had been granted to court favourites.

Manwood had defined a royal forest as 'A certain territory of woody grounds and fruitful pastures privileged for wild beasts and fowls of Forest chase and warren to rest and abide there in the safe protection of the King for his delight and pleasure.' If this was accepted, it followed that when new enclosures were made they must not be allowed to restrict the roam of the deer. No fence should be erected that was high enough to keep out a doe with her fawn.

In practice these conditions were relaxed, but the enclosing landowners could never obtain any clear definition of their rights to this new land. In 1875 the Royal Commissioners found that the inhabitants of Loughton had from time immemorial possessed and exercised the right of lopping trees in the parish for firewood. They maintained that this right was still valid at law. There was also the ancient right of pasturage, which apparently remained valid. Thus the lords of the manors concerned could not prevent the ratepayers of Loughton either lopping trees or pasturing cattle on the land they had enclosed.

The rapid enclosure of a large part of the Forest began with the disafforestation of Hainault Forest, carried out by Act of Parliament in 1851. Its wastes were quickly brought under cultivation. Before the illegality of these enclosures had been established, nearly three thousand acres of Forest land had been fenced in. The first step towards restoring these acres was taken in 1870, when the House of Commons presented an address to the Crown, 'praying that her Majesty would take such measures as in her judgment she might deem most expedient in order that Epping Forest might be preserved as an open space for the recreation and enjoyment of the public.'

In consequence of Her Majesty's gracious concurrence, the Epping Forest Act of 1871 was passed. This and later Acts are summarized by Sir Robert Hunter in his introduction to *The Epping Forest Act, 1878, with an Introduction, Notes, and an Index.* The long fight for the freedom of the Forest had begun.

There was by no means unanimity about the value of the Forest as an open space. Some were against enclosure; some for it. Coller, in *The People's History of Essex*, published in 1861, says, under the heading 'Loughton':

'The proximity of the Forest, and the pretext of procuring firewood by means of the loppings of the trees, which the inhabitants claim a right to cut during the winter months, encourage habits of idleness and dislike of settled labour, and in some cases give occasion for poaching, all of which are injurious to the morals of the poor. Enclosures, however, seem to be commencing in the neighbourhood, which will probably check these irregular and, to a certain extent, demoralizing tendencies.'

The morals of the poor were a very grave anxiety in those days. As late as 1875 the Loughton Vestry, burdened by the same anxiety, passed the following resolutions:

1. 'That the existence of the alleged forestal rights causes great waste and demoralization, and that it is expedient that they should be abolished with due compensation.'

2. 'That the Epping Forest Commissioners be informed that the enclosure of lands granted from the waste during the last twenty years has been highly beneficial to the parish by enlarging the area for assessment, by providing labour for the industrious poor, and by conducing to the general health by drainage and cultivation, and that in the opinion of this Vestry it is very desirable that no attempts should be made to interfere with such enclosed lands.'

Unfortunately, this concern for the well-being of the industrious poor is not very convincing when we learn that some of the vestrymen were themselves benefiting from the enclosures. The rector himself, who was also lord of the manor, was the greatest offender. We must not condemn him too hurriedly. Hard things have been written about the enclosing landowners. But it has to be pointed out that they were actually pressed to purchase Crown rights in the Forest, under threat that if they refused the land would be offered to others, so determined had the Government become that this waste land should be cultivated. For these rights the lords of the manors paid, approximately, between four and five pounds per acre. When, however, in 1865, the lord of the manor of Loughton fenced in 1,316 acres of Forest, the whole of the land within his manor, apart from some fifty acres of roadside waste, and proceeded to cut roads through the woods, with a view to developing them as building sites, the inhabitants of the village realized that if the Forest was to be saved something must be done quickly.

At this point old Tom Willingale, a labourer of Loughton, struck his blows for the ancient rights. Many accounts of what followed have been published, the most reliable being that of Mr. Percy Thompson, of Loughton, published in the *Essex Naturalist*, vol. xxi, pp. 157–69. Contrary to what has been alleged, Tom Willingale himself, an old man of over seventy at the time, never went to prison. He had been summoned to court in 1865 for injury to the Forest trees, but the case was dismissed. The old man's son, Samuel, along with Alfred Willingale, the old man's nephew, and William Higgins, another relative, were summoned to Waltham Abbey police court in March 1866 for lopping, and were fined 2s. 6d. each, with 11s. costs and damage, or in default of payment, seven days' imprisonment. All three refused payment, and were sent to Ilford jail. In December 1872 the Corporation of London took proceedings against a member of the Willingale family for felling a tree, in contravention of the Order of the Epping Forest Commissioners. He was bound over and cautioned.

The ancient right of lopping had been jealously guarded in Loughton, and it was therefore inevitable that it should not be given up without a struggle. In former centuries it had been a considerable privilege. We realize this when we discover than in 1764 a woman was publicly whipped by the common hangman for cutting down wood in Enfield Chase, only a short distance away from the Forest.

There was a tradition that this lopping should start as the clock struck twelve on St. Martin's Eve. The villagers would assemble on Staples Hill, where they would light a fire and celebrate the occasion lustily with beer. From twelve to two the axes flashed in the firelight. The branches cut were heaped, and afterwards drawn away on sledges, the first load drawn by white horses. An old story relates that during the eighteenth century the lord of the manor of Loughton tried to upset this ceremony. He invited all the villagers to a banquet, and plied them with ale in the hope that not a single man would be fit to begin lopping when the clock struck midnight. One of the company, however, kept a clear head, and walked proudly into the Forest at the appointed hour.

Local feeling in Loughton ran extremely high over the Willingale case. The Willingales, on the one side, were a large family, while the lord of the manor, on the other side, was also rector of the parish. It was said that the rector had tried to turn old Willingale out of his cottage, and force him to leave the village. Mr. Percy Thompson goes into the rights and wrongs of this old quarrel, and shows that neither the rector nor the labourer was as black as his enemies painted him. The rector was loved and respected by most of his parishioners, and old Tom Willingale had been left a legacy, as a token of appreciation, by his employer, Sir George Carrol, a Loughton resident and former Lord Mayor of London.

Finally, the cause of the commoners was taken up and fought by the Corporation of London, one of the many landowners in the Forest. When the future of the Forest was discussed in Parliament, widespread interest was aroused. In July 1874 the Master of the Rolls gave judgment, and 'affirmed the case of the Corporation on all its main points of contention, and granted an injunction against the lords of the manors, prohibiting them from enclosing in the future, and requiring them to remove all fences erected within twenty years before the commencement of the suit.'

When the Forest passed to the people in 1878, and was vested in the Corporation of London, the Act did not compensate the inhabitants of Loughton for their lopping rights. Later, seven thousand pounds was paid, part of which was spent in building Lopping Hall, the public hall in Loughton, which is still the social centre of the village. Without wishing to take sides in the old dispute between the Willingales and the rector, we cannot help smiling when we discover that the latter, the Rev. John Whitaker Maitland, pronounced a blessing on this hall, purchased with money paid in compensation for rights he had tried to deny, and of which his vestry had so strongly disapproved.

Though the Forest is now no longer a Royal Forest, the Crown continues to appoint a ranger. When Queen Victoria declared it open in May 1882 she appointed the Duke of Connaught to that office. The present ranger is the Duke of Gloucester.

CHAPTER XXXII

THE old inns of the Forest, once the haunts of highwaymen and
deer-stealers, now became the favourite resorts of London citizens
who came out to enjoy the country. The road through Leytonstone and Woodford was still bordered by green hedges and
ditches, with open fields behind them. Only a few old mansions
and low, weather-boarded cottages were seen between the
villages themselves.

One of the Forest inns, 'The Reindeer' at Loughton, famous for
the good fare provided by the innkeeper, so took the fancy of a
well-to-do visitor that he bought it and converted it into a country house for himself. It is now known as The Warren, and is
the residence of the superintendent of the Forest. After the
death of the first owner The Warren was occupied by General
Grosvenor, who erected the obelisk seen from the Epping New
Road to the charger he rode at Waterloo. Wellington himself
visited The Warren, and an oak in the grounds is still called
Wellington's Oak. Under its branches the duke and the general
would sit, fighting their battles over again in the quiet shade.

But it is not of dukes we think now. The Royal Forest has
become the People's Forest. The saturnalia that had been suppressed under Fairmead Oak on the Epping side of the Forest,
and under Fairlop Oak on the Hainault side, sprang to life again
on Chingford Plain every bank holiday. Nowhere is this new
saturnalia described more hilariously than in Somerset Maugham's
Liza of Lambeth.

Readers may remember how Liza rushed into her mother's
room calling: 'Mother! Mother! I'm goin' to Chingford!'
How she ran out into the street, scrambled up the steps of the
brake, and fell into Tom's lap. On reaching the Chingford road
they caught up with the rest of the odd assortment of vehicles
making their way to the Forest.

The huntsman's horn no longer sounds for kings and their

courtiers. Lord mayors and lords of the manors have lost their hold. It is the irrepressible cockney who survives.

But when the beer bottles have been emptied, the sausage-rolls, pork-pies, cherry-tarts, and all the other tasty things have been gulped down, the Lizas and Sallys, with their Toms and Harrys, go back to Lambeth, Bow, or Bethnal Green, and the Forest falls back into its ancient peace. The merriment of men may add a splash of colour here, their sadness a shadow there, the Forest outlives it all. Though at week-ends and bank holidays the open spaces near the Forest inns and villages are thronged with gay crowds, these rarely penetrate deep into the untracked wastes and thickets. The deeper Forest is left to those who love wild and solitary places. Chingford Plain, where Liza and her crowd beered and skittled, runs up to Pole Hill, where T. E. Lawrence dreamed one of his many dreams.

Lawrence had a friend in the Forest, Vyvyan Richards, a master at Bancroft's School, who had a retreat—'a little cloister with a diving-pool and garden'—on Pole Hill. It was here that Lawrence and Richards planned to set up a printing press. The idea of printing his own books fascinated Lawrence. He and Richards even discussed the possibility of printing *The Seven Pillars of Wisdom* themselves, and making enough money from it to provide them with two hundred pounds a year each. Again the Forest had cast its spell upon a mind imbued with the love of handcraft, spontaneity, and individual creation. Many of Morris's ideas were shared by the two friends, and discussed by them as they planned to build a timbered hall on Pole Hill. It was Richards who took care of Lawrence's books for him, and of these the most treasured were from the pen or press of William Morris.

One day Richards received a telegram informing him that Lawrence had bought the land on which the hut stood, and where the hall was to be built. Though Lawrence never actually lived on Pole Hill, he visited Richards there frequently, and came to regard the hut as in some sense his as well as his friend's. Sitting over the fire they would talk about the hall they intended building, and make designs for it. It was to have two walls round it, so that the temperature could be kept even. Richards says: 'Its walls were to be quite three feet thick; two walls with a space between.' There was to be no ceiling under the roof timbers, and the fire was to be of peat. In the garden a flagged walk was to form a cloister, surrounding greensward, with a pool in the centre. There were to be neither flowers nor animals, because neither appealed to Lawrence. Probably he was not so much lacking in appreciation of these as repelled by the sentimentality others showed towards them. The greensward was to be cut with a scythe; no lawn-mower was to be used. When Lawrence decided not to make any profit from his book the scheme was dropped.

Vyvyan Richards, in his *Portrait of T. E. Lawrence*, has told the story of this friendship, and given us glimpses of Lawrence in Epping Forest that are now woven into the tapestry of the Forest scene. In one we see him near the school, squatting with Richards and some of his boys in a bell tent filled with brushwood, over which rugs have been flung. The guys of the tent have been thrown back, so that it is half open. In front of the group a great log fire is blazing. It is a winter night, with the moon shining down on the Forest trees, thickly hung with snow. There we see them: Lawrence, the teller of tales, a slight, youthful figure in the firelight, with the eager faces of the boys, wide-eyed and excited, fixed on him in rapt attention.

The Forest has been a place of healing for many tired minds. The thought of Lawrence as a teller of tales reminds us that Rudyard Kipling came into the Forest as a boy, following a nervous breakdown. He had been at Southsea for six years, living in an establishment that passed as a school for children whose parents were in India. The husband of the schoolmistress was a naval captain. Kipling and he went walks together, and were on excellent terms. The wife was of a different kind. She was a fanatical evangelical, obsessed by visions of hell and revelling in torment. The children entrusted to her care were beaten and cowed. If Kipling had not had relations in England his life might have been blighted at the start by this excessively god-fearing woman. But each year another house was open to him for one blessed month. It was the home of his uncle and aunt, Sir Edward and Lady Burne-Jones, with whom love and happiness abounded, and the fires of hell were shut out. There he met also an honorary uncle, William Morris, whom the children called 'Uncle Topsy.'

The frightened boy came to imagine he saw terrible things that were not there. When his eyes were examined he was found to be half blind. Miseries crowded upon each other till at last his mother came over from India. When she went into his room to kiss him good night, he shot up his arm automatically to ward off the expected blow. Mrs. Kipling, of course, took him away at once.

It was in this state that Rudyard Kipling came to Loughton, where he made his home with a farmer on Golding's Hill, and ran wild in the Forest for several months. At Loughton he found everything he needed. The farmer's wife was kind and motherly; her niece, Patty—who lived in Loughton till she died at a great age quite recently—the postman, and the farm-boys were all his friends directly, and the place of the captain in his life was taken by a gipsy named Saville, who told the boys tales of his skill in selling horses. The farmer was less friendly than the others when he discovered that young Kipling had taught one of the cows to stand and be milked in the field. But apart from the farmer's occasional frown, there were few restrictions either in or out of doors, and there was always a full dairy, not too strictly guarded. The farmhouse has now disappeared; it was opposite Golding's Hill pond, where two cottages now stand.

Young Stanley Baldwin came down to stay with his cousin Rudyard, and the farmer's worries were doubled. When those two got together, he said, you could be sure they were up to no good. Their favourite haunt was the island in Golding's Hill pond. It was their own especial bit of Forest land. Kipling always remembered, and no doubt Lord Baldwin still remembers, how one day they attacked a wasp's nest there with switches of broom.

At The Outlook, Park Hill, Loughton, and afterwards at Feltham House, Loughton, lived another master of the short story, W. W. Jacobs, one of the few worthy to be mentioned along with Kipling. Jacobs was a superb craftsman, brief and vivid. Like many other true humorists he was a quiet, serious-looking man who talked little. Many who remember him in Loughton even use the word 'dull' in describing him. When someone brightly suggested to him that the wide view from his windows must inspire him in his work, he replied:

'Oh, dear me, no! I always get away from the window. In fact I turn my back to it, and write at a table facing a blank wall.'

In his old age Jacobs took a sombre view of life—not, perhaps, surprisingly to those who understood him, for his humour was always half compassion; but this gravity could be disconcerting to those who did not know him. The editor of a literary paper once asked him for an article on humorous literature, expecting something unusually good. But Jacobs only lamented the immorality of the modern world as revealed in its literature. When reminded that his own Bob Pretty was a liar, a trickster, and a thief, he shook his head sadly.

A friend of Jacobs, Arthur Morrison, author of *Tales of Mean Streets*, lived at High Beach. At High Beach, also, the poet Edward Thomas was stationed during the First Great War, in huts erected close to the King's Oak. The beauty of the Forest surprised and delighted him, and some of our lovely Essex place names are found in his poems. His wife, Helen Thomas, rented one of the two cottages close to what was then Paul's Nursery. It was the farther one from the road. These cottages are still to be seen between the 'Robin Hood' and the King's Oak, though the nursery has gone. Helen Thomas had little reason to remember the Forest with any pleasure.

John Drinkwater is usually associated with the Cotswolds; but he was born at Leytonstone in 1882, and a memorial to him may be seen in the library there. Passing references to the Forest, such as those in the letters of Winifred Holtby, are found in numerous collections of modern letters and memoirs. As Epping is now the People's Forest, it is, perhaps, fitting to recall that it was here that the spirit of romance came to those patient scholars, Sidney and Beatrice Webb, inveigling them into a partnership so fruitful to knowledge.

Articles on the Forest are scattered through all our popular magazines and papers. Some, like that by H. M. Tomlinson on Forest fungi, should not be lost. The associations of the Forest with modern literature are too numerous to include here. Time's winnowing fan must go over them before they become matter for Forest history. An association with art, however, must be mentioned. Jacob Epstein has had a cottage at Loughton for more than twenty years. It was in the shed in his garden overlooking Monk Wood that 'Rima' was carved during the winter of 1924–5. During the following year 'The Visitation' was modelled in the same place, and Epstein said how much he would have liked this figure with the folded hands, so expressive of humility, to remain standing on a knoll above the trees, looking across the Forest that had been so much in his mind while he worked. In 1933 he painted nearly a hundred water-colours of the Forest.

Any week-end you may see Epstein wandering in the Forest, humming to himself, and not suspect you are in the presence of such genius as his unless his measuring and appraising eyes chance to meet yours. There cannot be other such eyes in England. You will find yourself warmed by the radiance of a smile of rare sweetness and simplicity. Instinctively you will respond. You will feel quickened and excited, and then suddenly almost frightened by the searching intensity of the eyes that have penetrated and dissected you.

That melancholy Scot, John Davidson, found in the Forest as much pleasure as it is given to a man of his temperament to find anywhere. He celebrated his pleasure in poems published in *Liverpool Street Station*:

> Turf that whispered moistly to the tread;
>   Bursts of laughter from the shuffled leaves;
> Pools of light in distant arbours spread;
>   Depths of darkness under Forest eaves.

The Forest is open to all. Most of its villages are part of Greater London now; but others remain green and forgotten by Time—Upshire, with its wide greens and old cottages, Epping Upland and Epping Green, even Epping itself on market day. And if to name is not to kill, Aimes Green, so hidden and so remote that few men ever find it.

Most of the old halls have been rebuilt more than once. We have visited one or other of the Copt Halls and Loughton Halls several times in the course of this survey. Both have been rebuilt twice. When Loughton Hall was gutted by fire in 1836, a fine library of ten thousand volumes and many rare manuscripts was destroyed. The financial loss was estimated at between twenty and thirty thousand pounds. That year Mr. Maitland doubled his customary Christmas gifts, in gratitude for the help he had received from at least two hundred of his poorer neighbours while the fire was raging. In 1879 the present hall was built by the Rev. John Whitaker Maitland, the first clerical lord of the manor since the last abbot of Waltham, Robert Fuller, signed the deed of surrender in 1540. Crossing the Roding valley, we see Sir Thomas Smith's Hill Hall again. Four hundred years have gone by since we looked in upon that good knight there. His memorial is still to be seen in the village church. His hall, though altered, is still occupied, but no longer by members of his own family. The surrounding countryside has

changed less than most. Sir Thomas has been dead all these long
centuries, but his parkland is still alive. Each spring it breaks
into leaf again, and each autumn the leaves fall. The life of man
is still but threescore years and ten. He may leave a few marks
of his labour and thought behind. Most of them are quickly
effaced.

In Sir Thomas's old house a few years ago there was a visitors'
book, in which might be read the names of distinguished guests:
J. M. Barrie, Mr. and Mrs. Rudyard Kipling, Augustine Birrell,
and scores of others. Queen Mary was there to lunch on 29th
June 1926. She stayed the afternoon and planted a tree.

Many distinguished men have passed through those rooms since
Sir Thomas built the house. They have sat round the great fire-
places at night, discussing many of the same problems from
generation to generation. They have passed on, leaving the
problems unsolved, while the old Forest is content to reflect the
sunlight through the long summer days, to shelter the timid deer,
and bare its branches to wind and rain in winter.

The Forest has its own life. The dull green of its beeches turns
to gold without the help of man. The yellow hawthorn and the
evergreen holly do not owe their berries to him. The birds of the
Forest have their own life, from the garrulous throng in cottage
gardens to the lonely heron, still to be seen occasionally on the
banks of one of the Forest's many ponds, or the kingfisher,
uttering his sharp, shrill notes as he darts upstream. The deer,
too, have their own life, untamed creatures that flee at our
approach as though they had some inherited memory from days
when kings hunted them by day and commoners stalked them by
night. Only the village dogs chase them now. Sometimes they
may be seen, hunting in pairs, one to tease and confuse a terrified
doe by darting in front of her whichever way she turns, the other to
leap at her and tear her flesh. Normally she has a fair chance of
escape, but she may be in fawn, or in winter she may be swollen
with the bark she has eaten while the ground has been covered
with snow. No creature can be more helpless. Finally the dog
will fasten on to her throat, and the blood will gush down her
brown body. Sated, the dog will slink away. The red streak of
lust and cruelty remains in the Forest.

But while the Forest and all its creatures have their own independent lives, they have also a common life, and the lives of all
who have lived in its villages, and walked across its heaths, are

part of that life.   Its associations are part of the Forest itself.
A few of our Forest tales have been told in these pages—those
connected with men and women whose lives are remembered.
Other tales are suggested by names on the Forest map—names
that remain when the tales are forgotten: 'Hangboy Slade,'
'Monk Wood,' 'St. Thomas's Quarters.'   The old inns, too, bear
signs that link past and present romantically together: 'The Green
Man,' 'The Merry Fiddlers,' the 'Crowns' and the 'King's Heads,'
the 'Cocks,' the 'Bulls,' and the 'Owls'; the 'Thatched Houses'
that are no longer thatched.   Names of old families, too, are not to
be forgotten: the Willingales, the Ranns, and the Tredgetts.   We
find the name of Henry VIII's falconer on a tradesman's signboard.
Thus the lives of men are bound up with the life of nature, and
the life of the green Forest is bound up with our life.

As the last of our poets to be named, Gerard Manley Hopkins,
who was born in 1844 at The Grove, Stratford, reminds us:

> O if we but knew what we do
>   When we delve or hew—
> Hack and rack the growing green!
>   Since country is so tender
> To touch, her being só slender,
> That, like this sleek and seeing ball
> But a prick will make no eye at all,
> Where we, even where we mean
>   To mend her we end her,
>   When we hew or delve:
> After-comers cannot guess the beauty been.
>   Ten or twelve, only ten or twelve
>   Strokes of havoc únselve
>   The sweet especial scene,
> Rural scene, a rural scene,
> Sweet especial rural scene.

TOPOGRAPHICAL NOTE

PARIS has her Forest of Fontainebleau, with the palace of Louis XIV, Napoleon, and Louis Philippe at the heart of it; London's once famous forest is now a narrow stretch of waste measuring less than six thousand acres, with sprawling boroughs of Greater London on its southern borders. Its former glory has passed from it; its area is only one-tenth of what it was when its boundaries were fixed by the Long Parliament, soon after the death of Charles I. Yet what remains is a beautiful piece of natural woodland, much of which has never been enclosed or cultivated, extending nearly twelve miles between Forest Gate on the south and Thornwood on the north, with the Lea on the west and the Roding on the east.

When we cross its heaths, skirt its marshes, and thread our way through its thickets, we see what much of the English countryside was like before it was ploughed or cultivated. A forest was not all woodland. In Edward the Confessor's grant of lands to the monastery of Waltham, which included the forest manors of Woodford and Loughton, 'fields, feedings, meadows, woods, and waters,' were mentioned. Even then there were such open spaces as Waltham Marsh, Honey Lane Common, and Wanstead Heath. When we cross the Forest to-day from Loughton, Chingford, Theydon Bois, or Epping, we see the same diversity of scene.

Most of the towns and villages that belonged to the Forest when it stretched across its sixty thousand acres have lost all trace of their once silvan character. Many of them, however, retain features of interest, and a few are still rural. Epping remains a typical small Essex town, where cattle and poultry are sold in the street on market day. Waltham Abbey has lost little of its old-world appearance. Part of Harold's church, dedicated in 1060, may be seen to-day. (What is called 'Harold's Bridge' is probably fourteenth century.) John Foxe's house has gone, but several fifteenth- and sixteenth-century buildings are worth inspecting. Over the lich-gate into the churchyard is an overhanging storey of the fifteenth-century Welsh Harp Inn.

Naturally the buildings associated with the earlier chapters of this book have long since disappeared. The reader will waste

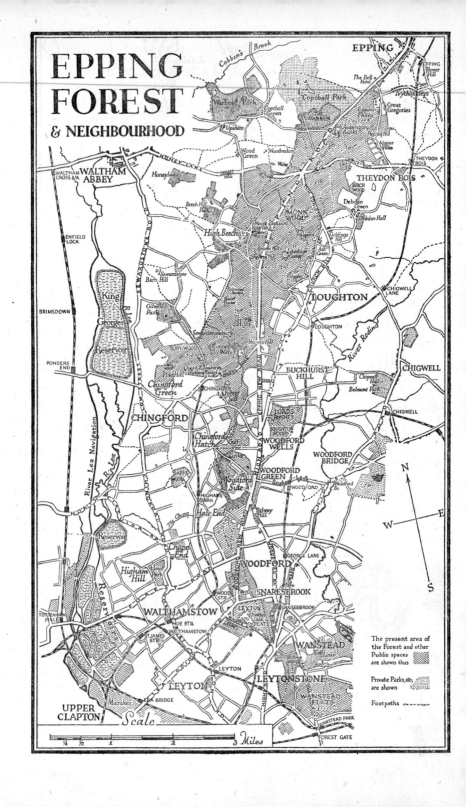

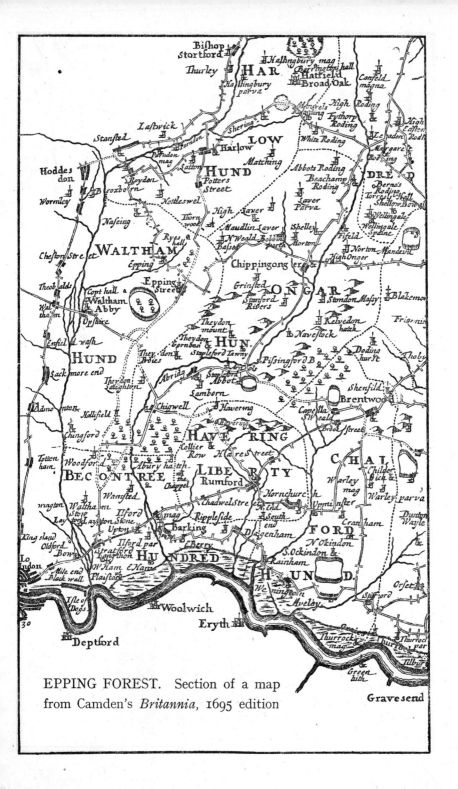

EPPING FOREST. Section of a map
from Camden's *Britannia*, 1695 edition

his time if he goes in search of Havering Palace, though in the
parish church at Havering-atte-Bower, dedicated to St. John the
Evangelist, is a twelfth-century font of Purbeck marble taken
from the old church, which formed part of the palace.   Of Barking Abbey, only the 'Fire-bell' or cemetery gate, and part of
the precinct wall remain.   The site was excavated in 1910,
bringing the lay-out of the main building to light.

Several of the sixteenth-century buildings mentioned are still
to be seen.   Queen Elizabeth's Hunting Lodge, now a museum,
is only a few minutes' walk from Chingford station; Pimp Hall,
another timber-framed and plastered building, is near.   Anne
Boleyn's Castle in Green Street, East Ham, is to be seen with
extensions.   The red-brick tower, referred to in the second chapter,
remains.   And at Nether Hall, Roydon, the red-brick ruins of the
gatehouse give some impression of what the fortified manor house
of the Colts was like.   Salisbury Hall Farm, Walthamstow, where
Roger Ascham lived, stands to remind us of days when Walthamstow was a favourite resort of poets, statesmen, and men of
learning.

The great abbeys of the Forest have gone, but some of its tiny
churches are still places of pilgrimage.   Of these the most famous
is the parish church of St. Andrew at Greensted.   The eleventh-
century nave is probably the timber chapel built when the body
of St. Edmund rested there about 1013.   The monks of Bury St.
Edmunds, fearing the Danes might steal their saint, carried the
body to London for safety.   On their return they rested a night
at Ongar, and an old chronicle tells us: 'His body was likewise
entertained at Aungre, where a wooden chapel erected to his
memory remains to the present day.'   The walls of the nave are
built of split oak logs, set upright.   When the church was repaired in 1848, the lower ends of the logs were found to have
suffered from their centuries of exposure.   They were shortened
and set on a low wall for protection.

The Forest has two prehistoric camps, both pre-Roman.   Both
can be reached easily from the main Woodford to Epping road,
and are marked on most maps.   Tradition would have us believe
that Ambresbury Banks marks the place where Boadicea fought
her last battle against Suetonius, but there is no evidence in
support of the story.   Numerous fragments of British pottery
were found when a trench was cut through the rampart and fosse.
Loughton Camp, two miles south-east from Ambresbury Banks,

lies on a ridge of the Forest, overlooking Debden Slade. In shape it is an irregular oval, and again the fragments of pottery found were all of early British origin. Mr. Hazzledine Warren of Loughton, who has studied the prehistory of the Forest for many years, thinks it possible that the interesting pillow mounds, on the slope in front of the King's Oak at High Beach, may be connected with these two camps on the plateau behind them. Their situation is certainly suggestive. They are on the brow of a hill overlooking the Lea valley, from which attack might be expected. They are also at the head of a stream which the approaching enemy might use for a passage. It does not seem at all unlikely that a battle was fought on this hill, and that these pillow mounds mark the funeral pyres of the slain. An account of Mr. Hazzledine Warren's excavations will be found in the *Essex Naturalist*, vol. xxi, pp. 214–26.

But for one person who comes to the Forest in search of such features as these, a thousand come to enjoy the beauty of its glades and clearings. Most of the paths are well marked, and in dry weather present no problems. The characteristic tree of Epping Forest is the hornbeam, but in Epping Thicks and above Fairmead Plain, magnificent beeches may be seen. There are stout oaks behind Connaught Water, and at High Beach both fine beeches and groves of silver birch. Each part of the Forest has its own particular beauty, which the forest-lover will delight to discover for himself.

At first the visitor may be afraid to venture far from the roads. After a few rambles he will become familiar with the well-known landmarks, of which the most prominent is the spire of High Beach Church. As the best parts of the Forest are about High Beach and 'Wake Arms,' it is wise to discover that particular landmark first.

INDEX

EPPING FOREST

*

A VIEW FROM HIGH BEACH

SILVER BIRCHES, EPPING FOREST

BEECHES, EPPING FOREST

NETHER HALL, ROYDON

THE GATEWAY, BARKING ABBEY

From a drawing by W. Deeble, 1818

ARCHBISHOP HARSNETT
From a brass in Chigwell Church

CHIGWELL SCHOOL
From an old drawing

WALTHAM ABBEY CHURCH
From a drawing by G. B. Campion, 1831

NORMAN NAVE, WALTHAM ABBEY CHURCH

From a drawing by F. Nash, 1804

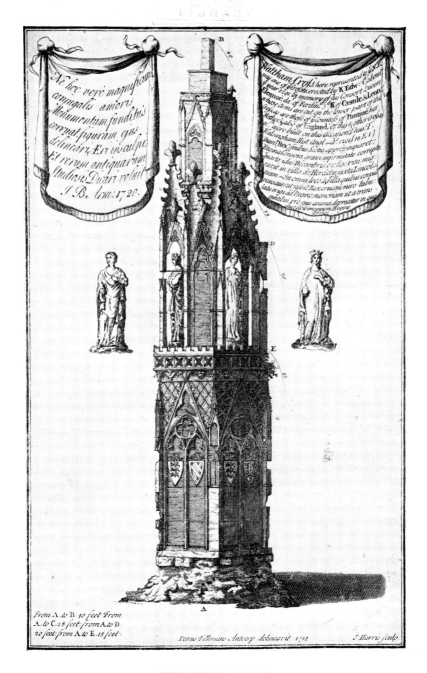

Næ licet verè magnificum
conjugalis amoris
Monumentum funditis
corruat, figuram ejus
delineari, Æri insculpi.
Et rerum antiquarum
studiosi Devari voluit
J. B. Arm: 1720.

Waltham Crosse here represented as it is
now, one of y[e] glorious erected by K. Edw[d]. I the
year 1291. in memory of his Consort Queen
Eleanor da: of Ferdin[d]. K[g] of Casule & Leon
whose arms are cut on the lower part of this
Ines, as also are those of y[e] countess of Pontue her
Mother, as also of England. Of this & other Crosses
were built on this Occasion. Thus T.
Walsingham Hist. on this Occasion. Thus T.
Dum [Rex] imibus Scotie appropinquaret:
Regina consors, gravi infirmitate correpta,
quarto idus Decembris ex hac vita mig-
ravit in villa de Herdeby juxta Lincoln-
iam. In cujus loco, & villa quibus corpus
pausaverunt jubet Rex crucem miro labo-
ratu erigi, ad Reginæ memoriam ut a trans-
euntibus pro ejus anima deprecetur in evum.
Cujus fit [?] inquient Regina

From A. to B. 40 feet. From
A. to C. 28 feet: from A. to D.
20 feet: from A. to E. 15 feet.

Petrus Tillemans Antverp. delineavit 1713   J. Harris sculp.

WALTHAM CROSS

ROMFORD MARKET

From a drawing by G. B. Campion, c. 1830

HARLOW BUSH FAIR

From a water-colour by Thomas Rowlandson, 1816

HARLOWBURY CHAPEL, HARLOW

COPT HALL

From a drawing by W. Bartlett, published 1832

CASTLE HOUSE AND MOAT, ONGAR

From a drawing by W. Bartlett, published 1832

CHIPPING ONGAR

From a drawing by W. Bartlett, published 1832

**

ROLLS PARK, CHIGWELL

From a drawing by J. P. Neale, published 1826

EAGLE POND, SNARESBROOK

From a drawing by T. M. Baynes, published 1832

WANSTEAD HOUSE

By S. Scott.   By courtesy of Captain Spencer-Churchill

DANCING AT WANSTEAD HOUSE

From 'The Wanstead Assembly', by William Hogarth

'WATCHMAN'S BOX,' WANSTEAD

LAMBOURNE CHURCH

ALFRED WILLINGALE
1843–1934
Photograph taken 1925

TURPIN'S CAVE, HIGH BEACH

OLD TEMPLE BAR, THEOBALD'S PARK

Originally erected in Fleet Street. Designed by Sir Christopher Wren

BIRCH AND BRACKEN, EPPING FOREST

INTERIOR OF WALTHAM ABBEY CHURCH

WALTHAM ABBEY CHURCH

THE GATEWAY, WALTHAM ABBEY

'HAROLD'S BRIDGE,' WALTHAM ABBEY

AN ESSEX LANE NEAR TOOT HILL